A Sermon in the Desert

A Sermon in the Desert

*Belief and Behavior in Early
St. George, Utah*

Larry M. Logue

University of Illinois Press
Urbana and Chicago

This book is printed on acid-free paper.

Library of Congress Cataloging-in-Publication Data

Logue, Larry M., 1947–
   A sermon in the desert.

   Bibliography: p.
   1. Mormons—Utah—Saint George—History—19th
century. 2. Saint George (Utah)—History. 3. Family—
Utah—Saint George—History—19th century. I. Title.
F834.S15L64   1988   979.2'48   87-19181
ISBN 0-252-01474-X (alk. paper)

For My Parents

Contents

List of Tables and Figures

TABLES

FIGURES

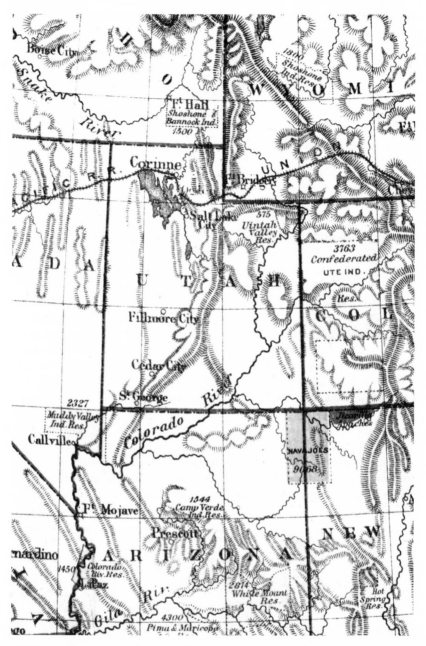

1874 map showing the location of St. George, Utah. Western History Collections, University of Oklahoma.

Preface

A recent commentator on American community history has suggested that its practitioners may "know more about how to do local history than about why it should be done."[1] This comment recognizes that historians of communities are straying ever further from tests of the frontier thesis and the *Gemeinschaft-Gesellschaft* taxonomy. Depending on one's viewpoint, this trend is either an "eclectic empiricism . . . content with lower-order generalizations" or a corrective to the tendency to make local studies into national history writ small.[2]

But this rising diversity also signals a maturation of the community study. In addition to testing received theory, local studies are increasingly recognized for their ability to *generate* theory.[3] Lower-order such theory may be, but it both points us toward improved theory-making and underscores the reason for studying communities. We require theories in history to be well-grounded explanations of the evidence we have before us; theories must at bottom account for "the common-sense meanings used by the actor and by the social structure within which [the evidence] was produced."[4] We can know communities and their common-sense meanings in ways that it is not humanly possible to know nations. The *why* of community studies is their ability to support theories about the past with evidence that is convincing in its scope because the subject is limited in its scale.

This study of St. George, Utah, is likewise meant to be purposefully eclectic. I will examine theories about past American family life, such as parents' role in marriage-making, that need to be assessed in places outside the eastern seaboard. Theories about the Latter-day Saints that also need testing, such as the marginality of plural marriage, will be evaluated here as well. But the central project of this study is to explain as fully as possible the people who lived for a time in southwestern Utah and produced records that we can examine. This requires sometimes using existing theories, sometimes piecing together new ones to account for why these Mormons believed and behaved as they did. Family life was at the heart of nineteenth-century Mormons' existence just as it was the cornerstone of their church's theology. This book will investigate how seriously the people of St. George took their theology and how much theology and family behavior shaped each other. It aims to probe the enigmatic tension between nineteenth-century American culture and anti-American separatism that ruled the lives of these Latter-day Saints and makes their past intriguing to us today.

As with all such projects, this book has had considerable help along the way. My first draft benefited from the insights and criticisms of Melvyn Hammarberg and Michael Zuckerman, and from an idyllic yet productive year at the School of American Research generously provided by the Weatherhead Foundation. In its second incarnation this study has been further improved by invaluable help from Elinor Accampo, Ben Bennion, Dean May, Murray Murphey, and in ways both tangible and immeasurable by Barbara Logue.

Staff members at research libraries always take much of the aggravation out of archival scouring. Archivists and librarians provided assistance at the Historical Department of the Church of Jesus Christ of Latter-day Saints, the Huntington Library, the Bancroft Library of the University of California, Berkeley, the Harold B. Lee Library of Brigham Young University, the Marriott Library of the University of Utah, the Utah State Historical Society, and the Western History Collections of the University of Oklahoma. Good editors likewise make life easier at the end of the process, and I was lucky enough to work with especially skilled ones in Elizabeth Dulany and Lori Drummond. Special thanks also go to Lynne Clark, who provided some of the pictures in this book. And finally, the determination of the Mormon people to know their past has been the indispensable catalyst that made this study possible.

NOTES

1. Robert R. Dykstra and William Silag, "Doing Local History: Monographic Approaches to the Smaller Community," *American Quarterly* 37 (1985): 425.

2. Ibid., p. 424; Kathleen Neils Conzen, "Community Studies, Urban History, and American Local History," in Michael Kammen, ed., *The Past Before Us: Contemporary Historical Writing in the United States* (Ithaca, N.Y.: Cornell University Press, 1980), p. 290.

3. Darrett B. Rutman, "Assessing the Little Communities of Early America," *William and Mary Quarterly*, 3d ser., 43 (1986): 163–78; Clyde Griffen, "Community Studies and the Investigation of Nineteenth-Century Social Relations," *Social Science History* 10 (1986): 315–38.

4. Aaron Cicourel, quoted in Paul Rock, "Some Problems of Interpretative Historiography," *British Journal of Sociology* 27 (1976): 355. See also Murray G. Murphey, *Our Knowledge of the Historical Past* (Indianapolis: Bobbs-Merrill, 1973), chaps. 1–2.

"Dixie" is a monument—a sermon in the desert—a fulfil-
ment of prophecy—an indisputable evidence of the actual
power of a living unity permeating our organization. . . .
Our Dixie people have been thus true—redeeming the
earth is a part of our belief.

—Joseph F. Smith and
Claudius V. Spencer,
Deseret News, May 22,
1867

1

St. George and Its People

Why did Mormons remain Mormons? As we will soon see, there are plenty of reasons why nineteenth-century Americans *became* Mormons, but conversion was not the only critical point in their lives. Converts in the 1830s and 1840s joined a group that was habitually at war with the larger society. Expelled from Ohio, then from Missouri, and then from Illinois when Joseph Smith was killed, the Latter-day Saints finally endured a march to the Salt Lake Valley. Later converts similarly put up with hunger, disease, and exhaustion to "gather" to Utah. Why? Some Mormons did simply drop out, and others started splinter sects. Yet thousands of other Americans and Europeans suffered persecution in the United States, the misery of a long march, and famine in early Utah partly because their leaders said they must. But obedience explains only part of why they endured all this; the Mormon people probably expected actual benefits from their odyssey. Self-interest can clearly be a compelling incentive for obedience, but it takes careful scrutiny to find what early Mormons had to gain.

Yet there is an ideal place to look—the settled Mormon town under stress. Mormonism's disordered first years were clearly aimed at survival, and any rewards for members had to wait at least until there was a peaceful gathering place; in the Great Basin, Mormons could finally practice their religion unmolested. But to avoid confusing commitment to Mormonism with complacency about comfortable circumstances, we need a place to examine where faith was continually tested, where people had to have good reasons to remain Mormons. No Utah community of any size remained settled longer under more faith-trying hardships than the town of St. George. The "capital" of southwestern Utah, St. George has existed since 1861 in spite of conditions that repeatedly strained the commitment of its residents.

Ironically, St. George came into being when tests of faith were apparently fading into the past for Salt Lake Valley Mormons. The 1850s finally brought some relief from the uncertainties that had long ruled

Mormons' lives. Harvests were better than in the first years of settlement, Utah was profiting from gold-rush traffic to California, and families like Robert Gardner's found themselves actually prospering. Lumber was in demand, and Gardner's sawmill near Salt Lake City began to make him a comfortable living. But in 1857 the church sent him to Canada to oversee emigration to Utah; when he returned, the city had been evacuated as federal troops approached to install the first non-Mormon governor. That crisis ended peaceably and Gardner moved back home, but his millstream was soon cut to a trickle by upstream usage. He and his brother finally relocated the mill and once again Gardner began to earn a good income. By the autumn of 1861 his neighbors were congratulating Gardner on his renewed prosperity, but he could take nothing for granted. Gardner recalled saying, in answer to the compliments, "I am almost afraid of another fall." And then, "In a few hours sure enough news came of another fall. My neighbors reported that they had heard my name called with others to go south on a mission to make new settlements and raise cotton. I was to start right away."[1] At the semi-annual general conference, church leaders had announced the names of three hundred families expected to make new homes in "Utah's Dixie," an area three hundred miles south of Salt Lake City.

The name Dixie does not suggest a wilderness, and indeed the southwest corner of Utah was not precisely a wilderness when the 1861 call went out. Southwestern Utah is the state's lowest and thus its warmest location. Brigham Young had long been intrigued by the area's potential for warm-weather crops, especially cotton; moreover, Dixie was on the Old Spanish Trail to California, a promising alternate route for immigrants and supplies. The church periodically sent groups of families to the area in the 1850s, and they raised encouraging cotton crops in their small settlements. When the Civil War threatened the cotton supply to Utah, it seemed the perfect time to have Dixie live up to its name.

But the southern colonies were in fact struggling and demoralized, and knowing their problems further distressed Gardner and his fellow recruits. Indeed, Utah's Dixie showed little resemblance to its namesake. People raised in the eastern United States or Europe, as most adult Mormons were, could adjust to the Salt Lake Valley's landscape, but they were unprepared for the starkness of southern Utah's arid volcanic ridges and sandstone cliffs. One Mormon leader showed an Easterner's reaction when he described southwestern Utah as "showing no signs of water or fertility; . . . a wide expanse of chaotic matter presented itself, huge hills, sandy deserts, cheerless, grassless plains, perpendicular rocks, loose barren clay, dissolving beds of sandstone . . . lying in inconceivable confusion."[2] Only along the area's few streams was there any substantial vegetation. Moreover, summers were miserably hot, with temperatures climbing daily past one hundred degrees; summer's low humidity made the heat more bearable but it also helped to wither crops. Irrigation was a continual problem because desert cloudbursts swept away all manner of irrigation dams. Half or more of the southern colonists in the 1850s eventually abandoned their settlements and returned north with tales of hardships that did not cheer future recruits.

However, three hundred families had been called by the man they considered God's living prophet, and also by his apostles, a command that could not be dismissed by faithful Mormons whatever their circumstances. John and Margaret Moody were even more upset than Robert Gardner at being called for the Dixie mission. John Moody recalled having "heard such discouraging accounts of the country. . . . I felt as though I could not do it," and Margaret had also been told that "we can never make a living in that country, and I was inclined to beleave it my self." But Moody prayed for help in deciding what to do and was answered with a hymn running through his mind, convincing him that his mission to the south "was called by the spirit of God." Afterward, "those bad feelings began to leave me and soon I was entirely free from them," and so apparently was Margaret.[3]

There was in fact no real way of forcing compliance with the call. Those who asked were usually excused from the Dixie mission, but the church's leadership made it clear that shirkers would ultimately be punished. George A. Smith, the apostle who superintended colonization in southern Utah, marveled at the "diseases [that] appear in men that had heretofore been considered healthy," the sufferers claiming that "I have always been sick in a warm country." He warned such followers that their negligence "will linger around you, it will haunt you and will be like a canker worm gnawing at the root of your felicity."[4] The Gardners, the Moodys, and over two hundred other families, on the other hand, eventually decided to go south. They sold their land and houses, packed their belongings, and left in the last months of 1861 for a mostly unknown land.

Most settlers traveled in small groups, riding or walking alongside wagons pulled by their cattle. Robert Gardner and William Lang had faster mule teams, and their families traveled together and camped with companies as they overtook them. Two weeks after starting out, the two families reached the turnoff for the road to the new townsite of St. George, named for George Smith. Though most of the settlers had instructions to head for St. George, Gardner and Lang noticed that travelers ahead of them had followed the trail leading toward the existing settlements farther up the Virgin River and its tributaries. Faced with a choice between the unknown new site and the small comfort of settled villages, Gardner and Lang "felt a little lost for a moment." But according to Gardner, Lang decided they should "go where we are told to go, and help make a track."[5]

At Washington, an early cotton-raising village on the way to St. George, Gardner reconsidered the decision. The residents were in tatters and obviously suffering from malaria, which "tried me harder than anything I had seen in all my Mormon experience. Thinking my wives and children, from the nature of the climate, would look as sickly as those now surrounding me." But once again, Gardner would "trust in God and go ahead."[6] The Gardners and Langs covered the last few miles of rugged volcanic rock interspersed with wagon-stopping sand. At the top of the lava ridge overlooking the new townsite they met Erastus Snow, one of the two church apostles assigned to lead the southern mission. The small group went down around the ridge to join the two families that had reached the wide valley a week earlier.

Erastus Snow had helped Brigham Young lay out Salt Lake City, and he knew how to set up a Mormon town. As companies of settlers arrived throughout December and January, Snow put a number of them on committees to locate a plot for the town, to map out irrigation routes, to find accessible timber, to arrange for cattle-herding, to set up a town government, and so on. The town was to be laid out on the standard Utah plan: all dwellings were to be in blocks, eight lots to the block, blocks separated by wide streets with ditches alongside to carry household water. The residents would make gardens and build stables on their town lots, but crop and grazing land was to be at a distance, along the Santa Clara Creek and on whatever acreage could be irrigated from the Virgin.

About 130 families huddled in tents and under inverted wagons in the unusually wet first months of 1862, waiting for a survey to mark their property. As awareness of their isolation eroded the resolve to fulfill their mission, something akin to this book's central question must have occurred to these settlers—how could they have come to be shivering in the rain in this hostile place?

The backgrounds of most of these pioneers are available in considerable detail (see appendixes), and they show the features that make early Utah Mormons at once familiar and alien to those who study nineteenth-century Americans. The group at St. George would not, at a casual first glance, look out of place in most settlements in the United

States. The average husband was in his early forties and the typical wife was near her mid-thirties. They had with them three children, and one more had died in childhood. Their speech had varied accents: about a third of the adults were born in the British Isles, another two-fifths in the northeastern United States, one-fourth in the South and the Midwest, and a few more on the European continent. Most had moved often: Robert Gardner was born in Scotland, spent his youth in Canada, and lived in two places near Salt Lake City before coming to St. George. None of this especially distinguishes this group from other Americans.[7] Moreover, some of the settlers enjoyed a smoke or a drink, and a day between rains in their makeshift camp might find them organizing a dance to pass the time until they could start making a town. The first residents of St. George were in many ways barely distinguishable from other American pioneers.

Yet other American migrants traveled to what they believed were better places to make a living, while most of these Mormons had given up relatively comfortable circumstances to go to a place where they knew life would be hard. Not only that, but they also had puzzling habits, like calling each other "brother" and "sister" and, among some of the men, having two or even three wives. Throughout the camp, one-fourth of the husbands were polygamists, their plural wives either with them or, like Robert Gardner's first two wives, waiting in the north to be brought later.

The Latter-day Saints' ambiguous relationship with nineteenth-century America has invited comparisons with the New England Puritans, who likewise withdrew from what they believed was a benighted society to practice a purer religion while they remained loyal Englishmen and -women.[8] The analogy is useful, but we must go beyond it if we are to understand Mormonism's appeal to the nineteenth-century people who settled St. George.

Most analyses of Mormonism's attractiveness take as their model Joseph Smith's own experience, focusing on his family's economic problems and his own spiritual restlessness. Smith's parents were never far from poverty, losing a farm in Vermont and then another in western New York, and no one in the Smith family could find real comfort in the religious sects that competed for converts. Joseph was especially distressed by local revivalists' "strife of words and . . . contest about opinions." His solution was to "ask of God," and he received the first of the visions that led to publication of the Book of Mormon.[9]

Analysts have agreed that subsequent conversions to Mormonism generally followed Smith's prototype: socially marginal people, adrift in the moral uncertainty of the nineteenth century, seized Mormonism's offer of a temporally relevant divine authority. Potential converts, it is argued, were disoriented by the post-Revolutionary weakening of the community leadership once exercised by established church and local gentry; nor had they benefited from the economic success that swept the new republic. Such people needed guidance, in the form of direct, plain reassurances that God still cared for his people and still planned their salvation. In this view, unambiguous authority was what attracted prospective Mormons, and a modern prophet who promised that he could still make Zion a reality amid the turbulence of the nineteenth century exactly fit their needs.[10]

Some Mormon conversion accounts do indeed resemble Joseph Smith's experience, partly by design. Smith's quest for eternal truths was part of Mormon lore, described in official church history and retold in sermons.[11] Their prophet's account made an ideal model for a discovery of faith, and Mormons who recalled their conversion often followed Smith's format. Whether they were converted in England or in America, many St. George residents described an initial confusion over competing doctrines, ending finally in the conviction that the Mormon priesthood preached the truth; occasionally the conviction was confirmed by a divine visitation.[12] Moreover, some accounts describe a particular vulnerability caused by poverty and spiritual uncertainty. Hosea Stout, an early St. George settler, wrote to his sister before his conversion in 1833, asking, "What shall I do? I feel like a poor out cast without a friend to council or assist me or even to communicate my troubles to."[13] Henry Eyring said he had "about exhausted my funds" in 1854, and exposure to Mormonism came "at the right time, when my mind was susceptible to good impressions."[14] Other converts like Henry Bigler had lost parents in childhood, and Bigler recalled his grandfather declaring that "if your Mother had been alive you never would have joined the Mormons."[15] Seeking and finding truth in the Latter-day Saints' doctrine clearly fits the accepted model of disorientation resolved by submission to the Mormons' authoritarian practices.

But in its focus on the vulnerability of converts, this model overlooks another thread that runs through the St. George conversion stories. The nineteenth century brought more than economic ups and downs and the decay of traditional authority. There was also a "revolution in choices," the realization by most Americans that, to some extent, they could control their fate.[16] Ordinary people had pushed their elite guardians off center stage by about 1820, taking to themselves the right to determine experience. Americans began to want accountability as well as leadership from their politicians; they started in large numbers to limit their fertility; they took a new interest in their health and reappropriated health care from physicians; and they increasingly demanded a choice among the paths to spiritual salvation. This last demand, of course, led to the confusing competition among sects cited by Smith and subsequent Mormons, but it ultimately gave them the chance to choose for themselves the way to heaven.

The enduring value of this ability to decide is clear in St. George conversion accounts. Robert Gardner recalled going to Mormon meetings "to hear and judge for myself," and he "compared their doctrine with the [Methodists'] doctrine of Christ and his Apostles" before deciding to join the Latter-day Saints in 1844.[17] John Moody converted in 1853 when, "after Much investigation, I at last became satisfied that not only the doctrine [the Latter-day Saints] taught was entirely scriptural, and the only one, but that it was also true. There fore I made up my mind, that I would some day obey it."[18] His second wife, Elizabeth, raised as a Mormon, proudly recalled rejecting alternatives to the church because "I never douted the truthfulness of the Mormons."[19] Hosea Stout turned to Mormonism only after long sessions with a Mormon elder spent "investigating our religious tenats . . . refering our opinions wherever we differed to the Bible."[20]

Reasoned comparison of doctrines hardly fits the picture of people with "weak, weary hearts, tossed and troubled, who have wandered from sect to sect, seeking in vain for the primal manifestations of the divine power."[21] The evident contradiction between enlightened choice and confused grasping for guidance is less puzzling when it is seen as complementary versions of the same event. As analysts, we stress Mormons' recollections of vulnerability because they demonstrate the nineteenth century's social dislocations: Mormonism appealed especially to people who were frustrated with their lives, those for whom the expanding American commercial empire and the growing British industrial economy meant little more than "misfortune . . . at every attempt to make an honest & respectable living."[22] With "truth" serving as a code for restored traditional authority, converts were willing to endure much hardship for the Mormon church so long as the church avoided a vacuum of authority.

But for the converts themselves, the need for guidance was matched by their desire to make their own choices. From the distance of years, they may well have overstated the rationality of what at the time was a choice driven by helplessness, but if so the overstatement itself is revealing. What to us seems a desperate choice became *to the converts* evidence of self-determination. In their retrospective accounts, St. George residents underscored the ultimate importance to them of choosing a doctrine to live by, and they identified joining the church as the result of that choice. The converts may indeed have been victims of a topsy-turvy society, but they were at the same time participants in the revolution in choices, fully aware of their ability to act on their own behalf. To be sure, they accepted a church with a complex hierarchy and rules covering all manner of activities. Yet as they saw it, they did not join the church simply as an act of refuge, but instead freely gave their consent to be governed. Mormon converts found in their new religion the crucial balance between dependence and self-determination that the Shakers or the Methodists or other sects did not seem to offer.

If anything made the Mormons who settled St. George doubt the wisdom of this choice, it was their experience in the town's early years. The rains ended in February of 1862 and the settlers moved to their lots and began building houses, digging irrigation ditches, and clearing rocks and brush from potential farmland. Trouble soon arose: digging the canal to bring water from the Virgin River was slow going, and it would not be finished for that year's planting. Moreover, the soil itself was poor, loaded in many places with plant-choking alkali. The settlers nonetheless managed to raise about fifty tons of cotton along other streams in 1862, and supplies they had brought with them plus a modest grain harvest provided food into the mild winter.

By February of 1863, however, the mission's historian reported that already "provisions are none too plentiful with some of the settlers," and by the end of the next summer the magnitude of the southern mission's problems was clear.[23] Tools wore out and replacements were far away, animals found little forage, and floods repeatedly destroyed irrigation dams and canals. Because of these conditions and because farmers turned increasingly to subsistence crops, the cotton yield was half the previous year's amount. The official crop report was an understated "crops are very light," underscored by an unofficial "in fact I might say a failure owing to the want of water."[24]

The following winter the food shortage became alarming. Some families in St. George had already given up and returned to the north, and those that stayed had diets which increasingly relied on carrot greens, the plant called pigweed, and bread made of sugar cane seed.[25] Erastus Snow took an inventory in March of 1864 which showed the extent of both out-migration and poverty in St. George.[26] Fifty-four families appear in the inventory, less than half the original settlers, and eighteen had less than twenty-five pounds of flour each to last to the midsummer harvest. On the other hand, another eighteen families had 200 or more pounds on hand, and loans by some of these against the next crop eased the shortage. Another solution was trade with the north, and twenty-six families contributed to a stock of goods to be exchanged for food in the more affluent northern settlements. The contributions were primarily livestock and cotton; by this time cotton had begun to be a burden, because such textile mills as there were lay far to the north. Residents appointed as traders took these possessions and exchanged them for provisions, but organized trade with the north was no answer to the food problem. The settlers' underfed animals and surplus cotton did not impress their northern neighbors, causing George Laub of St. George to complain that "the Northern Brethren took the Advantage of our Necesity . . . and we were obliged to Sell our wagons and cattle at a Sacrifice to obtain bread."[27] The next year, when there was again "a very scanty crop . . . our moveable prosperity [again] began to go for the purchase of bread Stuff from private individuals," but once more "goods [in the north] are dear."[28]

St. George's food problems were more effectively eased when, with the assistance of the church's leadership, shipments from the north were sought as donations rather than trade. Local tithing offices and individuals sent several tons of flour to the southern mission in 1865, giving relief "in our greatest extremity."[29] And by now there was an end apparently in sight for the problems of St. George and its drain on northern resources. The Virgin is a tributary of the Colorado River, and Brigham Young had begun to talk in earnest about a river route from Utah to California. The plan cheered the residents of St. George, who began to predict that "[we] will soon be filling our Store houses with the commodities of the world. This will much change affairs in our midst. . . . St. George will become a whole Sale mercantile port" for the whole of Utah.[30]

The railroad soon came to Utah and eliminated the river-route scheme, but by this time the residents had a new purpose. Brigham Young had authorized a permanent house of worship for St. George in 1862, committing the tithing receipts of all towns in southern Utah to the construction, but progress on the tabernacle was slow until 1867. Young had been sending new settlers south at nearly every fall church conference, and he increased the number in 1867 and 1868 and assigned many of them to work on the tabernacle.

New residents, supplies from the north to support the workers, and the emerging tabernacle itself kept spirits up in St. George, but there was still an undercurrent of insecurity. After good harvests in 1866 and 1867, grasshoppers and frost damaged crops the next two years, and crop reports collected by the federal census-taker in 1870 underscored southern Utah farmers' troubles. Washington County raised four bushels of grain per capita that year, less than half the nearly nine bushels produced in all of Utah, and far below the national production of over thirty bushels per person. The county had more livestock per capita than the rest of Utah, but animals were still miserably fed: Washington County produced less than a hundred pounds of hay per head of livestock versus half a ton for all of Utah. Most other crops showed the same shortfall.[31]

There were now over 1,100 people in St. George, and work on the tabernacle would not provide church-paid income for large numbers of people much longer. Brigham Young had no intention of giving up this southern outpost, and he had begun spending winters in St. George as one form of support. Another form was his proposal in 1871 for a temple in St. George. The temple is the focus of Mormon spirituality: it is not a place for worship but instead for the Latter-day Saints' ordinances of endowment (a dramatization of man's eternal progress and ceremony of devotion), baptism for the dead, eternal sealing of marriages, and other rituals. If it was finished before the slowly rising Salt Lake City temple, this would be the first temple built since the Mormon exodus from Illinois in the 1840s (Salt Lake City had a temporary "Endowment House" for temple ordinances). The St. George temple would also be an even larger public works project than the tabernacle; this prospect especially gladdened men like Isaiah Cox, who "rejoiced greatly at the news [of plans for the temple], as I now could feed my families."[32]

More families, supplemented by a force of temporary workers, moved in to work on the temple, and supplies came from throughout Utah until construction ended in 1877. In addition to this source of income for residents, silver mines opened twenty miles away, and the non-Mormons there provided jobs and markets for such surpluses as St. George could produce, notably local wine. All this smoothed the caprices of farming, which continued with a "deficiency in grain and forage" in early 1875 and a summer so dry in 1877 that George Laub's corn was scorched because "the water is Drying up verry fast in the Streams."[33] In 1880, despite a 38 percent population increase, Washington County raised less grain than ten years earlier, falling still further behind the rest of Utah. The only real improvement in agriculture was the widespread use of alfalfa to feed livestock in the 1870s; farmers in the county raised well over 400 pounds of hay per head of livestock in 1880, and meat and dairy products began to improve residents' diets.

In the early 1880s, though Brigham Young was no longer alive to see to its welfare, St. George had a stability of its own. It had the only temple in Utah until 1884, and Mormons who earlier had had to go to Salt Lake City's Endowment House could now come to St. George for temple ordinances. The population numbered over 1,300, and the pell-mell out-migration of the early years was over. Half the original families were still in St. George in 1880 (or had returned; some of those missing in the 1864 inventory had moved to nearby settlements and eventually came back), and two-thirds of the 1870 households stayed on.[34] Subsidies from the north had been mostly withdrawn and the nearby silver mines were nearly played out, but two decades of surviving floods, droughts, and frosts made lean years less disastrous.

But soon a different set of problems shook daily life in St. George. Anti-Mormon sentiment in the United States, fed by indignation over polygamy, climaxed in the 1880s when new federal laws paved the way for prosecution of polygamists. Federal authorities had focused on arresting Brigham Young and other principal church officers in the 1870s, but now they began to jail all the polygamists they could find. Marshals came to a number of towns, including St. George, gathering evidence on polygamists from wives and children and attempting to arrest the husbands. The "Raid," as the anti-polygamy campaign in Utah was known, had husbands hiding among haystacks by day and racing out the back door while deputies came in the front door at night.[35] At least a thousand men were jailed in Utah, and Mormons responded by forming an "underground" to hide polygamous husbands and their families; they also started settlements in Mexico to avoid U.S. authorities. The Raid was a time of profound disruption for Mormons, involving monogamous families who sheltered fugitives as well as polygamists themselves. Indeed, St. George's principal farmlands went uncultivated at the height of the persecution.[36] In 1890 the church officially discontinued polygamy and most of the harassment ended, but it will be seen that the discontinuance itself caused other problems for the residents.

The winter before polygamy was renounced, in spite of the latest reinforcements of the irrigation system, heavy rains once again caused "much loss in this country on the River Virgen and Santa Clara Rivers. Dams, ditches, bridges, and land washed away."[37] St. George remained an uncertain place to make a living, and in 1900 an official assessment admitted that "notwithstanding the strenuous efforts of the people to raise sufficient wheat to supply the inhabitants with bread stuff, the farmers so far have not succeeded."[38] Most people in St. George still depended in one way or another on nature: although less than a fourth of the household heads in 1880 actually described themselves as farmers, most families had a plot in the town's farmland plus a garden and livestock to supplement their other earnings.

Since nature's unpredictability continued to keep St. George from being a comfortable place, the central question surfaces again. Why did people who took pride in their rational choices endure living in this place? Of course their church wanted them to stay and work at building a kingdom of God: Brigham Young had commanded the settlers to go south, and the leadership combined a strategy of "kindly spirit and influence" with warnings about "our lack of a self sacrificing spirit, and murmuring against the providences of God" to get them to stay.[39] But can docility explain the willingness of hundreds of families to endure repeated periods of isolation and discomfort?

From evidence of everyday life in St. George, this book will explore the effects of the townspeople's worldview on their behavior, as well as the influence of the residents' circumstances on their beliefs. The residents' attitudes and behavior under obvious stress will suggest why Mormons went through so much for God's kingdom and why, paradoxically, they seem to have relinquished the kingdom so willingly. Some analysts of turn-of-the-century Mormonism point to the Latter-day Saints' eager conformity with the American society they had recently struggled against: their festivals, for example, now represented "a sincere expression of middle-class American values and habits," and "farmers were seeking the good life in commercial enterprise."[40] This apparent change from defiance to conformity came, it is often argued, because the Mormon people had grown disaffected with separatism; Mormonism itself, in its emphasis on American ideals of individual achievement and self-control, held the seeds that finally destroyed opposition to non-Mormon America.[41] In this view, the cessation of polygamy was an inevitable bow to reality and was greeted with relief by most Latter-day Saints. In St. George, where the strains on obedience to the church were particularly severe, there should have been especially strong pressure to give in to the outside world. Yet in the remainder of this book will be seen a community whose belief system nourished both self-determinism and continuing defiance of non-Mormon America.

NOTES

1. "Journal and Diary of Robert Gardner," in Kate B. Carter, comp., *Heart Throbs of the West* 10 (1949): 311.

2. Parley P. Pratt, quoted in Andrew Karl Larson, *Erastus Snow: The Life of a Missionary and Pioneer for the Early Mormon Church* (Salt Lake City: University of Utah Press, 1971), p. 317.

3. Journal of John Monroe Moody, in Family Record of John Monroe Moody, Huntington Library, San Marino, Calif., pp. 6–7. All material from Huntington Library cited by permission.

4. Quoted in Andrew K. Larson, *"I Was Called to Dixie": The Virgin River Basin—Unique Experiences in Mormon Pioneering* (Salt Lake City: Deseret News Press, 1961), pp. 104–5; quoted in Larson, *Erastus Snow*, p. 412.

5. "Journal of Robert Gardner," p. 313.

6. Ibid. The discussion of St. George's history that follows is based primarily on Larson, *I Was Called* and *Erastus Snow*; Leonard J. Arrington, "The Mormon Cotton Mission in Southern Utah," *Pacific Historical Review* 25 (1956): 221–38; James G. Bleak, "Annals of the Southern Utah Mission," 2 vols., Brigham Young University Library.

7. The median ages of adult men and women (over age twenty) in the 1860 census were in the thirties, the average family had three children, and Britain had been the largest source of immigration to the United States. Though Americans' geographical mobility has been overstated in some studies, they nonetheless had a propensity to migrate; see Donald H. Parkerson, "How Mobile Were Nineteenth-Century Americans?" *Historical Methods* 15 (1982): 99–109. This comparison of St. George's settlers to other Americans is not an argument that the town was America in microcosm, but rather that a traveler through America at mid-century would not have been instantly struck by most of the settlers' characteristics.

8. Perhaps the first and best known of these comparisons is Emerson's remark that Mormonism was "an after-clap of Puritanism." See James Bradley Thayer, *A Western Journey with Mr. Emerson* (1884; reprint ed., Port Washington, N.Y.: Kennikat, 1971), p. 39. More recent linkings of the two groups are in David Brion Davis, "The New England Origins of Mormonism," *New England Quarterly* 26 (1953): 147–68; Leonard J. Arrington, *Great Basin Kingdom: An Economic History of the Latter-day Saints, 1830–1900* (Cambridge, Mass.: Harvard University Press, 1958), chap. 1; Klaus J. Hansen, *Mormonism and the American Experience* (Chicago: University of Chicago Press, 1981), chaps. 2, 7.

9. Brigham H. Roberts, ed., *History of the Church of Jesus Christ of Latter-day Saints*, 7 vols. (Salt Lake City: Church of Jesus Christ of Latter-day Saints, 1932–51), 1: 3, 4.

10. See Mario S. DePillis, "The Quest for Religious Authority and the Rise of Mormonism," *Dialogue* 1 (Spring, 1966): 68–88; Hansen, *Mormonism*, pp. 160–63; Davis, "New England Origins." On backgrounds of English converts, see P. A. M. Taylor, *Expectations Westward: The Mormons and the Emigration of Their British Converts in the Nineteenth Century* (Ithaca, N.Y.: Cornell University Press, 1966), chaps. 2, 7.

11. The "History of Joseph Smith" was published in the 1840s in two church newspapers, the *Deseret News* and the *Millenial Star*, before it was included in Roberts, ed., *History of the Church*. For examples of sermon references to Smith's quest, see *Journal of Discourses by Brigham Young . . . and Others*, 26 vols. (1854–86; reprint ed., Los Angeles: Gartner, 1956), 12: 334, 353, 14: 140–41. The anti-rationalist basis of Mormon doctrine is described in Richard L. Bushman,

Joseph Smith and the Beginnings of Mormonism (Urbana: University of Illinois Press, 1984), pp. 183–85.

12. For examples of confirming visions, see the initial section of the Journal of Henry Eyring, Library-Archives, Historical Department of the Church of Jesus Christ of Latter-day Saints (hereafter cited as LDS Church Archives); Autobiography and Journal of Henry William Bigler, Huntington Library, p. 15.

13. "Autobiography of Hosea Stout," *Utah Historical Quarterly* 30 (1962): 252.

14. Journal of Henry Eyring.

15. Journal of Henry Bigler, p. 16.

16. "Revolution in choices" is from Robert H. Wiebe, *The Opening of American Society: From the Adoption of the Constitution to the Eve of Disunion* (New York: Knopf, 1984), chap. 8. See also Robert V. Wells, *Revolutions in Americans' Lives: A Demographic Perspective on the History of Americans, Their Families, and Their Society* (Westport, Conn.: Greenwood Press, 1982), chap. 5; Richard D. Brown, *Modernization: The Transformation of American Life, 1600–1865* (New York: Hill and Wang, 1976); Nathan O. Hatch, "The Christian Movement and the Demand for a Theology of the People," *Journal of American History* 67 (1980): 545–67. On the antecedents of this revolution, see James A. Henretta, *The Evolution of American Society, 1700–1815: An Interdisciplinary Analysis* (Lexington, Mass.: D. C. Heath, 1973), pp. 211–14; Henry Glassie, *Folk Housing in Middle Virginia* (Knoxville: University of Tennessee Press, 1975), chap. 8; Michael Zuckerman, "Dreams That Men Dare to Dream: The Role of Ideas in Western Modernization," *Social Science History* 2 (1978): 332–45. For a reminder, however, of the considerable residue of fatalism, see Lewis O. Saum, *The Popular Mood of Pre-Civil War America* (Westport, Conn.: Greenwood Press, 1980).

17. "Journal of Robert Gardner," p. 272. Similar comparisons of doctrines are in Autobiography of Milo Andrus, Huntington Library, initial passage; Diary of Charles Smith, LDS Church Archives, pp. 1–2; Autobiography of Joseph Orton, Washington County Library, St. George, Utah, p. 2; Synopsis of the Life of Easton Kelsey, Mormon Biographies File, Bancroft Library, University of California, Berkeley, initial passage. The Bancroft file is a copy of originals in the Library of Congress.

18. Journal of John Moody, p. 2. See also Biography of William Atkin, Mormon Biographies File, Bancroft Library, pp. 2–5; Journal of Henry Eyring.

19. Autobiography of Elizabeth Moody, in Family Record of John Monroe Moody, Huntington Library.

20. "Autobiography of Hosea Stout," p. 257. Similar investigations by eventual Mormon leaders are noted in Jan Shipps, *Mormonism: The Story of a New Religious Tradition* (Urbana: University of Illinois Press, 1985), p. 28; Leonard J. Arrington and Davis Bitton, *The Mormon Experience: A History of the Latter-day Saints* (New York: Knopf, 1979), pp. 28–29. A "thirst for knowledge" was characteristic among people who were attracted to millenarian movements. See J. F. C. Harrison, *The Second Coming: Popular Millenarianism, 1780–1850* (New Brunswick, N.J.: Rutgers University Press, 1979), chap. 8.

21. John Greenleaf Whittier, quoted in Harrison, *Second Coming*, pp. 191–92.

22. "Autobiography of Hosea Stout," p. 251.

23. Bleak, "Annals," 1: 131.

24. Ibid., 1: 139; A. Karl Larson and Katharine M. Larson, eds., *Diary of Charles Lowell Walker*, 2 vols. (Logan: Utah State University Press, 1980), June 21, 1863, 1: 241.

25. Most autobiographies and local histories include descriptions of diets so poor that embellishment with time becomes a question. There are, however, contemporary reports of southern Utah food production that could only meet part of the town's needs, and the well-known song "Once I Lived in Cottonwood," which tells of subsistence on "carrot tops and lucern greens," was written in the 1860s. Lester A. Hubbard, *Ballads and Songs from Utah* (Salt Lake City: University of Utah Press, 1961), pp. 429–30. See also *Journal of Discourses*, 11: 156; Journal of Allen Joseph Stout, Huntington Library, entries for 1866–67; [George A. Burgon], article on conditions in St. George, in "The Verprecula" (St. George manuscript newspaper), Brigham Young University Library, Oct. 15, 1864; [Guglielmo Sangiovanni], "A View of Dixie," ibid., Mar. 15, June 1, 1865; Larson and Larson, eds., *Diary of Charles Walker*, Aug. 21, 1864, July 4, 1869, 1: 244–45, 294; *Deseret News*, Apr. 5, 1865. Charles Smith took his family to Salt Lake City for a time in 1869 "because they needed very much to have more wholesome diet." Diary of Charles Smith, July 2, 1869.

26. Bleak, "Annals," 1: 151–53.

27. Journal of George Laub, Huntington Library, Dec. 30, 1864.

28. [George A. Burgon], in "The Verprecula," Oct. 15, 1864; [Guglielmo Sangiovanni?], article on conditions in St. George, ibid., Jan. 1, 1865.

29. [Guglielmo Sangiovanni?], "A View of Dixie," ibid., June 1, 1865.

30. [Sangiovanni?], "A View of Dixie," ibid., Apr. 1, 1865.

31. The major exceptions were products such as wine and molasses, which were unsuited to the rest of Utah, and cheese, a specialty of the European converts who settled near St. George. The reported cash value of all crops in Washington County was actually higher per capita than in Utah ($27 versus $23), but this probably reflects the value of labor and other costs that went into raising a crop rather than the well-being of the residents.

32. Quoted in A. K. Hafen, *Beneath Vermilion Cliffs (Historic St. George)* (St. George: privately published, 1967), p. 14.

33. Bleak, "Annals," 2: 383; Diary of George Laub, Huntington Library, June 25, July 1, 1877.

34. There was, however, an underlying outward movement of sons and daughters seeking jobs and chances for new households (see chaps. 3 and 4). On residential persistence in St. George, see Appendix B.

35. See, for example, Larson and Larson, eds., *Diary of Charles Walker*, 2: Aug. 14, 1887, June 16, 1888, 2: 683, 691.

36. Larson, *Erastus Snow*, pp. 550–51. On estimates of polygamists jailed, see Phillip R. Kunz, "One Wife or Several? A Comparative Study of Late Nineteenth-Century Marriage in Utah," in Thomas G. Alexander, ed., *The*

Mormon People: Their Character and Traditions (Provo: Brigham Young University Press, 1980), p. 56. On the Raid in southern Utah, see Nels Anderson, *Desert Saints: The Mormon Frontier in Utah* (Chicago: University of Chicago Press, 1942), chap. 12; L. W. Macfarlane, *Yours Sincerely, John M. Macfarlane* (Salt Lake City: privately published, 1980), chap. 21; Larson, *I Was Called,* chap. 35; William Mulder and A. Russell Mortensen, eds., *Among the Mormons: Historic Accounts by Contemporary Observers* (Lincoln: University of Nebraska Press, 1973), pp. 412–15; Biographical Record of Martha Cox, Washington County Library, pp. 45–48, 53–55.

37. Larson and Larson, eds., *Diary of Charles Walker,* Feb. 16, 1890, 2: 713. See also Albert E. Miller, *The Immortal Pioneers: Founders of City of St. George, Utah* (St. George: privately published, 1946), pp. 72–74; Larson, *I Was Called,* chap. 21.

38. Andrew Jenson, "St. George Ward," LDS Church Archives.

39. Erastus Snow, quoted in Bleak, "Annals," 1: 279; Brigham Young, quoted in ibid., 2: 157.

40. Howard R. Lamar, "Statehood for Utah: A Different Path," *Utah Historical Quarterly* 39 (1971): 326; Charles S. Peterson, "The 'Americanization' of Utah's Agriculture," ibid. 42 (1974): 111.

41. Hansen, *Mormonism,* chap. 7; Richard D. Poll, "An American Commonwealth," in Richard D. Poll, Thomas G. Alexander, Eugene E. Campbell, and David E. Miller, eds., *Utah's History* (Provo: Brigham Young University Press, 1978), pp. 669–80; Grant Underwood, "Re-visioning Mormon History," *Pacific Historical Review* 55 (1986): 403–26. For a dissenting view, see Jan Shipps, "The Principle Revoked: A Closer Look at the Demise of Plural Marriage," *Journal of Mormon History* 11 (1984): 65–77; Shipps, *Mormonism,* p. 63.

2

Mormonism and the Worldview

To study the worldview in a Mormon town is to explore the relationship between official and popular religion. It is not enough to assume that the two forms of religion do not fully match. The intent here is to show *how* they diverged in a community of believers. Departures from official doctrine are important ways believers make religion work in difficult times. It is equally important, on the other hand, to recognize popular conformity with official doctrine where it occurs. The worldview in St. George was in fact an irregular reflection of Mormon theology, now mirroring, now modifying church teachings.

It is hardly surprising to find Mormon theology intertwined with the personal and social worlds of St. George's residents. Virtually all of the town's families were Mormons; we have already seen that Americans turned to Mormonism partly because of their need for reliable authority, and the church responded with doctrine and activities meant to shape the rhythm of life. Sunday was naturally the centerpiece of this rhythm, with worship services in the tabernacle followed by meetings in St. George's four wards. But other days were part of the spiritual calendar as well. There was a periodically varying schedule of weeknight meetings for the male priesthood and the Female Relief Society; sessions of a prayer circle for men and Bible classes for women; meetings of the discussion group called the School of the Prophets; sessions of the judicial High Council; home teaching, which was priesthood visitation aimed at "keeping the [ward's] bishop informed of the spiritual progress of the congregation"; and other activities.[1] The first Thursday of each month was fast day, with its own meeting and offering for the poor. When the St. George temple opened in 1877, certain weekdays were designated for baptisms and other ordinances for residents' ancestors.

But the church's influence went far beyond explicitly spiritual activities. A social hall was one of the first buildings planned for St. George, and the church supervised its construction and use. Parties and dances were held on any appropriate occasion, watched over by the bishopric as spiritual events. As a Mormon historian put it, "dancing was blessed to the point of being a type of sacrament."[2] Rehearsals for the town's drama club opened and closed with a prayer, and Erastus Snow reminded performers that they were to be "a pattern to our bretheren and sisters for genteel manners, Piety, moralaty, and saintlike demeneour."[3] There were also a choir and a band, whose leader was sent on a two-year mission from Salt Lake City.

Doing business also meant encountering the church. The local tithing office was bank and general store combined; it collected and dispensed contributions in a largely cashless economy, and it was a reminder that work served God's purposes as well as one's own. Church officials also supervised the committees that ran cooperative ventures like irrigation, livestock herding, and merchandising. In the 1870s the church went still further, implementing a largely unsuccessful attempt at a more overt communal economy known as the United Order.[4]

True to its authoritarian image, Mormonism thus offered an encompassing program for daily life. But it would be a mistake to infer a Mormon worldview solely from the Latter-day Saints' theology and institutions. The form of Mormonism urged in doctrinal expositions and expressed in organizations was not necessarily the form held by ordinary Mormons. The Latter-day Saints had their share of contention and indifference, and even complaisant members did not always have the same concerns as the leadership in Salt Lake City. Residents of Dixie were no exception: Lorenzo Brown thought Sunday meetings were "long and tedious," calling one of Erastus Snow's jeremiads a "snow squall"; John Moody, accused of neglecting his High Council duties, told its members that "I did not put my self [on the Council] . . . and they were perfectly welcome to put some one else there."[5]

Yet discord is outweighed in residents' journals and diaries by signs of the church's importance in their lives. One clear sign is participation in the town's spiritual rhythm. Some diarists, from the tone and subject of their entries, were obviously active Mormons; they represent the upper end of a scale of participation. Charles Walker, an early settler of St. George, and Mary Whitehead, who came to the town in 1877, are two such residents. In a typical year Walker might attend a hundred worship services and priesthood gatherings and Whitehead would go to nearly as many worship meetings, Bible classes, and Female Relief Society sessions.[6] This is less than two meetings a week, but it allows for sickness, travel, and suspension of some activities in the hot months.

At the other end of the scale is William Nelson, who, like Walker, held the church rank of Seventy, a middle-level office named for Christ's first seventy missionaries. Nelson, however, was brought before the High Council in 1888 and threatened with excommunication for apostasy.[7] But he continued to take part in church activities: he attended thirty-one worship services that year, went to choir practice weekly, and regularly played the fiddle at dances. This was not a marked change from Nelson's participation in previous years, suggesting that spiritual activity varied over a relatively narrow range and included those judged to be lax as well as enthusiastic churchgoers.

Quantity of participation does not by itself indicate its meaning to St. George residents, but their diaries show in other ways the significance of sacred activities. Diary-keeping itself was encouraged by the church, and townspeople responded with records that highlighted their spiritual lives.[8] Even habitually brief entries like William Nelson's usually indicate who spoke at Sunday meetings, and they sometimes include an evaluation, noting a "very good" ward meeting or someone who "Spoke Well" at a Sunday service; this was more detail than Nelson usually gave to work or socializing.[9] Other diarists summarized sermons, preserving the spiritual lessons of their leaders.[10] Still others used diaries to work out their own discourses for worship meetings.[11] Whatever their amount of detail, almost all the diaries devote special attention to religious affairs. Public worship and other spiritual gatherings were times of particular intensity, when residents were especially attuned to what happened and were equally sensitive to their own responses.

These responses were as important as Mormon theology in shaping the worldview in St. George. As we have seen, people who became Mormons were acclimating to their century's offer of control over life. They sought self-determination as well as a regimen of authority, so there is plenty of variation in the details of their views. But there are also overarching themes in the concepts residents used to make sense of daily life. The soul's potential on earth and its fate after death, their relations with God and sometimes with Satan, and their dealings with each other and the non-Mormon society were among the townspeople's critical concerns.

The Self

Mormonism teaches that humans are composed of body and spirit. Spirits, which have resided with God since he "organized" the universe, are eventually embodied and born into the mortal phase of their development. Spirits are conscious before coming to earth, but their preexistence is forgotten at birth. There was no consensus in Dixie about the nature of the preexistence, just as there is no consensus among Mormons today.[12] Wandle Mace copied into his journal an apostle's description of covenants that spirits made in heaven: parents and children, husbands and wives all arranged their relationships before birth.[13] But Martha Cragun, who had been raised as a Mormon, had never heard of such arrangements when they were mentioned to her just before her marriage.[14] Wandle Mace and Charles Walker both reported Mormon leaders' declarations that all spirits came to earth untainted by sin. Walker wrote that this claim "was new to Me," and Mosiah Hancock of nearby Kanab related a dream in which certain spirits, about to be embodied, agreed to uphold God's law but others refused.[15] Dixie residents apparently treated the details of the preexistence as the arguable concepts that they remain today.

There was no uncertainty, however, about the spirit's earthly project. Now equipped with a body, the spirit could either act materially to improve itself or else waste its capacities in destruction and dissipation. The agent of choice was the will, which was "the *Spirit* of man claiming its prerogatives of thought and volition through its proper organs of the body."[16] The will was in fact the centerpiece of God's plan of salvation. Each person freely chose to act righteously or to sin, thus helping to determine his or her fate.

There was little disagreement in St. George about the efficacy of the will. A Mormon aphorism promises that mortals can be as God now is, and the same logic of progress shaped the residents' view of human purpose. Sermons reminded residents that since "we had come down to this earth to gain an experience, to learn to overcome our weakness and train our Spirits to the Mind and will of God . . . we ought to advance."[17] The townspeople responded by viewing life as a continuous program of self-improvement. Martha Cox told of her resolve to "reach a higher plane" by improving children's minds as a teacher; Samuel Miles, another early settler, reported in 1865 that he was "trying to improve and make me a comfortable home"; Charles Walker wrote that he could "see a small advancement in myself as pertaining to my religion"; Henry Eyring described his family's efforts "to gradually work ourselves up out of extreme poverty" in early St. George.[18] Lorenzo Brown and John Moody, despite their occasional dissatisfaction, saw their lives in the same light. Brown tried "to perfect myself in every part," and Moody worked "to improve as circumstances would permit" in spite of his troubles with church officials.[19]

Obstacles, of course, stood in the way of self-improvement. Chief among these was the body, which without the will's discipline could lead a person to "blaspheme his maker, debauch himself day by day, cheat, lie, swear, [and] commit whoredoms."[20] This "weakness of the flesh," as sermons called it, was in a sense a powerful impulse against which the spirit must struggle mightily. Indeed, speakers described the body-spirit relationship as a combat, the spirit's obligation being to "overcome" the body's tendencies. The church likewise promoted the Word of Wisdom, its program to curtail use of tobacco, alcohol, tea, and coffee, as a way of controlling sinful impulses. But most of the concern with sin remained with the leadership; the introspective sin-seeking that occupied the New England Puritans is largely missing from St. George diaries. Even Brigham Young's revivalistic warning that Dixie residents "will go to hell, lots of you, unless you repent" had little apparent impact on residents' assessment of their lives.[21] The townspeople would not be turned aside from the nineteenth century's more tolerant view of sin; they were evidently more impressed with Mormonism's promise of salvation for all but the most dedicated sinners and celestial glory for the truly faithful than they were by "snow squalls."[22] Regardless of how much they actually did indulge their weaknesses, St. George residents were more confident than their leaders that their efforts at self-improvement would overcome their sins.

And the townspeople paid little attention to their leaders' view of the spirit's fate after death. The Book of Mormon made clear to residents what happened to departed souls: all spirits "are taken home to that God who gave them life," and righteous spirits "are received into a state of happiness, which is called paradise, a state of rest, a state of peace, where they shall rest from all their troubles and from all care, and sorrow."[23] This rest was to last until the resurrection, when body and spirit would be rejoined for the millennium. Latter-day Saints would then redouble their temple work unhindered by death or enemies, to be rewarded with varying degrees of exaltation on Judgment Day.

But since Joseph Smith's death, Mormon leaders had begun to portray the period between death and the resurrection as a time of activity. Latter-day Saints' spirits now preached to non-Mormons in the spirit world, urging them to accept the posthumous baptism offered in Mormon temples. This view was known in St. George: Wilford Woodruff, church president and one of the strongest advocates of the active afterlife, told the people of St. George that dwellers in the spirit world were "all 'in a hurry,' " because they "had not any too much time to get things ready before the coming of the Son of Man and the ushering in of the great Millenium."[24] Erastus Snow likewise told Ann Jarvis, who like him had lost a school-age son in 1881, that "the boys are in a higher school" continuing their vital activity.[25] Two historians of

Mormonism have concluded that this emendation of the afterlife concept was one of the Latter-day Saints' key theological developments. By promising uninterrupted activity after death, Mormonism reduced death's mystery and terror to the extent that "death itself was, for the Saints, a minor event."[26]

Yet the leadership's redefinition of death had little impact on St. George residents' reaction to deaths around them. Although its age and sex patterns were somewhat different, death had much the same considerable presence in St. George as in other nineteenth-century places.[27] Dying was not trivialized in the town; instead, the townspeople registered typical human anguish over the deaths of loved ones. When Cynthia Bigler died in 1874, her fourteen-year-old son "was so over come with greaf that . . . he fell to the floor with anguish filled with exceeding pain of Sorrow tears streaming like rain and could not be composed," and the death of Adolphus Whitehead caused "great sorrow and affliction" in his family.[28] The death of Charles Walker's infant daughter brought "a shriek and wail [from her mother] that seemed to go thro me and chill my heart's blood," and Walker himself wrote "Oh, God, how can I stand to have the little cherub torn from me by the hand of Death."[29] Despite Erastus Snow's reassurances, Ann Jarvis's grief over her son's death did not soon fade: "Oh, that trial! I thought that it would kill me. It helped to destroy my health"; Hannah Romney "felt that I could not bear the loss of my baby" in 1867.[30] Allen Stout reported that after his wife's death "I often exclaim, O how can it be that she is dead and I am left again to mourn alone in this wicked world."[31] Poems written at parents' request typically recognized grief with lines such as "Thy heart was well nigh broke with grief / The silver cord night cut in twain."[32] Anguish over death is clearly one of the central themes linking St. George diaries.

The townspeople did take comfort from their religion and thus managed to control their grief, but this comfort had little to do with a continually active afterlife. They believed that God had his own reasons for death's timing, one of which was to strengthen the living. Erastus Snow wrote to his wife that the death of their daughter should be "a lesson in humility and deep dependence on God." Snow recalled "that good and patient man Job when his vast property and his ten sons were all swept away in a single day. Ought we not . . . to try to imitate his noble example of resignation?"[33] Having lost eight children, Charles Smith wrote that "of all trials that fall to the lot of us Mortals these are the hardest to bear, as they come nearest the heart," but "my own cup has never been so bitter but what I have been able to drink it, through the blessing of the Lord, and to thank God for his blessing and mercy." Smith delivered a sermon at a child's funeral in which he spoke of "the necessity of Mortals drinking the bitter cup on earth that they might appreciate the sweet. Showed that those who were capable of suffering the most intense and going thru jury trials here would receive the greater exaltation in Celestial Kingdom of our Father."[34] Ann Jarvis also ultimately bowed to God's wisdom after her son's death. "I knew it was wrong to be shelfish even in grief," she recalled, "and although I kissed the rod and thought the Lord wanted to chastize me, yet I know the Lord did comfort me, and ruled it for my good."[35] Charles Walker often used the phrase "the Lord giveth and the Lord taketh away: Blessed be the name of the Lord," and on one occasion he wrote that "it seems in the kindly dealings of providence I am called to drink [from the bitter cup] the fourth time; the Lords will be done."[36] Submission to God's wisdom is a basic religious response to death and is hardly a peculiarly Mormon attitude. Indeed, "Christian resignation" was still common among antebellum American mourners, and its persistence in St. George reminds us of the Latter-day Saints' enduring links to their origins.[37]

But St. George residents sought more than conventional religious solace about death. Instead of keeping anxious deathbed vigils for signs of grace, Mormons confidently assumed salvation and concentrated on the spirit's departure to a different world.[38] Church leaders, in stressing continued activity in the spirit world, hoped that that world's similarity to life would cheer their followers. In St. George, however, it was the spirit world's *difference* from this world that was the main source of comfort. The spirit world's special appeal was its restfulness: there, adults exhausted by hard work, hunger, and disease could peacefully wait for the resurrection with their deceased relatives and friends. For deceased infants, the spirit world was a return to the innocent sleep of childhood and an escape from the torment of their last waking hours.

Residents' references to death resonate with the assurance that departed spirits were resting in a better world. Allen Stout kept with him a poem he had written when his first wife died in 1848, including these lines:

> But she alas! is gone to some more healthful clime
> Where she can rest in peace while I am left behind,
> To finish out the work we had just begun.[39]

Martha Cragun, to console a family mourning an infant son, wrote

> Gentle mother, cease your weeping,
>   For thy little one so dear;
> He is calmly, sweetly sleeping,
>   Freed from every worldly care.[40]

When Brigham Young's nephew died, Charles Walker wrote a hymn which was sung at the funeral and buried with the body. The hymn urged mourners to

> Weep not for the departed
> 　He's resting with the blest;
> He sweetly sleeps with Jesus,
> 　In Heaven's sweet place of rest.
> Mourn not for his departure,
> 　He's free from death and pain,
> And would not, if permitted,
> 　Come back to earth again.

Another of Walker's funeral poems assumed that

> Oh, yes, that rest will be complete,
> Pure, unalloyed, and by God given,
> When husband, wife and children meet,
> And realize sweet rest in heaven.

When Walker himself died in 1904, Sarah Atkin read this memorial:

> Guard the Temple! Guard it well—
> As faithful as the one who fell
> In peaceful slumber, and has fled,
> To mingle with the worthy dead.[41]

Even Erastus Snow and Wilford Woodruff, speaking at a funeral in St. George before Woodruff became church president, described death as "but a short nap" until the resurrection; Snow later underscored death's contrast with life when he wrote that "those once released from Earth [are] ushered into the society of the Righteous spirits in Paradise."[42] When Joseph Johnson died shortly after moving to Arizona from St. George, his funeral hymn promised that "There is sweet rest in Heav'n."[43]

Yet there were occasional mentions of activity in the spirit world. Charles Walker, noting the death of three missionaries, wrote that "they will continue their labors on the other side of the vail."[44] Allen Stout, thinking about his own death, expected that "I shall then commence a greater and more glorious work, and not be loaded down with this mortal clay."[45] When his father died, Francis Moody believed that "the Lord wanted him to work and fill a position behind the veil to help forward his work."[46] But these were minority views, and they were exceptional in other ways. The deceased missionaries mentioned by Walker were men in their twenties who had been interrupted in their search for converts, and resumption of the mission after death was clearly appropriate. John Moody, though he was sixty-one when he died, was an active partner with his son in establishing a Mormon colony in southern Arizona; Francis still saw him as an able worker. Indeed, Erastus Snow's and Ann Jarvis's above-mentioned sons also died in the middle of important work, since schooling has always been a key obligation for Latter-day Saints. Such deaths were rare in St. George: between early childhood and old age, mortality in males was unusually low for the nineteenth century. More than a fourth of all males born would not see their fifth birthday, but the rest could expect to live past their mid-sixties, comparable to men in present-day America.[47] As previously noted, a few people did die at the "healthy" ages, but it is far more important that so many *did not* die in the active years. Death in St. George, especially for men, was primarily a phenomenon of the very young and the old.

Allen Stout was seventy-one when he wrote about his expected activity after death, and he considered his life's work nearly done. As detailed earlier, Stout himself had earlier assumed that his wife had gone to rest, so he is part dissenter, part confirmer of St. George residents' view of the immediate afterlife. Except in the rare case of men prematurely interrupted in vital church duties, those who died were presumed to be at rest. At the resurrection they would renew their work for God, but until then they made the most of their escape from the world's demands.

St. George residents thus adopted a view of death that made sense of mortality as they encountered it. Buoyed by the optimism of their doctrine and undoubtedly influenced by the romanticism about death that was supplanting resignation elsewhere in America, they assumed the preresurrection fate that best suited the individual and the church.[48] If continued activity was sensible, then that was the presumed fate; and there is no reason why this fate could not include women as well. The church clearly valued women's contributions to God's kingdom, but it seldom directly gave them an assignment. If a woman died on an explicit mission, such as attending medical school at Brigham Young's behest, it is possible she would have been assumed to be still working; the evidence is simply incomplete.[49] But the question seldom arose: most residents died before their work had begun or after it had ended, and they went to a fate that gave comfort and hope to the living.

On the other hand, there is every indication that the people of St. George saw the resurrection as their leaders did—as the start of renewed activity after death's "short nap," the chance to finish, under perfect conditions, humanity's work on earth. Anthony Ivins, a teenager raised in St. George, received his patriarchal blessing from eighty-year-old

William Perkins in 1871. In his blessing, an informal ritual conducted
by a declared descendant of the biblical Jacob, young Ivins was assured
that he would "see the graves open and the dead come forth. You will
witness the return of the Ten Tribes" in the resurrected world of fulfilled prophecy and sacred activity. Ivins reported "the profound
impression made on my mind by this blessing," with its explicit promises of a miraculous future.[50] George Laub copied into his diary Brigham
Young's assurance that "Jesus will Shurely come to Reign ere long . . .
and many are here in this hous that will See him and Speak to him
face to face."[51] Allen Stout wrote that he received baptisms for his
ancestors so that "they may come forth in the first resurrection and be
made partakers of eternal life."[52] Charles Walker's funeral poems often
included lines promising that

> He's gone, but will not tarry long,
> He yet will come to earth again;
> Yea, with the great angelic throng,
> A thousand years with Christ to reign.[53]

The spirit's rest would end when earth was again Eden, when humans would be "just the same as we are now only increased in intelligence, without Sin, and all the effects of the Fall removed."[54] As
will soon be discovered, the imminence of the millennium was regularly confirmed for St. George residents by the increasing derangement
of the outside world. The dazzling prospect of a promised earthly
paradise plus the clearly observable evidence of its approach made the
resurrection the "living, tangible reality" that church leaders hoped it
would be, and gave extra solace to those mourning the dead.[55]

Spirit Beings

It was not only after death that Mormons expected to encounter God
directly. They regarded God, plus Christ, the Holy Ghost, the angels,
Satan, and other deities as actual beings with whom people frequently
interacted. Evidence of spirit beings' existence was all around, in answered prayers, Satanic tricks, and the like. Moreover, it was possible
to have a sensory experience of a spirit being: some Mormons reported
revelations in which divinities appeared or spoke to them. The impact
of deities on the lives of these people was real, and to fully understand
the residents of St. George it is necessary to explore the way they dealt
with their spirit beings.

God himself was the deity with whom the townspeople had the
most interaction. Mormon doctrine portrayed a God who was ap-

proachable because he and mortals were fellow laborers, a "father and his children engaged in an eternal task."[56] A church official wrote that humans could "draw nigh to their Father, as to an endearing parent, and ask for blessings, as a son would ask for bread, and be confident of receiving."[57] St. George diaries let us see the outline of the towns-people's dealings with this divine parent. Most interactions with God were requests for help with specific problems; chief among these, and deserving most of our attention, were prayers for recovery from disease or injury.

The existence of injury and disease strains many belief systems, since they must explain why a deity who embodies all that is good presides over a world filled with capricious suffering. One analysis of Mormon theology has noted, however, that Mormonism is uniquely able to resolve this paradox. Mormon doctrine views God as having certain limitations: he did not, for example, create the universe *ex nihilo* but instead assembled it from existing materials. This view implies that God must struggle against the miseries of the world along with humans, since the causes of suffering may have been among the elements and therefore not of God's doing.[58] But nowhere is the gap between the theological implications of a belief system and everyday practice clearer than in St. George residents' response to suffering.

If accidents and disease were really seen as natural phenomena to be mastered, in much the same way, for example, as a river is tamed, the expected attitude among ordinary Mormons would be commitment to eliminating suffering with all practical means at hand. Brigham Young made it clear that humans could indeed help God struggle against suffering. Although he repeatedly denounced physicians (especially non-Mormon ones), Young also criticized exclusive reliance on faith-healing and urged Mormons to study disease and self-prescribe natural remedies; such pronouncements were known in St. George.[59] Some St. George residents demonstrated their conviction that disease was hu-manly curable by using Mormon physicians.[60] Others, however, saw injury and disease in a different light. In their view, God could and did influence human suffering. Charles Walker summarized this atti-tude in a sermon, arguing that "the Lord could if he choosed let the earth bring forth in its fullnes and could hinder pain, sickness and death, and other miseries that we are heir to by reason of the Fall. But it would not benifit us but would tend to make us of little worth and we should know very little of our selves and the overcoming of our weakneses and besetments."[61] Human distress in this view was part of God's plan of salvation, another trial to test the spirit. The strength of this belief lessened faith in non-religious ways of easing suffering:

even residents who used physicians often doubted their effectiveness or regarded them as a last resort.[62] When illness or injury struck a household, it was usually dealt with first by asking God's help, not that of mortals.

In fact, requests for divine help often worked. Residents' diaries occasionally report direct appeals to God, as Henry Bigler's did when his daughter had a fever. Bigler wrote that he "placed one of my hands on the child's head and prayed the good Lord to have mercy and rebuke the fever and preserve the Child from the distroyer. He heard my humble prayer and the child sleept well all night."[63] But when solitary prayer was ineffective or when the suffering was serious, residents asked for an "administration." Several members of the priesthood would anoint the sufferer with consecrated oil, then place a hand on him or her and invoke God's healing power. St. George residents often reported giving or receiving administrations, with enough successes to sustain their trust in faith-healing.[64] Although medicine had made some inroads into this reliance on administering to sufferers, the importance of faith-healing makes it clear that God was seen as the principal reliever of suffering, if not the only one.[65]

And yet God was not seen as the entire cause of individual suffering. There are no instances, for example, of the soul-searching that occurs when disease is seen as punishment for sins.[66] The administration rites were likewise not attempts to placate an angry God, but were rather a means of getting his attention, to persuade him to send his "angel of health" to end a case of suffering.[67] Charles Walker's reference to "besetments" is critical to understanding St. George residents' concept of suffering. The townspeople assumed that God had included pain and suffering in the plan of salvation to test the spirit further, but the test operated more or less randomly in the individual case. If, however, one or more members of the priesthood attested to God their belief that an individual had suffered enough, he would consider their petition and if it suited him would end the affliction.[68]

When prayer and ritual failed to stop suffering, there was no apparent effort to blame it on inadequately observing custom. For example, when Walker's infant daughter was dying, he was satisfied that it was not due to his lack of effort: "Felt calm. I have done all that lay in my power. Had the Elders administer to her; had her prayed for in the Temple and the Doctor [h]as done what he thought best for her, yet she keeps sinking in a dull heavy stupor."[69] In such passages St. George residents recognized a mystery that confounds the followers of most religions. At the moment they abandoned their efforts to persuade God to heal a sick or injured person, the townspeople acknowledged God's responsibility for this case of suffering. God's act was not in causing the misery, but in refusing to provide the healing that was clearly within his power. The unpredictability of God's actions ultimately heightened the residents' sense of subordination. Healing prayers were occasions of humility for Henry Bigler, and Francis Moody acknowledged in praying for his father's life that "not as I will, but as thy will all things will be done."[70] While Charles Walker prayed for his wife's recovery, he "felt small like a worm of the ground and the tears trickled down my face while I yet strove with the Lord."[71] Physical suffering impressed on the residents God's power and mystery, rather than the accessibility promoted by official doctrine.

What *really* happened when someone fell ill in St. George is not an issue here. Miraculous recoveries were more than part of the town's folklore; they were part of residents' lives. The townspeople obviously were often silent about failed administrations, and they undoubtedly overlooked some recoveries attributable to medicine. But this is less important than the residents' consistently demonstrated conviction that they could invoke a deity who might directly intervene in a crisis.

Residents appealed to God for other kinds of help, and in these cases they did act as fellow laborers. Francis Moody, for example, in praying to find a lost horse, assumed that since "no one ever had a greater desire to do or perform their duties more than I did there fore the lord would answer my prayer."[72] John Moody reminded God that he had "come down heather to surve thee, and keep thy commandments," and asked for guidance in a dispute with Erastus Snow.[73] Charles Walker asked God to "loose my tongue that I might speak to his names honor and glory" at a worship service.[74] Undoubtedly modeled on their prophet's question-and-answer relationship with God, these prayers sound more like polite bargaining than trembling appeals. They suggest that God was seen as more approachable and responsive in the cooperative effort of building his kingdom than in the healing of sick individuals. But appeals for health are much more common in St. George diaries and journals than this bargaining; the extent of sickness in the town, especially among children, was a continual reminder that the residents' sometimes accessible God was more often a stern master of the human character.

Following Judeo-Christian tradition, Mormons believed that God's antithesis was Satan, who had been driven from heaven after opposing God regarding the plan of salvation. Satan had fought against the inclusion of free will in the plan, and now he continued the fight by corrupting humans' free will and harassing God's kingdom. Sermons warned St. George residents that they must be on guard against Satan's ploys. He lured people into sin by giving false revelations or deceiving through false prophets or pandering to the appetites, especially the taste for liquor.[75] But leaders warned that Satan's most insidious attack on God's work was his disruption of the Latter-day Saints' unity. Brigham Young declared that the devil "would get into the hearts of some and break up the bonds of union that God wished to see planted among the saints."[76] Such statements impressed George Laub, who feared the "many fals Brethren making their apearance for Saten is working for his kingdom & Marshaling all the hosts of hell against these Saints."[77]

But just as they were relatively unconcerned with their own sins, so residents refused to be intimidated by Satan. Shielded by their church and strengthened by their determination to improve themselves, the townspeople enjoyed ridiculing the devil and his intrigues. Henry Bigler gleefully noted in 1879 that "the St. George Temple is finished and the devil is mad [because temple ceremonies are] hateful to him!"[78] George Laub quoted Brigham Young's defiance of a satanic windstorm: "let old [Satan] Blow for I presume he has fresh hands at the [bellows] and we can stand the dust and Sand for we can wash those of[f]."[79] Allen Stout, though he blamed Satan for breaking his wife's leg "to hinder [us] from administering for the dead," knew "the Lord will overrul to His own glory, and we will yet be able to do some good, if we are only faithful to our covenants."[80] There was less alarm about Satan than church officials wanted; he was as much a foil as he was a menace. If residents approached God with less confidence than the fellow-laborer image suggests, they regarded Satan with the assurance of people convinced that they could master sin.

The Social World

The human environment for St. George residents was sharply divided into two parts—the Saints and the World. The Saints were, of course, all believing Mormons, identifiable by their common purpose of preparing the earth for God's direct rule at the millennium; the World was almost everyone else, identifiable by their opposition to the Saints' cause.

An attempt to replicate the family on a social scale is frequently at the center of communitarian religion.[81] The Latter-day Saints were among the most deliberate of groups in making the family the model of relationships among members. The Mormon ideal of the family itself originated in Victorian domestic culture. In a world where choice and self-determination were gaining importance, the family now had to leaven its discipline with encouragement of individuality.[82] Two items from the church's publication on families reveal Mormons' view of the delicate balance this task demanded. A poem reminded parents that

> Glorious, bright-eyed, romping childhood
> By each harsh blow is defiled;
> Oh! then treat the darlings gently—
> Spoil the rod and spare the child.[83]

But an editorial warned that "there is an inclination with some to leave children too much to their own ways, to give them too much independence of action, to permit them to make choices in matters in which they are entirely inexperienced, and to encourage a feeling that they are wiser than their parents and are not required by the law of God to give them proper honor and due obedience."[84] Families were expected to encourage as well as to repress, to teach by example while controlling by punishment.

It was the extent to which this concept was to rule public as well as private life that set groups like the Mormons apart. The Mormon church meant to take a thoroughgoing parental role with its members. Latter-day Saints were to use the family as a metaphor for their social and ecclesiastical relations, and for the most part they did. Most diarists in St. George used the terms "brother" and "sister" to refer to anyone from the next-door neighbor to Brigham Young; "father" was used for revered elderly men, and venerated women were sometimes called "aunt." Responding to Erastus Snow's role as the town's spiritual leader, diarists occasionally called his sermons "fatherly."[85] Home teaching, with its regular exchange of aid and surveillance, likewise encouraged familial feelings among Mormons. Charles Walker's description of the teacher's responsibilities reflected both their purpose and his view of the results. His job, as he saw it, was "to cheer and instruct the saints," and he "felt blessed" while doing it.[86]

But families must also cope with disputes and disobedience, and when friction arose between residents the family metaphor became most visible. Church officials wanted members to come to them for parental advice rather than for settling intractable quarrels themselves. George Laub showed his willingness to do so when he found squatters from St. George on a remote piece of his land. They refused his request to leave, and Laub's rejoinder was that "we Should have an Investigation Either by committee or by high Council or by law." Two days later Laub went to Erastus Snow, who advised him to ask the squatters once more to leave; if they were again "not Reasonable then to Sight [the father of one of the squatters] . . . and have him tried for his fellowship."[87] The squatters eventually left without official action. Special committees, home teachers, and the High Council often did step into disputes, using patient guidance backed by the threat of ostracism. Charles Smith reported a High Council session at which "the Council labored with [an accused drunkard] to Shew him his error that he might quit it."[88] Charles Walker, after a visit to settle a domestic quarrel, gave this account: "After showing the order of the Kingdom and preaching explaining and showing them their duties as Husband and wife for about 2 hours, we got them to promise to do better. We then prayed with them and gave them some good counsel and exhortations and left them with a good influence around them."[89]

Of course these attempts at mediation did not always work. When Charles Walker was an arbitrator, he interpreted failed arbitrations as rejections of familial guidance. Walker reported that one person, for example, "did not manifest a teachable spirit," and another lacked "much of the spirit of reconcilliation."[90] Such complaints echo the official warning cited earlier about children who felt "that they were wiser than their parents." Some residents remained defiant in spite of the threat of excommunication, and the unrepentant were occasionally struck off.[91] The chore of continually acting *in loco parentis* strained the authorities as well. Charles Smith, for example, was dissatisfied with having to repeatedly lecture miscreants on their sins.[92] Nonetheless, the church managed to keep a firm hold on civil as well as spiritual discipline. The realistic option for people who rejected the family as a community model was to leave the town; recalcitrance by those who remained was an occasional ripple in a calm sea of cooperation.

In this cooperation the townspeople partly repressed the self-determination that they asserted when they differed from the church regarding sin and death. But only partly: the United Order, which included an attempt to extend the familial metaphor into a full-scale system of common ownership and sometimes communal living, lasted only a year or two in most places. Mormons accepted the family metaphor as an aid to mutual survival in a hostile place, but they insisted on a clear line between private and public families. Individuals and their families continued to guard the ability to ultimately decide their own fate within a culture of mutual cooperation and supervision.

If the Saints usually expected familial behavior from each other, they expected just the opposite from the World. An analysis of the *Pearl of Great Price*, a Mormon sacred document, has found a "Kingdom/World" dichotomy which it suggests was a major determinant of the Mormon identity.[93] The narrative in this document foreshadowed Mormon separatism, it is argued, by portraying an escalating struggle between Joseph Smith and society; Smith and the Kingdom ultimately win by destroying the World's institutions. The analysis contends that by symbolizing a dialectical relationship between their prophet and non-Mormons, the narrative fostered a Mormon self-image based on opposition to the larger society.

It is clear that the church's leadership wanted Mormons to define themselves as a group by their awareness of this opposition. Indeed, persecution by the outside world was the dominant theme at general church conferences from 1860 to 1890.[94] Brigham Young likewise told the St. George residents that "our enemies at present were like a thousand hungry wolves surrounding a Forest in which was one sollitary little Lamb at which they were howling, yelping and barking at[,] . . . all thirsting for its Blood."[95] Another sermon detailed "the endeavors of the wicked to overthrow the people of God."[96] Erastus Snow remarked that "it seems that the Saints must be hated, cast out and reviled by the wicked and unbelieving world."[97]

The leaders explained the Saints' conflict with the World as, in a sense, an aggregate version of individual suffering. Brigham Young insisted that "the Lord has his design in this [persecution by the World]. . . . You all know that the Saints must be made pure, to enter into the celestial kingdom."[98] Like disease and injury, persecution purified the spirit and prevented self-satisfaction. In another sense, however, official doctrine differentiated the Saints/World conflict from individual suffering. As previously mentioned, Mormon theology implied that ill health was a problem solvable by human effort and knowledge, thereby hinting that man might someday earn exemption from this trial. But declarations on Gentile persecution argued that God permitted persecution as a necessary part of the plan of salvation. Oppression had always followed God's chosen people, and "hatred and persecution have been the lot of every man that ever lived upon the earth holding the oracles of the Kingdom of Heaven."[99] But trials would make the Saints stronger, Brigham Young insisted. "Every time you kick 'Mormonism,' you kick it upstairs; you never kick it downstairs. The Lord Almighty so orders it."[100] Oppression was thus to be endured as a necessary ordeal.

But this view of oppression was overwhelmed by St. George residents' conviction that the World's actions heralded the millennium. Persecution by the outside world was part of a final orgy that would soon end in the evildoers' destruction. The harsher the World's persecution and the worse its other vices became, the closer its annihilation as Armageddon approached. Some church leaders actively encouraged this view. The apostle George Smith, for example, called on God to "pour out on [our enemies] the wrath which thou hast in store for them . . . if they will not repent," and asked God to give anti-Mormons a foretaste of the apocalypse: "Control the President of the United States, and those in authority, who purpose evil against thy people; put hooks in the jaws of the enemies of Zion, and turn them from their wicked purposes."[101] Dixie residents were confident that God would indeed do so. Allen Stout wrote that "the days of calamity of the nations of the earth . . . [are] now at hand," because non-Mormons "have turned a deaf ear to the warnings and maltreated the servants of God who have been sent to them; but they will be left without excuse when the judgments of God shall sweep them off." Stout was convinced that the World's oppression of the Latter-day Saints "can only hasten their own destruction."[102] Lorenzo Brown believed that non-Mormons "do cherish and nourish animosities . . . [and] are yet wishing to bring a war of extermination in our midst," but he felt "assured that come what may it will be for the advancement of the Saints, and the Kingdom of God will increase & shine."[103] Commodore Liston, commenting on famine and wars overseas, wrote that "the world is ripe in iniquity, the gosple has come & the world do reject it & wo unto them."[104] The World still concerned St. George residents in 1894, when Charles Walker composed a poem received with "rounds of applause" at the annual Pioneers' Day celebration:

> What Mean these strange sounds of Riots we hear,
> Of bloodshed, and murder, man's hearts fill'd with fear,
> Of floods, fires, and cyclones that sweep oer the Land?
> 'Tis but a begining of those close at hand.
>
> . . .
>
> They've often been warn'd by God's voice from on high,
> To repent, for the Day of his coming was nigh;
> They've regected the Gospel, shed innocent blood
> And will soon feel the wrath and anger of God.[105]

The Saints/World conflict proved to St. George residents that the Saints were God's people and the World was the Devil's. As we have seen, George Laub called anti-Mormons "the hosts of hell," and Charles Walker made clear who supported them:

> They've been fretting their lives
> 'Bout the Mormons and wives
> And neer think of their own social evil,
> But advise guns and arms
> To bring us to terms
> And are backed by their Master the Devil.[106]

The more the World raged, and the more the Saints trusted in God, the sharper the contrast between the two sides became. Possibly because the residents felt that suffering from disease was trial enough, they deemphasized Brigham Young's contention that persecution purified the Mormon character and stressed instead another purpose of the conflict: God allowed the oppression to escalate so that his enemies had a full chance to expose their true natures. Non-Mormons as well as Mormons were considered masters of their own fate, and letting non-Mormons do what they would was God's way of ensuring that they earned their final judgment. As in the *Pearl of Great Price* narrative, the chief concern in St. George about the World was maintaining a clear distinction of right and wrong between Mormons and the outside world. The antagonism between the World and the Saints further defined the residents' role as part of God's select family, reassured them of the rightness of their struggle against persecution, and signaled that the struggle would soon end in victory over their tormentors.

Conclusion: The Mosaic of Beliefs

The people of St. George, applying their free will to their beliefs as well as to their actions, made their worldview a mosaic of official doctrine and popular emendations. Residents accepted the church's familial model for social relations, but they saved space for individual action and resisted when the church encroached on that space. Building on the fundamental optimism of nearly universal salvation, St. George residents sometimes surpassed their leaders in favorably interpreting their lives. Reminders of their sins found a generally unashamed audience, as did suggestions that persecution was a chastisement. With the eager anticipation of committed millenarians, they put great hope in the resurrection as an ideal time of sacred work and relief from enemies and disease. Non-Mormons' self-destruction and persecution of the Saints were unmistakable signs that this long-awaited time was near.

But optimism could not cope with all of life's trials. God was comparatively approachable in Mormon doctrine, but in reality he repeatedly let people suffer and die even when the priesthood petitioned for help. Suffering in fact provoked the kind of resignation and humility that the leadership could not. Residents likewise refrained from inappropriate kinds of optimism. Uninterrupted activity in the spirit world made little sense for most deaths. Instead, the Book of Mormon's declaration that spirits rested until the resurrection far more frequently comforted mourners for the dead.

Their certainty about the efficacy of the will and their uncertain daily existence were the key reasons why St. George's residents modified Mormon theology for their own use. The townspeople felt that they had nearly unbounded potential for good or evil, so they concentrated on their capacity for self-improvement and put limits on social regulation of their behavior. Yet the continuous presence of suffering and death intruded on residents' optimism, tempered their self-assurance about God, and discouraged them from accepting new ideas about the afterlife. No belief system, no matter how deeply held, is immune from the conditions of daily life.

NOTES

1. Leonard J. Arrington, Feramorz Y. Fox, and Dean L. May, *Building the City of God: Community and Cooperation among the Mormons* (Salt Lake City: Deseret Book Co., 1976), p. 255.

2. Nels Anderson, *Desert Saints: The Mormon Frontier in Utah* (Chicago: University of Chicago Press, 1942), p. 422.

3. Reported in A. Karl Larson and Katharine M. Larson, eds., *Diary of Charles Lowell Walker*, 2 vols. (Logan: Utah State University Press, 1980), Mar. 21, 1866, 1: 254 (hereafter cited as Walker Diary).

4. See Arrington et al., *City of God*, chap. 8. Although the Order's communal experiment ran aground on Mormons' individualism, it has been noted that an important Order accomplishment was temple-building, including the temple in St. George. See Leonard J. Arrington, *Great Basin Kingdom: An Economic History of the Latter-day Saints, 1830–1900* (Cambridge: Harvard University Press, 1958), pp. 337–41.

5. Journal of Lorenzo Brown, Huntington Library, San Marino, Calif., Dec. 21, 1862, Jan. 11, 1863; Journal of John Monroe Moody, in Family Record of John Monroe Moody, Huntington Library, p. 11. All items from Huntington Library cited by permission.

6. Walker Diary; Diary of Mary G. Whitehead, in Sketch of the Life of Adolphus Rennie Whitehead and Diary of Mary G. Whitehead, Brigham Young University Library.

7. Journal of William Nelson, Huntington Library, Mar. 28, 1888.

8. See Appendix A.

9. See, for example, Journal of William Nelson, Jan. 6, 1878, Mar. 6, 1887. See also Diary of Mary Whitehead, passim.

10. See Sketch of the Life of Adolphus Rennie Whitehead, Brigham Young University Library; Diary of George Laub, Huntington Library; Journal of George Laub, Huntington Library; Diary of Charles Smith, Library-Archives, Historical Department of the Church of Jesus Christ of Latter-day Saints (hereafter cited as LDS Church Archives); Autobiography of Francis W. Moody, in Family Record of John Monroe Moody, Huntington Library; Journal of Henry Eyring,

LDS Church Archives; Diary of Henry Sudweeks, Huntington Library—all passim.

11. See Diary of Charles Smith, Nov. 22, 1866, Jan. 13, 1869; Walker Diary, Apr. 26, 1864, Aug. 19, 1879, 1: 243, 490. For a description of Mormon worship services and sermons, see Davis Bitton, "Early Mormon Lifestyles; or the Saints as Human Beings," in F. Mark McKiernan, Alma R. Blair, and Paul M. Edwards, eds., *The Restoration Movement: Essays in Mormon History* (Lawrence, Kan.: Coronado Press, 1973), pp. 300–301.

12. See George T. Boyd, "A Mormon Concept of Man," *Dialogue* 3 (Spring, 1968): 55–72; Rodney Turner, "The Moral Dimensions of Man: A Scriptural View," ibid., 72–83; Kent E. Robson, "'Man' and the Telefinalist Trap," ibid., 83–97.

13. Autobiography of Wandle Mace, Huntington Library, pp. 238–39; see also Life Story of Mosiah Lyman Hancock, LDS Church Archives, pp. 71–74.

14. Biographical Record of Martha [Cragun] Cox, Washington County Library, St. George, Utah, p. 28.

15. Autobiography of Wandle Mace, p. 239; Erastus Snow's sermon and Charles Walker's reaction in Walker Diary, Oct. 28, 1883, 1: 619; Story of Mosiah Hancock, pp. 71–74.

16. [Joseph Orton], "The Will," in "The Verprecula" (St. George manuscript newspaper), Brigham Young University Library, June 1, 1864 (emphasis in original).

17. James G. Bleak, reported in Walker Diary, Sept. 11, 1870, 1: 317. A contributor to "The Verprecula" wrote that a man "who improves his time and makes the best of every thing, enjoys life perhapse to a greater degree than any other class of man." [Guglielmo Sangiovanni], "Happiness," June 1, 1865.

18. Record of Martha Cox, p. 25; Life History of Samuel Miles, Washington County Library, p. 17; Walker Diary, Dec. 31, 1873, 1: 380; Journal of Henry Eyring, entries for 1862.

19. Journal of Lorenzo Brown, Jan. 23, 1892; Journal of John Moody, p. 11.

20. Diary of Charles Smith, Nov. 22, 1866.

21. James G. Bleak, "Annals of the Southern Utah Mission," 2 vols., Brigham Young University Library, 2: 509. Charles Walker was an exception: he sometimes made physical and spiritual inventories reminiscent of William Byrd of early Virginia, and he did worry about his occasional sins. See Walker Diary, Dec. 25, 1859, Mar. 12, Sept. 27, 1860, Aug. 24, 1861, Jan. 27, 1867, Aug. 30, Oct. 25, Nov. 18, 1868, Apr. 10, 1869, July 4, 1874, 1: 100, 111, 140, 195, 279, 290, 291, 293, 389. He stands alone, however, among St. George diarists in this concern about sin, and like Byrd his internal evaluations were overwhelmingly positive: roughly three-quarters of Walker's assessments were remarks like "Feel well in body and spirit," and in only a small fraction of the times when he felt "solemn" did he blame it on his sins. For Byrd's daily assessments, see Louis B. Wright and Marion Tinling, eds., *The Secret Diary of William Byrd of Westover, 1709–1712* (Richmond, Va.: Dietz Press, 1941). Cf. "Diary of Cotton

Mather, 1681–1708," *Massachusetts Historical Society Collections,* 7th ser., 7 (1911).

22. On the optimism of the "new theology," see H. Shelton Smith, *Changing Conceptions of Original Sin: A Study in American Theology since 1750* (New York: Charles Scribner's Sons, 1955), chap. 8. On the Mormon view of salvation, see *Doctrine and Covenants,* sec. 76.

23. Alma 40: 11–12.

24. Reported in Walker Diary, June 13, 1892, 2: 742. A poem in the church's *Juvenile Instructor* described the fate of a slain missionary:

> In spirithomes, at times 'mong pris'ners there,
> Teaching the principles of life and truth,
> How grand his mission in that world will be,
> Which in this life he scarcely had begun;
> Preparing captives thence to be set free,
> A savior blest; our called and chosen one.

"Called and Chosen," Oct. 15, 1889.

25. Autobiography of Ann Prior Jarvis, Brigham Young University Library, p. 22.

26. Mary Ann Meyers, "Gates Ajar: Death in Mormon Thought and Practice," in David E. Stannard, ed., *Death in America* (Philadelphia: University of Pennsylvania Press, 1974), p. 133. See also Klaus J. Hansen, *Mormonism and the American Experience* (Chicago: University of Chicago Press, 1981), pp. 109–12. Mormon leaders were in fact not alone in envisioning an active afterlife; some Protestant liberals likewise embraced the concept. When Lyman Abbot's wife died, for example, he pictured her "in her accustomed place, doing her Master's work with her accustomed enthusiasm." Quoted in James J. Farrell, *Inventing the American Way of Death, 1830–1920* (Philadelphia: Temple University Press, 1980), p. 86.

27. See chap. 5 for details on mortality in St. George and other places in the nineteenth century.

28. Autobiography of Henry William Bigler, Huntington Library, Nov. 7, 1874 (Bigler was still living near Salt Lake City at the time); Diary of Mary Whitehead, Feb. 28, 1895.

29. Walker Diary, Mar. 1, 1879, 1: 477.

30. Autobiography of Ann Jarvis, p. 21; Autobiography of Hannah Hood Hill Romney, Huntington Library, p. 4.

31. Journal of Allen Joseph Stout, Huntington Library, Sept. 21, 1888. See also Minerva Snow to Erastus Snow, Dec. 22, 1882, in Andrew Karl Larson, *Erastus Snow: The Life of a Missionary and Pioneer for the Early Mormon Church* (Salt Lake City: University of Utah Press, 1971), p. 661; Autobiography of Francis Moody, entry for 1879; Journal of Henry Eyring, Dec. 31, 1882.

32. Poem "inscribed to Sister K—— by request" in Charles Lowell Walker, Book of Verse, Mormon Biographies File, Bancroft Library, University of California, Berkeley, p. 43. This file is a copy of originals in the Library of Congress.

See also [Martha Cragun], "Lines Written by a Lady of St. George [on the death of Monroe D. Moody]," *Deseret News*, Aug. 21, 1867.

33. Erastus Snow to Julia Snow, Mar. 3, Aug. 10, 1886, in Larson, *Erastus Snow*, pp. 711, 713.

34. Smith to Henry Eyring, Oct. 25, 1866, in Diary of Charles Smith, p. 7; sermon reported in Walker Diary, Dec. 20, 1882, 2: 598.

35. Autobiography of Ann Jarvis, p. 21.

36. Walker Diary, Feb. 2, 1887, 2: 674. See also Erastus Snow to Julia Snow, Aug. 10, 1886, in Larson, *Erastus Snow*, p. 713.

37. See Lewis O. Saum, *The Popular Mood of Pre-Civil War America* (Westport, Conn.: Greenwood Press, 1980), chap. 4.

38. See ibid.; Farrell, *American Way of Death*, chap. 1; Phillippe Ariès, *Western Attitudes toward Death: From the Middle Ages to the Present*, trans. Patricia M. Ranum (Baltimore: Johns Hopkins University Press, 1974), pp. 37–39; Gordon E. Geddes, *Welcome Joy: Death in Puritan New England* (Ann Arbor: UMI Research Press, 1981), chap. 3.

39. Journal of Allen Stout, p. 35.

40. "Lines Written by a Lady of St. George," *Deseret News*, Aug. 21, 1867.

41. "Funeral Hymn," "He is Gone," "In Memoriam," in Walker, Book of Verse, pp. 19, 43, 128.

42. Sermons by Snow and Woodruff, reported in Walker Diary, Dec. 24, 1876, 1: 439; Erastus Snow to Julia Snow, Mar. 3, 1886, in Larson, *Erastus Snow*, p. 711. A frequent contributor to the *Juvenile Instructor* wrote in a collection of stories about a heaven where "the pure in heart rest from their labors." Augusta Joyce Crocheron, *The Children's Book . . . a Mormon Book for Mormon Children* (Bountiful, Utah: privately published, 1890) p. 72.

43. Rufus David Johnson, *J[oseph] E[llis] J[ohnson]: Trail to Sundown* (Salt Lake City: Deseret News Press, 1961), p. 470. "Sweet Rest in Heav'n" is actually the refrain in "Farewell, All Earthly Honors," a hymn which also promises that the dead will "minister in glory / Before the throne of God"; it is revealing, however, that the hymn is remembered in Johnson's biography for its peaceful refrain. At least one of the speakers at Johnson's funeral was also from St. George.

44. Walker Diary, Oct. 17, 1892, 2: 751–52.

45. Journal of Allen Stout, Mar. 13, 1887.

46. Autobiography of Francis Moody, entry for 1884.

47. In 1964, five-year-old boys in the United States could expect to live to age sixty-nine, whereas boys in St. George from 1861 to 1880 could expect to live to sixty-six. See Samuel H. Preston, Nathan Keyfitz, and Robert Schoen, *Causes of Death: Life Tables for National Populations* (New York: Seminar Press, 1972), p. 768, and Table 15 below. These are *period* mortality measures, which give the lifetime experience of a population if it had the same death rates as our briefly observed population. See chap. 5 and Appendix B.

48. See Farrell, *American Way of Death*, chap. 3; Karen Halttunen, *Confidence Men and Painted Women: A Study of Middle-class Culture in America, 1830–1870* (New Haven: Yale University Press, 1982), chap. 5; David E. Stannard, *The*

Puritan Way of Death: A Study in Religion, Culture, and Social Change (New York: Oxford University Press, 1977), chap. 7.

49. On Young's program to encourage women in medicine and other professions, see chap. 5.

50. Journal of Anthony W. Ivins, University of Utah Library, p. 19. See also the blessing given in 1846 to Lorenzo Brown (Journal, Feb. 13, 1846).

51. Diary of George Laub, Mar. 29, 1874.

52. Journal of Allen Stout, Feb. 1880.

53. "He Is Gone," in Walker, Book of Verse, p. 43.

54. Sermon by Brigham Young, reported in Walker Diary, June 8, 1862, 1: 230.

55. M. F. Cowley, *Cowley's Talks on Doctrine* (Chattanooga: B. E. Rich, 1902), p. 168.

56. Thomas F. O'Dea, *The Mormons* (Chicago: University of Chicago Press, 1957), p. 132.

57. John Taylor, *The Government of God* (Liverpool: S. W. Richards, 1852), p. 30.

58. See Sterling M. McMurrin, *The Theological Foundations of the Mormon Religion* (Salt Lake City: University of Utah Press, 1965), pp. 99–109.

59. Linda P. Wilcox, "The Imperfect Science: Brigham Young on Medical Doctors," *Dialogue* 12 (Fall, 1979): 26–36; Walker Diary, Feb. 2, 1873, 1: 360.

60. See Diary of Charles Smith, May 31, 1862, Sept. 2, 1872, Mar. 26, 1883, Sept. 30, 1893; Journal of Daniel H. McAllister, Huntington Library, Oct. 10–11, 1877; Autobiography of Elizabeth Moody, in Family Record of John Monroe Moody, Huntington Library, entry for 1869; Journal of William Nelson, Feb. 6–7, 1878; Walker Diary, Feb. 28, 1879, 1: 477; L. W. Macfarlane, *Yours Sincerely, John M. Macfarlane* (Salt Lake City: privately published, 1980), p. 271; Journal of Allen Stout, Aug. 1866.

61. Walker Diary, Aug. 2, 1877, 1: 463.

62. Before coming to St. George, Henry Bigler had brought in physicians for his father, but "they have done him no good. They don't know what his sickness is." Autobiography, June 22, 1859. Ann Jarvis declared that "I have never employed a doctor but twice in my life for my children, once in England, but I did not let my child taste the medicine, I threw it away." Autobiography, p. 23. See also Journal of Allen Stout, Aug. 1866.

63. Autobiography, Feb. 1, 1891. See also Walker Diary, July 15, 1866, Mar. 28, 1871, Feb. 27, 1873, Dec. 4, 1878, May 31, 1879, Oct. 24, Nov. 7, 1880, Dec. 5, 1883, Aug. 7, 1884, July 23, 1885, 1: 263, 327–28, 366, 472, 486, 2: 506, 508, 623, 634, 652; Autobiography of Francis Moody, entry for 1884.

64. Henry Bigler reported twenty administrations for the sick, with two failures to improve health. Autobiography, passim. Charles Walker reported the results of twenty-nine administrations, nine of which failed. Walker Diary, passim. See also Autobiography of Francis Moody, entry for 1884 (one recipient improves after administration, another dies); Journal of Allen Stout, Feb. 15, 1888 (recipient unchanged); Diary of Charles Smith, Oct. 4, 1863 (recipient dies), June 16, 1879 (recipient improves), July 24, 1879 (recipient dies); Journal

of John Daniel Thompson McAllister, LDS Church Archives, Dec. 22, 1876 (recipient dies), Feb. 23, 1877 (recipient gives birth safely), Mar. 24, 1877 (recipient gives birth safely), July 14, 1878 (recipient improves), July 23, 1878 (recipient improves); Autobiography of William Lang, LDS Church Archives, Sept. 1–5, 1880 (rebaptized for health, improves); Journal of William Nelson, Mar. 24, 1878 (recipient improves); Life of Adolphus Whitehead, Nov. 2, 1879 (recipient dies), Dec. 22, 1879 (recipient improves).

65. In St. George's cemetery records, an attending physician was the reporter in 80 percent of deaths giving the name of the reporting party through 1880. This suggests that physicians played a role in life-threatening disease, if only as pathologists. St. George City Cemetery Records, St. George Branch Genealogical Library.

66. See, for example, Cotton Mather's speculation on the sins that might have caused his toothache, in "Diary of Cotton Mather," July 6, 1681. See also Alan Macfarlane, *The Family Life of Ralph Josselyn, a Seventeenth-Century Clergyman* (Cambridge: Cambridge University Press, 1970), pp. 172–76.

67. Angels as well as the Holy Ghost helped to execute God's will. See Walker Diary, March 28, 1871, July 1, 1887, 1: 328, 2: 678.

68. The Mormon scripture that authorizes administrations specifies that "the elders of the church, two or more, shall be called, and shall lay their hands upon [sick persons] in my name; . . . he that hath faith in me to be healed, *and is not appointed unto death,* shall be healed." *Doctrine and Covenants* 42: 44, 48 (emphasis added).

69. Walker Diary, Feb. 28, 1879, 1: 477. Similar reports are in Autobiography of Henry Bigler, Nov. 5, 1874; Autobiography of Francis Moody, entry for 1884.

70. Autobiography of Francis Moody, entry for 1884.

71. Walker Diary, Mar. 28, 1871, 1: 328.

72. Autobiography of Francis Moody, entry for 1881.

73. Journal of John Moody, p. 13.

74. Walker Diary, June 28, 1879, 1: 487.

75. See ibid., Jan. 5, May 20, Dec. 23, 1860, June 29, 1862, 1: 102, 123, 153–54, 232. Satan's agents are described in [Guglielmo Sangiovanni], "Association of Ideas," in "The Verprecula," May 15, 1865.

76. Reported in Walker Diary, June 1, 1876, 1: 425. See Erastus Snow's similar warning, reported in ibid., Aug. 11, 1875, 1: 413.

77. Diary of George Laub, June 10, 1874.

78. Autobiography of Henry Bigler, Aug. 4, 1879.

79. Diary of George Laub, Mar. 27, 1870.

80. Journal of Allen Stout, May 15, 1885.

81. See Lawrence Foster, *Religion and Sexuality: Three American Communal Experiments of the Nineteenth Century* (1981; reprint ed., Urbana: University of Illinois Press, 1984), pp. 237–40; Louis J. Kern, *An Ordered Love: Sex Roles and Sexuality in Victorian Utopias* (Chapel Hill: University of North Carolina Press, 1981), chap. 14.

82. On the nature of and expectations for the nineteenth-century American family, see Richard L. Rapson, "The American Child as Seen by British Travelers, 1845–1935," *American Quarterly* 17 (1965): 520–34; Carl N. Degler, *At Odds: Women and the Family in America from the Revolution to the Present* (New York: Oxford University Press, 1980), chap. 5; Robert H. Wiebe, *The Opening of American Society: From the Adoption of the Constitution to the Eve of Disunion* (New York: Knopf, 1984), chap. 14; John Demos, "Images of the American Family, Then and Now," in Virginia Tufte and Barbara Myerhoff, eds., *Changing Images of the Family* (New Haven: Yale University Press, 1979), pp. 49–55; Joseph F. Kett, *Rites of Passage: Adolescence in America, 1790 to the Present* (New York: Basic Books, 1977), chap. 5. On the Mormon family, see Leonard J. Arrington and Davis Bitton, *The Mormon Experience: A History of the Latter-day Saints* (New York: Knopf, 1979), chap. 10.

83. Francis S. Smith, "Spare the Child and Spoil the Rod," *Juvenile Instructor*, Apr. 1, 1889. See a similar statement by Erastus Snow, reported in Walker Diary, Feb. 4, 1883, 2: 606.

84. Editorial, *Juvenile Instructor*, June 1, 1889. See also [Joseph Orton], "Self-Government," in "The Verprecula," July 15, 1864.

85. See, for example, Journal of William Nelson, Feb. 25, 1883; Walker Diary, Nov. 4, 1882, 2: 593.

86. Walker Diary, Jan. 20, 1859, 1: 55.

87. Diary of George Laub, Oct. 12–14, 1874.

88. Diary of Charles Smith, Aug. 11, 1883. See also Journal of Henry Eyring, Feb. 5, 1885.

89. Walker Diary, July 14, 1859, 1: 80. This arbitration took place in Salt Lake City but did not differ from Walker's later sessions in St. George.

90. Ibid., Apr. 27, 1860, Mar. 8, 1879, 1: 120, 478–79.

91. See Anderson, *Desert Saints*, chap. 13.

92. Diary of Charles Smith, summer 1881.

93. Steven L. Olsen, "Joseph Smith and the Structure of Mormon Identity," *Dialogue* 14 (Autumn, 1981): 89–99.

94. Gordon Shepherd and Gary Shepherd, *A Kingdom Transformed: Themes in the Development of Mormonism* (Salt Lake City: University of Utah Press, 1984), p. 76.

95. Reported in Walker Diary, Sept. 15, 1870, 1: 318.

96. Bleak, "Annals," 2: 153.

97. Quoted in Larson, *Erastus Snow*, p. 666.

98. John A. Widtsoe, comp., *Discourses of Brigham Young*, (Salt Lake City: Deseret Book Co., 1925), p. 531.

99. Ibid., p. 535.

100. Ibid., p. 538.

101. Bleak, "Annals," 2: 124.

102. Journal, Dec. 5, 1886; entry for Oct. 1866. See also entries for July 4, 1863, Apr. 25, 1886.

103. Journal, Jan. 1, 1862.

104. Diary of Commodore P. Liston, Huntington Library, May 10, 1878. See also Journal of George Laub, entry for 1865; Diary of George Laub, Mar. 14, 1874, Jan. 10, 1875; Walker Diary, passim.

105. Walker Diary, July 24, 1894, 2: 774–75.

106. Ibid., Oct. 2, 1882, 2: 589.

3

Monogamy and Polygamy

Mormon theology has always put an extraordinary value on marriage. "No people hold more sacred the principle of marriage," wrote a church official at the turn of the century.[1] A Mormon theologian declared that "to marry and multiply is a positive command of Almighty God, binding on all persons of both sexes." To neglect this duty was "to fail to answer the end of our creation, and is a very great sin."[2] The church's publication on family life urged that "everything should be done that is possible to encourage marriages, and early marriages, too," warning against "the feeling that marriage must be deferred until comfortable homes and surroundings are secured."[3] Brigham Young assigned "each of the young men in Israel, who have arrived at an age to marry, a mission to go straightway and get married to a good sister."[4] The age to marry was in one's teens: Young insisted that "every man in the land over eighteen years of age take a wife," and on another occasion he reportedly lowered the age to sixteen for men and fourteen for women.[5]

Church leaders in St. George echoed the importance of marriage. Erastus Snow "exhorted the young men and women to get married and fulfill the measure of their creation for there were ten thousands of choice Spirits every year waiting to tabernacle in the flesh."[6] Snow told Joseph Orton, an unmarried shoemaker about to leave for a church conference in Salt Lake City, to "bring back a wife," and he did.[7]

But it was not enough simply to find a spouse. The church expected its members in good standing to marry more than one wife and to have all their marriages "sealed" for eternity. Joseph Smith had explained this duty: "We shall not marry . . . [in heaven] hence it is necessary for us to marry here, and to marry as much as we can, for then in heaven a man will take the wives whom he married on earth; . . . they will be his queens, and their children will be his subjects . . . hence we shall ourselves be gods!"[8] Mormon doctrine taught that through Smith, God had restored the biblical practice of plural marriage for patriarchs. Plural marriage was now a holy commandment for Latter-day Saints who hoped for distinction in this life and exaltation in the afterlife. Subsequent church leaders reaffirmed the eternal blessings of plural marriage, declaring that its purpose was for Mormon men to "have wives and posterity in the world to come and throughout the endless ages of eternity," and repeating Smith's promise that plural wives would become "queens in heaven, and rulers to all eternity" in the hierarchical heaven envisioned in Mormon doctrine.[9] And if they rejected the "new and everlasting covenant" that restored plural marriage, Mormons could expect at least two kinds of trouble. On the one hand, their fellow believers would view them with suspicion. One prominent Mormon, referring to another who refused to marry a second wife, admitted that "we look on [him] as only half a Mormon."[10] But there were also warnings of a more ominous punishment. The apostle George Q. Cannon declared in 1882 that "if I had not obeyed that command of God, concerning plural marriage, I believe that I would have been damned."[11]

The obligation to marry plural wives (known to Mormons and non-Mormons alike as polygamy) was likewise proclaimed in St. George. Erastus Snow insisted in a sermon "that in taking [plural] wives we were only doing as God commanded us, and all that entered into it and carried out the divine behest of the great Eternal would progress and would always be in advance forever and ever of those who had refused and neglected to obey this glorious principle."[12] Other sermons reminded men that monogamists were barred from holding important offices in this life and from glory in the afterlife.[13]

Mothers were told "to teach their daughters and encourage them in [plural marriage]," and all residents were warned that denouncing polygamy was "dangerous work."[14] Church leaders instructed John Macfarlane and Miles Romney to take second wives; though both men and their first wives objected, they eventually obeyed.[15] Marriage was clearly a sacred obligation, and plural marriage was a second and equally sacred duty for spiritually and socially aspiring Latter-day Saints.

How the people of early St. George ordered their marriage-making in light of their spiritual obligations and social circumstances will be examined below. The church had clearly spelled out its members' marriage decisions, but Latter-day Saints were inevitably influenced by the age structure of their population, economic opportunities for new families, and individual preferences.

Monogamous Marriages

The demographic data in this work extend from St. George's first settlement to 1880, and include nearly 400 monogamous men and women. Table 1 shows marriage-age data for these residents compared with other American populations. The "Mormon Demographic History" (MDH) sample includes several thousand monogamous couples from throughout Utah and the "Mormon Trail" that led from Illinois to the Great Basin. Like the MDH couples shown, St. George's monogamists married primarily from the 1840s through the 1870s. The table next shows marriage ages from five eastern states and estimated ages from

Table 1: Age at Monogamous First Marriage in St. George, Mormon Demographic History (MDH) Sample, and Other American Populations

	Mean Age at First Marriage	
	Men	Women
St. George monogamists, married before 1880	24.4	20.0
MDH sample, married 1846–80	24.9	20.4
Western rural areas, married before 1900	25.4	20.5
Kentucky, 1859	25.0	21.5
Massachusetts,		
1860	26.2	23.6
1875	26.4	23.9
Rhode Island, 1860	——	23.3
Vermont,		
1859	25.8	23.0
1870	25.5	23.0
New Jersey, 1868	24.8	22.4

Sources: Calculated from M. Skolnick, L. Bean, D. May, V. Arbon, K. de Nevers, and P. Cartwright, "Mormon Demographic History I: Nuptiality and Fertility of Once-Married Couples," *Population Studies* 32 (1978): 14; Thomas P. Monahan, *The Pattern of Age at Marriage in the United States* (Philadelphia: Stephenson-Brothers, 1951), pp. 157, 161, 174, 176, 207; calculated from Samuel H. Preston and Robert L. Higgs, *United States Census Data, 1900: Public Use Sample* (machine-readable data file), 1st ICPSR ed. (Ann Arbor: Inter-university Consortium for Political and Social Research, 1980). See note 16 below on the basis for estimating first marriages in this sample.

late nineteenth-century rural areas in the West.[16] Mormon men married one or two years younger than the easterners shown, whereas women married anywhere from one to nearly four years sooner than eastern brides. Women's ages in St. George and the larger Mormon region most closely resemble the average for the non-Mormon West.

The table suggests that women's ages were more sensitive to regional differences than were men's. Women married latest in the older and more urban Northeast, earliest in the newly settled rural West, and in between in Kentucky, which was relatively old but also mostly rural. Men's ages varied less systematically; the ratio of women to men, which went from a surplus of women in the Northeast to a small shortage in Kentucky to a considerable shortage in the West, is an intuitive explanation for this pattern. That is, the greater the excess of men, the more women were in demand as brides and the earlier they married.[17] We will see, however, that the explanation is decidedly more complex in the Mormon region.

The Incidence of Polygamy

For all its emphasis on plural marriage, the church did not intend polygamy to be universal among Latter-day Saints. In principle, plural marriage was carefully regulated by the Mormon hierarchy. Church policy required a man who wanted to take a plural wife to consult the president, who would await a divine revelation approving the marriage. Although in practice approval could be granted by lesser authorities, the desire for exclusivity is obvious. Brigham Young clearly specified which members should seek approval: "[Plural marriage] was never given of the Lord for any but his faithful children; it is not for the ungodly at all; no man has a right to a wife, or wives, unless he honors his priesthood and magnifies his calling before God."[18] One indication of good standing in the priesthood was a husband's having entered celestial marriage, that is, having had his marriage sealed by the priesthood so that the union would last through eternity. Although it was closely allied with polygamy in the marriage covenant revealed to Joseph Smith, this sealing was performed for first marriages as well. Celestial marriage was, however, restricted "to those members of the Church only who are adjudged worthy of participation in the special blessings of the House of the Lord."[19] It was thus governed by rules of fitness similar to those for plural marriage. Indeed, in many cases the sealing of a member's first marriage demonstrated his worthiness for a subsequent plural marriage.

In practice this system did not work entirely as intended. Until the St. George temple was finished in 1877, the only place in Utah where marriages could be sealed was the Endowment House in Salt Lake City; travel was thus a problem in having any temple ordinance performed for remote residents. But there is nonetheless a relationship between sealing and polygamy in the marriage data from St. George. Only two of the seventy-six polygamists with church data did not have any of their marriages eventually sealed.[20] Some of the marriages that were sealed showed slippage in the system of approval: eight first marriages were sealed after the second marriage, and five more men had the second marriage sealed but not the first. Yet all but two of the polygamous husbands proved at some time that they were worthy of one of the church's principal blessings. In contrast, 14 percent of monogamous marriages with church data were not sealed during the couple's lifetime. For one reason or another, these couples never obtained the priesthood's eternal sanction for their marriage. It is reasonable to suppose that the husbands in these marriages could not have gotten permission to take a second wife and were thus ineligible for plural marriage. The denominator, or the at-risk population for plural marriage in St. George, will therefore be figured in two ways to measure the prevalence of polygamy. One way will use the full population, to measure polygamy's impact on the whole community; the other will reduce the denominator by 14 percent to estimate the prevalence of polygamy among the population that actually qualified for plural marriage.

The numerator in a plural-marriage rate should simply be the number of polygamists, but simplicity is frustrated by incomplete data in censuses and biases in genealogies. Studies that have used federal censuses place the ratio of polygamists to all husbands at under 10 percent, but census schedules indicate only co-resident polygamous marriages.[21] Polygamy must, in the absence of other sources, be inferred from a census's listing of multiple wives in a household. Yet polygamists often maintained multiple households, some of which were in different towns. When a census is the sole source, name repetition among families makes linking of plural households difficult at best and nearly impossible where such households were in different towns. Former polygamists who at the time of the census had only one wife due to a plural wife's death would likewise be overlooked, as would those who were traveling with one or more wives, leaving one apparently monogamous wife in town.

The St. George data set, on the other hand, was compiled from family group sheets and published genealogies in addition to censuses, and the linkage of plural households is simple and reliable.[22] To calculate a rate similar to the census polygamy rates compiled in other studies, the households in the 1870 and 1880 St. George censuses were classified as monogamous or polygamous from the information in the data set of reconstructed families. Each household received the status of the husband at the time of the census;[23] husbands who maintained several households were counted once. The top half of Table 2 shows the census plural-marriage rates for St. George. Nearly 30 percent of St. George's households were involved in polygamy in 1870 and 33 percent in 1880. This is a much higher polygamous proportion than in any census study to date, but it is more reliable because it makes full use of the supplemental sources available for determining a husband's status. If the number of households is reduced by 14 percent to allow for husbands who were unlikely to enter polygamy because of their inactivity in the church, over 34 percent of all "eligible" households were polygamous in 1870 and nearly two in five in 1880. Either method of defining the denominator produces high rates of plural marriage.

Yet these high rates do not necessarily mean that St. George was atypically polygamous. If we identify polygamists from census schedules alone, without supplemental information, the apparent plural marriage rate in St. George drops dramatically. Twenty-one percent of the

Table 2: Plural-Marriage Rates for Census Households and Husbands

A. Census Households	1870	1880
Monogamous households	126	162
Polygamous households	53	80
Total households	179	242
Polygamous as % of all households	29.6	33.0
Polygamous as % of "eligible" households[a]	34.4	38.4

B. Husbands		
Permanent monogamists in data set		212
Ever-polygamous husbands in data set		101
Total husbands		313
Polygamists as % of all husbands		32.3
Polygamists as % of "eligible" husbands[a]		37.5

[a]Denominator reduced to estimate members who were "unapprovable" for plural marriage; see text.

town's households apparently had multiple wives in 1870, and less than 11 percent are identifiable as polygamous in 1880; the latter figure is quite close to the rates found in other census studies.[24] These rates are doubly misleading: not only are they too low, but they also suggest a falling polygamy rate in St. George when the actual rate shown in Table 2 was rising. Plural families in St. George increasingly split into separate households (which would be apparently monogamous to the analyst using only the census) as families grew and individual circumstances allowed; the actual prevalence of polygamy in the town did not drop. Much of the difference between other studies and St. George's incidence is thus due to the method of identifying polygamists. This is becoming clearer through the record linkage being done by Lowell Bennion for other Utah towns.[25]

Determining polygamy's incidence from sources other than censuses poses different problems. Published genealogies can be biased toward elites, and elite Mormons were especially likely to be polygamists. The analysts who found an incidence of 27 percent in one set of genealogies strongly suspected such a bias.[26] The St. George data set, however, includes nearly 90 percent of the families counted in the censuses and is essentially free of an elite bias.[27] The usual method of figuring polygamous incidence from genealogies is to follow a group of men through their lives, noting which ones took plural wives and which did not. In addition to the above-mentioned 27 percent incidence, two other historians who used genealogies found plural marriage rates of 12 percent and 17 percent of married men.[28] An analogous rate can be calculated for St. George by dividing the husbands in the data set into those who ever married plurally and those who remained monogamous before and after coming to the town. The bottom half of Table 2 shows these incidence rates. Again, just under a third of all men took a plural wife, increasing to 38 percent of all "eligible" men. The close agreement between the two methods shown in the table reaffirms, on the one hand, the unexpectedly high incidence of plural marriage in St. George and underscores, on the other hand, the point that census-only studies are affected by inadequate data.

The best measure of polygamy's prevalence that can be calculated for St. George has not been attempted elsewhere. The St. George data set includes an entry and exit date for each person who lived in the town from 1861 to 1880. It is simple to divide each individual's time in the town (that is, his or her person-years in St. George) into monogamy and polygamy. Table 3 shows the results of this division, which was done in the following ways: married years lived in St. George by a single-wife couple were counted as monogamous; if the

Table 3: Person-Years Lived in St. George by Monogamous-Polygamous
Status, 1861–80

	Husbands	Wives	Children
Monogamy	2041.9	1199.3	6125.3
Polygamy	933.2	1954.6	5923.6
Total	2975.1	3153.9	12048.9
Polygamous %	31.4	62.0	49.2
Polygamous % of			
"eligible" person-years[a]	36.5	72.1	57.2

[a]Denominator reduced to estimate members who were "unapprovable" for plural
marriage; see text.

husband took a plural wife, the status of all spouses changed at that
moment, and they were thereafter counted as polygamous; children
followed the status of their parents, except that they were dropped
from the count after age eighteen because monogamous-polygamous
status carries less meaning for young unmarried adults. If these individuals married and remained in the town, however, they were re-
entered into the tabulation as a new couple. To assess plural marriage's
prevalence among those eligible for church approval, the person-years
for husbands, wives, and children were reduced by 14 percent and the
polygamous rate was re-figured on this base.

Table 3 shows a polygamous incidence for husbands similar to those
found in Table 2. One-third or more of their person-years were spent
in polygamy, which again indicates that polygamy was more significant
than most analysts have assumed. The table also measures the polygamous experience of wives and children. Except for the town of Kanab,
where 30 percent of wives were in plural marriages, polygamy's incidence among women and children has usually been gauged by speculation rather than measurement.[29] The table shows that plural marriage in St. George deeply affected family life. Almost two-thirds of
all wives' experience in the town was in plural marriages, as were half
of all child-years. Taking only those marriages where the husband
could have expected to receive permission to enter polygamy, the data
are even more remarkable. When the husband "magnified his calling,"
almost three-quarters of wives' time was spent in polygamy, and well
over half of children's time was spent with a shared father. This indicates the profound familial impact of what was, for men, a minority
practice. Not quite two in five men in good church standing took plural
wives, but in doing so they transformed the experience of the town's
families. A shared husband was clearly the rule for wives; this meant

that most women were eventually subjected to the strains of divided attention, which led to occasional competition and jealousy among wives.[30]

It also meant, on the other hand, that most wives had the chance to try new household arrangements. The wives in Isaiah Cox's household, for example, "had our work so systematized and so well ordered that we could with ease do a great deal," since they had divided the domestic chores.[31] Having company undoubtedly increased the "sense of pride and importance" that plural wives felt about their status.[32] Polygamy's prevalence also helps to explain the self-assurance of the "system of mutual support" that plural wives formed to make "the difficulties [of plural marriage] more bearable" and to fight the non-Mormons' anti-polygamy campaign.[33] For example, one of St. George's leading plural wives could confidently proclaim that "it looks very odd to me nowadays to see a man living alone with one wife," a situation which she deemed to be "selfish, contracted, drawn up into a nut shell."[34]

A child, especially one born into the home of parents who had been granted the church's ordinances, was likely at some time to find one or more "aunts" and their children in the family. The varied relationships among children and adults in polygamous families is evident in the forms of address in John Macfarlane's household. The second wife's children called the first wife "Ma"; the first wife's children addressed the second wife as "Aunt," but called the third wife by her first name.[35] Table 3 shows that these unfamiliar situations were common among family members in St. George.

Measuring person-years has shown what the static analysis of censuses will not necessarily indicate—the accumulation of polygamous experience in families over time. If a family was monogamous at census time, it did not always stay that way; sooner or later most wives and at least half the children of St. George would be in plural marriages. One study of plural marriage's impact has concluded that its "new social patterns were never thoroughly embedded in the culture," because "monogamy remained the preferred choice of the majority."[36] The data from St. George indicate otherwise, showing that polygamy was deeply rooted in the townspeople's experience.

The Age Pattern of Polygamy

Robert Gardner and Jane McKeown, a nineteen-year-old Canadian woman, were married in 1841 when Gardner was twenty-one and still living in Canada. Ten years later, having moved to Salt Lake City and survived its first impoverished years, Gardner made a plural marriage to eighteen-year-old Cynthia Berry. He married Mary Ann Carr in 1856 and made his last marriage at forty-three to Leonora Cannon. Gardner's four marriages clearly would have raised the hackles of any non-Mormon crusader, but he was actually part of a small group of men who married more than two wives. Yet Gardner did not dramatically deviate from the age structure of plural marriage.

Table 4 shows that eventual polygamists typically made their first marriages at about the same age as monogamists, and they married women slightly older than monogamists' brides. A study that sampled genealogies of Utah pioneers shows similar ages for both brides and grooms. The differences between monogamists and polygamists are less impressive than their similarities: both groups made their first marriages at about the same age, men before their mid-twenties and women around their twentieth birthday.

Like Robert Gardner, most men of St. George waited a decade or more to make a plural marriage, and they ended their marrying by their early forties (Table 5). Only 20 percent of all eventual polygamists in St. George married a plural wife by thirty, but 75 percent of those who married three or fewer wives had all their marriages made by age forty-three; indeed, only two of the eleven men who took a fourth wife did so after forty-six (these figures are not shown in the table). This is a more distinct clustering than among the Utah pioneers, where the age difference between second and third marriages was over twice as

Table 4: Age at First Marriage for Polygamists in St. George and "Polygyny and Fertility" Study

	St. George Monogamists	St. George Polygamists	"Polygyny and Fertility" Polygamists
Men			
Mean	24.4	23.7	23.9[a]
Median	23.4	23.4	——
N	181	84	374
Women			
Mean	20.0	21.0	21.6[a]
Median	19.4	20.2	——
N	199	192	945

[a]In families with three or fewer wives only.
Source: Calculated from James E. Smith and Phillip R. Kunz, "Polygyny and Fertility in Nineteenth-Century America," *Population Studies* 30 (1976): 470.

Table 5: Husband's Age at Sequential Marriages, St. George
Polygamists and "Polygyny and Fertility" Sample

	Husband's Age	
Wife Number	St. George Polygamists	"Polygyny and Fertility" Polygamists
One		
Mean	23.7	23.9
Median	23.4	——
N	84	374
Two		
Mean	38.1	34.9
Median	37.3	——
N	75ᵃ	374
Three		
Mean	40.9	43.3
Median	39.2	——
N	41	147
Four		
Mean	43.9	——
Median	42.2	——
N	11	——

ᵃThere are fewer second than first marriages because some men never
brought their second wives to St. George and some of these had an
unknown marriage date.
   Source: Calculated from Smith and Kunz, "Polygyny and Fertility,"
470.

large as in St. George. It is clear that plural marriages in St. George
were, as a rule, made in a husband's late thirties and were seldom
made more than twice.

The compressed range of polygamous marriage age was probably
due to countervailing forces acting on would-be polygamists. On the
one hand, they undoubtedly felt the intense pressure by the church to
take plural wives. Men who wanted to rise in the church, and to rise
socially, needed to demonstrate the sooner the better their commitment
to God's purposes by becoming polygamists. Moreover, as will be seen
in the next chapter, husbands' heavenly standing depended in part on
the number of their progeny; the sooner they expanded their families
likewise the better. On the other hand, there were equally effective

forces delaying plural marriage. One, as already mentioned, was the need to obtain approval for polygamy. Before demonstrating his commitment to the church by taking plural wives, a man had to show the more basic forms of worthiness. These might include tithing, accepting church assignments, and participating in priesthood activities, all of which helped men qualify for temple ordinances and then for plural marriage. Making oneself known as a faithful Mormon took time, especially when Mormons were largely converts gathered from near and far. There was also a simple economic reason for waiting to marry again—supporting multiple households required money. St. George men who married a plural wife in their twenties were one-third wealthier than those who waited longer to marry plurally ($2,590 on average versus $1,975 in the 1870 census). A third reason for delay, the effective shortage of women in the town, will be discussed shortly. The late thirties were the balance point between hurrying and delaying pressures, when men who keenly felt their church's urging to form plural families had accumulated the spiritual credit and material resources to become polygamists.

Marriage and Parental Authority

Parents in the past controlled the marriage-making of their children in various ways. In colonial America, analysts have found that parents often regulated marriage by parceling out wealth to sons and "marrying off" daughters.[37] By controlling inheritances given to their sons and the choices of their daughters, parents were able to influence when and whom their children married. This influence lessened in some places in the nineteenth century: New England's "parental-run marriage system," for example, became "participant-run."[38] In contemporary Philadelphia, on the other hand, the nineteenth-century family still influenced marriage choices. Data from 1880 suggest that young adults in Philadelphia "did not feel prepared to marry until after they had discharged obligations to their family as well as accumulated some resources to support a family of their own."[39] Marriage data will likewise gauge the influence of parents' priorities versus other determinants of marriage in St. George.

The St. George data set includes about 300 sons and daughters who married from 1861 to 1880. This was a generation primarily born and raised in Mormon households; their parents, the settlers of St. George, were mostly converts who joined the church at various ages. Table 6 shows the timing and range of the children's marriages compared to first-married Philadelphians in 1880. These offspring of St. George

Table 6: Timing and Spread of Marriages, Children of St. George Parents, 1861–80, and Philadelphians, 1880

	Age at First Marriage	
	St. George	Philadelphia
Men		
Mean	23.4	——
1st decile	19.6	21.2
Median	22.8	26.8
Spread[a]	7.9	17.1
N	132	——
Women		
Mean	19.4	——
1st decile	16.7	18.5
Median	18.9	25.0
Spread	6.3	11.7
N	162	——

[a]Range of the middle 80 percent of cases.
Source: John Modell, Frank F. Furstenberg, Jr., and Theodore Hershberg, "Social Change and Transitions to Adulthood in Historical Perspective," *Journal of Family History* 1 (1976): 14.

parents are the youngest-marrying group we have seen: their average ages are even younger than those of the Mormon monogamists and polygamists shown in Tables 1 and 2, most of whom were of the previous generation.[40] The "period of preparation for adult responsibility" was considerably shorter in St. George than in Philadelphia. Sons and daughters in St. George began marrying earlier and concentrated their marriages in a much narrower range than did Philadelphia residents. The range of the middle 80 percent of cases was only half as large in St. George as in Philadelphia; 90 percent of St. George men who married were wed before age twenty-eight and 90 percent of women by twenty-three, whereas both sexes in Philadelphia were in their thirties before reaching the same proportion. Children of St. George families clearly timed their marriages differently from their Philadelphia peers.

St. George itself obviously differed from an eastern city, and we would expect that rural conditions would determine children's marriage-making in a western farming community. Marriage in pre-industrial societies is thought to be especially tied to parental mortality. The death of a father, for example, usually hastens inheritance and thus the chance to marry, but sometimes the death of either parent can delay marriage by requiring older children to care for the family. Whatever the direction of the influence, parental death is seen as a key determinant of marriage.[41] In St. George, however, orphanhood itself was unusual. Over 80 percent of St. George children had both parents alive when they married, a much higher proportion than in other places.[42]

Table 1 shows that parents themselves had married young; combined with residents' reasonably good health in adulthood (see chapter 5) and the even younger marriages of their children shown in Table 6, this meant that both parents usually lived to see most of their children married.

Marriages in St. George that did follow a parent's death must be interpreted cautiously, since it is necessary to subdivide the small number of children who had lost a parent to allow for the more likely orphanhood of older-marrying children whose parents ran a greater risk of dying. A tentative review of such marriages, excluding children who had lost parents after they reached twenty, shows mixed results. The death of the opposite-sex parent had only a slight effect on marriage age, but sons married a year and a half earlier if the father had died, as did daughters who had lost their mother.[43] If they held up with larger numbers, these results would point to inheritance and a "place" in the town's economy as incentives for sons' marriage. Early marriage of daughters without mothers, on the other hand, hints at their expendability when a stepmother or plural "aunt" was available to care for the younger children. When Mary Jane Laub died in 1872, for example, seven children were left in the household; a year later, the oldest daughter married just past her seventeenth birthday. But her father's plural wife lived next door, and the households were eventually combined. These circumstances were typical, since most widowed fathers had remarried or had plural wives by the time their daughters were wed. But the central point is that orphanhood seldom had a chance to affect marriage. Influenced by considerations other than inheritance or possible responsibility for orphaned siblings, most children married well before their family was broken.

Nor did birth order determine age at marriage. When parents deliberately use their wealth to establish their children in marriage, there are often differences in marriage ages between earlier-born children and later ones. Older children benefit from their access to a previously undivided estate and can thus marry sooner.[44] Table 7 indicates, however, that birth order made virtually no difference in marriage ages of either sons or daughters in St. George. The usual relationship between inheritance and marriage did not operate in typically measured ways.

A Sermon in the Desert

Table 7: Marriage Age by Birth Order,[a] Children of St. George Parents

| | Age at First marriage | | |
	First-born	Second-born	Later-born
Sons			
Mean	23.4	23.1	23.1
Median	22.9	22.5	22.8
N	59	37	36
Daughters			
Mean	19.5	19.3	19.3
Median	18.9	18.8	19.1
N	75	40	46

[a]Birth order refers to survivors to adulthood—first-born sons are first *surviving* sons, for example.

But control of marriage might have varied across social or economic classes of families rather than within families themselves. St. George's families were divided in three ways to examine this possibility. Wealth and occupation as reported in 1870 are the best available measures of economic standing in the town. Wealth was measured as real and personal property combined, and occupations were divided here into two broad groups. Professionals and farmers, the highest categories in the Philadelphia Social History Project's occupational ladder, are one group, and artisans and laborers, the lower occupations on the ladder, are the other group.[45] A measure of social and ecclesiastical standing is marriage status. As noted before, men who made plural marriages showed both their commitment to the church and their eligibility for advancement in this life and the next.

Each child who married was thus assigned the wealth, occupation, and marriage status of his or her father; the effects of these variables on marriage age are illustrated in Table 8. The measure of significance indicates whether we can be sure (that is, at least 95 percent certain) that our findings are not due to chance. In the case of wealth and father's marriage type we cannot in fact be certain: there is more than a 5 percent probability that the relationships with marriage age are simply random variation. In other words, neither wealth nor polygamous fathers had an important effect on marriage age, nor did the father's occupation influence a daughter's age. The delay for artisans' and laborers' sons is the only economic influence that is not statistically trivial. These men may have had to work longer than others until they

Table 8: Socioeconomic Variables and Age at First Marriage, Children of
St. George Parents

	MEN	
A. Father's Total Wealth, 1870 Correlation coefficient, wealth and marriage age	$-.15$	
Significance of correlation	$p > .05$	
	Professional or farmer	Artisan or laborer
B. Father's Occupation, 1870 Mean age at marriage	22.6	24.0
N	70	58
Significance of difference of means	$p < .05$	
C. Father's Marriage Type	Monogamous	Polygamous
Mean age at marriage	23.5	22.9
N	70	62
Significance of difference of means	$p > .05$	
	WOMEN	
A. Father's Total Wealth, 1870 Correlation coefficient, wealth and marriage age	.06	
Significance of correlation	$p > .05$	
	Professional or farmer	Artisan or laborer
B. Father's Occupation, 1870 Mean age at marriage	19.3	19.6
N	89	69
Significance of difference of means	$p > .05$	
C. Father's Marriage Type	Monogamous	Polygamous
Mean age at marriage	19.3	19.5
N	69	93
Significance of difference of means	$p > .05$	

felt ready to marry, but even this delay was not lengthy. Artisans' and laborers' sons married no older than the previous generation of St. George residents or any of the other men listed in Table 1. The data in Table 8 reaffirm the general absence of conventional pre-industrial forms of control over marriage-making. Parents did not, or could not, influence their children's marriage by the usual economic calculus; inheritance or other economic matters played no consistently critical part in the town's marriage patterns.

Nor did the larger economy of the town stand in the way of residents' determination to marry early. Though St. George was separated by a continent and a century from eighteenth-century New England towns, in most ways it resembled northeastern villages more than western settlements. Utah's towns underwent a compressed version of New England's history, cohering socially and spiritually in the beginning but soon showing the strains of overcrowding.[46]

Nowhere did these strains surface more quickly than in Utah's Dixie. Washington County had fewer than two people per square mile after two decades, but most of the county's terrain was wasteland. Only land that could be irrigated from a few streams was usable for farming. St. George found itself virtually from the start in the same position as New England towns did after several generations—too many people were dependent on too little farmland. Washington County's average farm size in the 1880 federal census was thirty-eight acres, third smallest in Utah and among the smallest in the United States. Even this average is deceptively high: 45 percent of all farms in the county were under twenty acres, which was barely adequate for an irrigated subsistence farm.[47] Nor was there much potential farmland around St. George. Unimproved land amounted to about eleven acres for each farmer, one-third the potential acreage for farmers in Massachusetts and Rhode Island, the most densely populated states in the nation.[48] Residents with other occupations also depended on farming, and their acreage, much of which was not listed in the census, was undoubtedly also squeezed to the limit.

St. George experienced high fertility in its first two decades (see chapter 4), and its ability to feed new families was clearly limited. From the New England example, we would expect a "safety valve" to have opened when the town's density outgrew its resources. The safety valve describes the drawing off of grown children from overcrowded towns to places where they could make a living.[49] And the valve did indeed open in St. George: the town grew from 1870 to 1880, but the young-adult population in 1880 was one-fourth smaller than the corresponding early-teen cohort in 1870. Young men went to the mines in Nevada or moved elsewhere in Utah to find tillable land or settled in the new Mormon colonies in Arizona, often taking with them wives from St. George. About half of the children who were still residents when they married set up households elsewhere. Yet the town made room for the other half of the newlyweds. As in other American communities, St.

George's growth was a complex process of accommodation as well as out-migration.[50] If the wrench of leaving the close-knit Mormon community was not enough to discourage out-migration, there were increasing problems with the Mormon region's safety valve. Utah's other towns were also filling to the breaking point, and conditions in the newest settlements in Arizona were if anything harder than in St. George.[51] Unless they were to leave Mormon communal life altogether, which most of these newlyweds did not, their chances of making a living might be just as good in town as elsewhere. As a result, St. George offspring started over a hundred new families in the first two decades (nearly 150 sons and daughters stayed in town, but about half married each other). A new husband typically made a living primarily by being mobile: hauling supplies to the silver mines, freighting other goods among the scattered Mormon settlements, or tending livestock, spending "the greater part of his time in the surrounding settlements going from one place to another, wherever he could get a job to work."[52] Having started a family on the earnings from this kind of work, he could hope for a more secure place in the town, perhaps even an inherited or purchased farm. The median age of farmers in St. George did not change from 1870 to 1880, which meant that new younger farmers partly offset the aging of current farmers (death and out-migration of older farmers offset it as well). There were thus some chances for generational continuity in an increasingly crowded town.

But such chances were hardly compelling reasons to start a family. A farm or a trade were still Mormon goals, and the wait for a more secure living, such as it was in an unpredictable desert, could be lengthy.[53] The typical farmer or artisan in St. George was in his late forties, and only rarely did a man have a productive farm or a blacksmith's shop by thirty. In the meantime, young husbands' migratory work strained families. Mary Ann Bentley, whose new husband was away most of the time, recalled living "in constant fear" from transients "coming in to ask for a meal or the privilege of sleeping in the barn" on their way to the nearby silver mines.[54]

Yet whether they waited for a decent living in the town or took their chances elsewhere, St. George's children married young. Male out-migrants and persisters alike typically married not long after reaching twenty-three, and women wed a few months after nineteen. Their marriages were even younger than among the western couples shown in Table 1, without the circumstances that apparently encouraged youthful marriages on the frontier. As we examined earlier, men who took Mormon community life seriously could not simply start a new household on unclaimed land, and opportunities in Mormon towns were limited; nor was there the shortage of women believed to have kept them in demand as brides elsewhere on the frontier.[55]

If economic security was at best an indifferent incentive to marry early, there was nothing indifferent about Mormons' sacred obligation to begin forming families. We have already seen the church's insistence on marriage, which along with the accompanying emphasis on polygamy exerted a double-acting pressure to marry. One way the pressure acted was to create a sense of spiritual urgency about marriage apart from the usual social reasons for finding a spouse. There is a hint of this urgency in a prayer by Francis Moody, single and in his mid-twenties, who asked God to "direct me to one that I might place my affections upon that would prove true."[56] Other residents revealed their awareness of the spiritual imperative when they talked about polygamy. Charles Smith told Henry Eyring that "I wish you were a Polygamist there is Something immensely Godlike in it," and Martha Cragun agreed to become a plural wife because she felt that its promise of celestial glory "was the only source through which I could attain salvation."[57] John Hafen of nearby Santa Clara maintained that he "complied with the celestial law of plural marriage in obedience to the church authorities and because the command was divinely inspired," and that his compliance "[has] brought great blessings."[58] First wives likewise overcame their resistance to sharing their husband by recalling plural marriage's sacred character. Hannah Romney, who "felt that was more than I could endure to have [my husband] divide his time and affections from me," finally "put my trust in my Heavenly Father" and admitted that "it was my duty to sustain [my husband in polygamy]."[59] Ann Jarvis, who was a monogamous wife but whose son was a polygamist, stated that "[I] knew by the Spirit of God that [plural marriage] was True . . . and [I] have always defended the principle."[60] Residents took seriously their church's teachings on the priority of first and plural marriages.

A second and equally potent result of these teachings was a heightened competition for brides. There was no shortage of women either throughout Utah or in St. George to push women's marriage age downward, but the marriage market did not consist solely of single men looking for single women.[61]

Unmarried men had to compete with married men looking for plural wives, and there was thus an *effective* shortage of women wherever polygamy was as common as it was in St. George. We would ordinarily suspect vanity in Mary Ann Hafen's reference to her numerous "young men callers" and in the claim that Margaret Jarvis had "quite an assortment of suitors," but the explanation that the suitors were "both among the single and married men" describes a very real competition. Hafen "was ready to say yes" and she married at nineteen and Jarvis wed at twenty, joining most of their peers.[62] Indeed, two-thirds of daughters of St. George sample families were married by age twenty. Brides were in demand, which made proposals of marriage both likely and urgent while women were still in their teens; it also meant, on the other hand, that most men had to wait for a bride. Only 12 percent of men raised in St. George's families married by age twenty, and the four-year difference between brides and grooms was larger than the difference in any of the eastern states shown in Table 1. Only in the rural West, where there was an actual shortage of women, was the age difference in couples greater than in St. George. This "marriage squeeze" against men reinforced the pressure of the church's urgings and helped create a powerful impulse to marry among St. George's residents.[63]

Conclusion: The Structure of Marriage-Making

Even allowing for hyperbole in their pronouncements, Brigham Young and other leaders clearly wanted Mormons to link marriage with growing up, to pair off and start their own families sooner rather than later. The leadership likewise wanted polygamy to be a goal for faithful Latter-day Saints. Like other nineteenth-century efforts at communal religion, the church attempted nothing less than to impose a public structure on private decisions to marry.[64] The evidence from St. George demonstrates that the church did succeed remarkably in influencing decisions within families. The most notable success was in encouraging polygamy. Measuring the incidence of plural marriage with all available records and not just the federal census shows that polygamy was much more common than previously supposed; this is undoubtedly true for other places as well as St. George. Excluding those families where the husband was probably ineligible for polygamy due to his relative inactivity in the church, almost two-fifths of all husbands' time, nearly three-quarters of all woman-years, and well over half of all child-years were spent in polygamy before 1880. Polygamy was therefore far from the marginal practice that previous studies have described.

But polygamy was not the church's only impact on marriage. Children raised in Mormon households and exposed throughout their youth to Mormon teachings married earlier than their parents, who were largely converts to the church; they also married earlier than in any eastern state with comparable data and earlier than their western neighbors. They did so without the usual incentives to marry early: economic chances were uncertain in the town and equally modest elsewhere in the Mormon region, and there was no sizeable imbalance in the sex ratio. Nor was parental death an important determinant of marriage. Those few who lost a parent in childhood did marry even earlier, but most children married from intact families. Parents' economic circumstances likewise had little to do with their children's marriage-timing.

What did affect their timing, however, was marriage's sacred character. Marriage properly sealed for eternity was a crucial step toward the earthly respectability and heavenly glory promised to faithful Mormons, and plural marriage compounded the benefits. Marriage was meant to precede rather than depend on comfortable circumstances, and so it did for most St. George residents.

Because married as well as single men felt their obligations keenly, young women in St. George could expect plenty of chances in their teens to meet their own obligation to marry. But they could not expect to live comfortably: they might have to endure a migratory husband or, as Martha Cragun did, marry "one of the poorest men and one who had already had two wives, and a family of seven children."[65] Material rewards, however, would come in time; meanwhile, residents simultaneously met their spiritual duty and increased their eternal standing when they married. Whenever residents called polygamy "Godlike" or referred to obedience and blessings in the same breath, they revealed their twofold reasons for marrying when they did. Marriage was obedience to authority, but it was also an act that shaped residents' future by insuring rewards of earthly admiration and heavenly glory. That future might be far off, but a step to take in the present appealed to nineteenth-century people who, as we have seen, were beginning to appreciate having the power to decide their own fate. Yet marriage was only an initial stage in the scheme of self-determination. Childbearing also played a key role in Mormon families' spiritual program.

NOTES

1. M. F. Cowley, *Cowley's Talks on Doctrine* (Chattanooga, Tenn.: Ben E. Rich, 1902), p. 179.

2. Parley P. Pratt, *Key to the Science of Theology* (Liverpool: F. D. Richards, 1855), p. 165. See a similar declaration by the apostle George Q. Cannon, in *Journal of Discourses by Brigham Young . . . and Others*, 26 vols. (1845–86; reprint ed., Los Angeles: Gartner, 1956), 24: 148.

3. *Juvenile Instructor*, Oct. 1, 1892.

4. John A. Widtsoe, comp., *Discourses of Brigham Young* (Salt Lake City: Deseret Book Co., 1925), p. 303.

5. Ibid.; French traveler Jules Remy's report, quoted in Raymond Lee Muncy, *Sex and Marriage in Utopian Communities: 19th-Century America* (Bloomington: Indiana University Press, 1973), p. 133.

6. Reported in A. Karl Larson and Katharine Miles Larson, eds., *Diary of Charles Lowell Walker*, 2 vols. (Logan: Utah State University Press, 1980), Aug. 14, 1881, 2: 564.

7. Autobiography of Joseph Orton, Washington County Library, St. George, p. 15.

8. Quoted in Julie Roy Jeffrey, *Frontier Women: The Trans-Mississippi West, 1840–1880* (New York: Hill and Wang, 1979), p. 163.

9. Wilford Woodruff and Brigham Young, quoted in Stanley P. Hirshson, *The Lion of the Lord: A Biography of Brigham Young* (New York: Knopf, 1969), p. 121.

10. John Taylor, quoted in ibid., p. 122.

11. George Q. Cannon, in *Journal of Discourses*, 23: 278.

12. Reported in Larson and Larson, eds., *Diary of Charles Walker*, Nov. 7, 1882, 2: 595.

13. Ibid., Apr. 26, 1884, Mar. 16, 1881, 2: 629, 543. The apostle George Smith declared that "God comanded [plural marriage] for the Glory and Exaltation of the Saints and all who do not abide his law will be damed." Sermon reported in Journal of George Laub, Huntington Library, San Marino, Calif., Mar. 27, 1870. All items from Huntington Library cited by permission.

14. James G. Bleak, "Annals of the Southern Utah Mission," 2 vols., Brigham Young University Library, 2: 177; Autobiography of Francis W. Moody, in Family Record of John Monroe Moody, Huntington Library, Nov. 4, 1884.

15. L. W. Macfarlane, *Yours Sincerely, John M. Macfarlane* (Salt Lake City: privately published, 1980), pp. 79–81; Autobiography of Hannah Hood Hill Romney, Huntington Library, p. 4. Romney lived in Salt Lake City at the time but moved to St. George later that year.

16. The estimate for the West is from a 1/750 sample of the 1900 census in places of 2,500 or fewer people in western states except Utah (Samuel H. Preston and Robert L. Higgs, *United States Census Data, 1900: Public Use Sample* [machine-readable data file], 1st ICPSR ed. [Ann Arbor: Inter-university Consortium for Political and Social Research, 1980]). The marriages in this subsample took place on the average in the mid-1880s. The actual mean age at marriage from the sample is 28.4 for men and 22.5 for women, but the marriage data in the census include *all* marriages, not just first ones. To allow for remarriages, the ratio of second to first marriages at each age from St. George was subtracted from the western data. The result is an estimate of first marriages by age for the western states, after marriages under age fourteen are excluded as misreporting and those after forty excluded as primarily remarriages. The estimate depends, of course, on the applicability of remarriage ratios from St. George to the rest of the West, but remarriage apparently happened as quickly in St. George as elsewhere on the frontier. For discussions of frontier remarriage, see James E. Davis, *Frontier America, 1800–1840: A Comparative Demographic Analysis of the Settlement Process* (Glendale, Calif.: Arthur H. Clark,

1977), pp. 54–56; Jack E. Eblen, "An Analysis of Nineteenth-Century Frontier Populations," *Demography* 2 (1965): 399–413. Other studies have found frontier ages at marriage similar to the estimate given here. A small sample from Texas in 1850 shows an average age of 26.3 for men and 19.4 for women at first marriage; the sex ratio in the twenties was 389. Calculated from Blaine T. Williams, "The Frontier Family: Demographic Fact and Historical Myth," in Harold M. Hollingsworth and Sandra L. Myres, eds., *Essays on the American West* (Austin: University of Texas Press, 1969), pp. 50, 57. Williams also questions the assumption of quick remarriage for widows on the frontier. A sample from late nineteenth-century Dakota Territory shows a median age at first marriage of 26.4 for men and 21.7 for women. John C. Hudson, "The Study of Western Frontier Populations," in Jerome O. Steffen, ed., *The American West: New Perspectives, New Dimensions* (Norman: University of Oklahoma Press, 1979), p. 45.

17. The average sex ratio in the northeastern states shown in the table was 91 men per 100 women in their twenties for the years shown; in Kentucky in 1860 the ratio was 107 men per 100 women; in the western rural areas in 1900 it was 153 and was probably even higher when the marriages occurred. For a discussion of the sex ratio's effects on society, see Marcia Guttentag and Paul F. Secord, *Too Many Women? The Sex Ratio Question* (Beverly Hills, Calif.: Sage, 1983).

18. Quoted in Gustive O. Larson, *The "Americanization" of Utah for Statehood* (San Marino, Calif.: Huntington Library, 1971), p. 40. See a similar declaration by Heber Kimball, in *Journal of Discourses*, 5: 30.

19. James E. Talmage, *A Study of the Articles of Faith*, rev. ed. (Salt Lake City: Church of Jesus Christ of Latter-day Saints, 1968), pp. 445–46.

20. Tabulations of church ordinance data for individuals excludes families reconstructed without a family group sheet. Such families are about one-fourth of all families in the St. George sample. See Appendix B.

21. Two studies have used censuses for determining polygamous incidence. Nels Anderson, *Desert Saints: The Mormon Frontier in Utah* (Chicago: University of Chicago Press, 1942), pp. 394–99, worked from manuscript census schedules for Washington County from 1860 to 1880. In 1860 this study finds that 8.5 percent of the county's households were polygamous; for 1880, the text (p. 394) refers to an 8 to 10 percent polygamy rate but the table on p. 399 produces a plural-marriage rate of 21 percent. James E. Smith and Phillip R. Kunz, "Polygyny and Fertility in Nineteenth-century America," *Population Studies* 30 (1976): 471, used aggregate census figures and an estimate of total polygamists to arrive at an 8.8 percent incidence.

22. See Appendix B.

23. Former polygamists who now had only one wife because of death or divorce are nonetheless counted in the table as polygamists, since the loss of a plural wife did not necessarily end the impact of polygamy on a family; for one thing, a widowed polygamist still had children of different wives in his household. There were only a few such cases in each census.

24. The 1870 census does not actually list the marital status of household members, so for this estimate all women over age twenty in a household were counted as wives. This inevitably includes a number of daughters as supposed plural wives; the 1880 figure is much closer to a "true" polygamy incidence calculated from the census.

25. Lowell "Ben" Bennion, "The Incidence of Mormon Polygamy in 1880: 'Dixie' versus Davis Stake," *Journal of Mormon History* 11 (1984): 27–42, shows five settlements in southern Utah and Nevada where more residents (men, women, and children combined) were in polygamous families than the 39.9 percent incidence he finds in St. George; in Davis County, north of Salt Lake City, five of the nine wards had more than 20 percent of their population in polygamy, though the county's average incidence was somewhat below the southern Utah figure. Other towns being surveyed show plural marriage rates that cover a wide range and occasionally exceed St. George's incidence.

26. Smith and Kunz, "Polygyny and Fertility," p. 470.

27. See Appendix B.

28. Stanley S. Ivins, "Notes on Mormon Polygamy," *Western Humanities Review* 10 (1956): 230 (Ivins's figure refers to Sanpete and Emery counties); Dean L. May, "People on the Mormon Frontier: Kanab's Families of 1874," *Journal of Family History* 1 (1976): 172. The incidence for Kanab, though it is based on genealogies, reports the current status of each household rather than whether it ever became polygamous. The author notes the possibility that the incidence may have actually been higher due to husbands with wives in other towns. Ivins's study has been especially influential, serving as the basis for the general belief among historians of Mormonism that polygamy involved 10 percent or less of men.

29. The figure for Kanab is in Leonard J. Arrington, Feramorz Y. Fox, and Dean L. May, *Building the City of God: Community and Cooperation among the Mormons* (Salt Lake City: Deseret Book Co., 1976), p. 229. May, "Mormon Frontier," 172, notes that 24 percent of *all* Kanab residents were in plural families, and Bennion, "Incidence of Polygamy," likewise gives polygamy rates for all residents. Speculation on women and children is found in Ann Vest Lobb and Jill Mulvay Derr, "Women in Early Utah," in Richard D. Poll, Thomas G. Alexander, Eugene E. Campbell, and David E. Miller, eds., *Utah's History* (Provo: Brigham Young University Press, 1978), p. 349, who estimate that 25 percent of women lived in polygamy; Leonard J. Arrington and Davis Bitton, *The Mormon Experience: A History of the Latter-day Saints* (New York: Knopf, 1979), p. 199, who estimate that 12 percent of women and 10 percent of children were in plural families; Jeffrey, *Frontier Women*, p. 165, who argues that "women in polygamous marriages were not typical . . . but extraordinary."

30. Jeffrey, *Frontier Women*, pp. 171–72; Kimball Young, *Isn't One Wife Enough?* (New York: Henry Holt, 1954), chap. 14; Autobiography of Hannah Romney, p. 5; Jessie L. Embry, "Effects of Polygamy on Mormon Women," *Frontiers* 7:3 (1984): 56–61.

31. Biographical Record of Martha Cox, Washington County Library, p. 32. See also Macfarlane, *Yours Sincerely*, p. 90; Jeffrey, *Frontier Women*, p. 169;

A Sermon in the Desert

"Journal and Diary of Robert Gardner," in Kate B. Carter, comp., *Heart Throbs of the West* 10 (1949): 311; Life Sketch of Mary Ann Mansfield Bentley, Brigham Young University Library, pp. 9–10; Stephanie Smith Goodson, "Plural Wives," in Claudia L. Bushman, ed., *Mormon Sisters: Women in Early Utah* (Cambridge, Mass.: Emmeline Press, 1976), pp. 103–4.

32. Lawrence Foster, *Religion and Sexuality: Three American Communal Experiments of the Nineteenth Century* (1981; reprint ed., Urbana: University of Illinois Press, 1984), p. 212.

33. Lobb and Derr, "Women in Utah," p. 350.

34. Artimesia Snow, quoted in Andrew Karl Larson, *Erastus Snow: The Life of a Missionary and Pioneer for the Early Mormon Church* (Salt Lake City: University of Utah Press, 1971), pp. 747–48.

35. Macfarlane, *Yours Sincerely*, pp. 81, 90.

36. Jeffrey, *Frontier Women*, p. 169.

37. Daniel Scott Smith, "Parental Power and Marriage Patterns: An Analysis of Historical Trends in Hingham, Massachusetts," *Journal of Marriage and the Family* 35 (1973): 419–28; Philip J. Greven, Jr., *Four Generations: Population, Land, and Family in Colonial Andover, Massachusetts* (Ithaca, N.Y.: Cornell University Press, 1970), chaps. 4, 6, 8; Daniel Blake Smith, "Mortality and Family in the Colonial Chesapeake," *Journal of Interdisciplinary History* 8 (1978): 403–27; Allan Kulikoff, *Tobacco and Slaves: The Development of Southern Cultures in the Chesapeake, 1680–1800* (Chapel Hill: University of North Carolina Press, 1986), pp. 49–56.

38. Smith, "Parental Power," p. 426. For evidence of a less controlled marriage structure developing earlier, see David Levine, " 'For Their Own Reasons': Individual Marriage Decisions and Family Life," *Journal of Family History* 7 (1982): 255–64; James M. Gallman, "Determinants of Age at Marriage in Colonial Perquimans County, North Carolina," *William and Mary Quarterly*, 3d ser., 39 (1982): 176–91.

39. John Modell, Frank F. Furstenberg, Jr., and Theodore Hershberg, "Social Change and Transitions to Adulthood in Historical Perspective," *Journal of Family History* 1 (1976): p. 18. For an argument that parental control continued in nineteenth-century rural America as well, see James A. Henretta, "Families and Farms: *Mentalité* in Pre-industrial America," *William and Mary Quarterly*, 3d ser., 35 (1978): 3–32.

40. The marriages of some of the children are counted in both Tables 1 and 6 because they stayed in town after marrying and thus became parents eligible for the data set. Nonetheless, more than two-thirds of monogamists and about 90 percent of polygamists in Tables 1 and 4 are in-migrant parents who married primarily in the 1840s and 1850s. St. George children were discouraged from making plural marriages by the "Raid" of the 1880s. See chaps. 1 and 6.

41. See G. Ohlin, "Mortality, Marriage, and Growth in Pre-industrial Populations," *Population Studies* 14 (1961): 190–97; D. B. Smith, "Mortality and Family"; D. S. Smith, "Parental Power"; Levine, "For Their Own Reasons." For an example of older children presiding over broken families on the American frontier, see Williams, "Frontier Family," pp. 60–62.

42. Less than one-third of children had both parents alive at maturity in two studies of colonial Virginia. See D. B. Smith, "Mortality and Family," p. 422; Darrett B. Rutman and Anita H. Rutman, " 'Now-Wives and Sons-in-Law': Parental Death in a Seventeenth-Century Virginia County," in Thad W. Tate and David L. Ammerman, eds., *The Chesapeake in the Seventeenth Century: Essays on Anglo-American Society* (Chapel Hill: University of North Carolina Press, 1979), p. 161. Only 38 percent of children had both parents alive at age twenty-one in eighteenth-century Prince George's County, Maryland. Kulikoff, *Tobacco and Slaves*, p. 170. In a nineteenth-century French village, just over a third of newlyweds had both parents alive. Katherine A. Lynch, "Marriage Age among French Factory Workers: An Alsatian Example," *Journal of Interdisciplinary History* 16 (1986): 422. About a fourth of brides and grooms in pre-industrial Shepshed, England, had lost their fathers. Levine, "For Their Own Reasons," p. 257. The comparable figure for St. George is 7 percent.

43. These are the average marriage ages for children with and without parents alive, excluding cases where a parent died after the child's twentieth birthday.

	Age at Marriage	N
Men		
Father dead	21.6	4
Mother dead	22.7	15
Both parents alive	23.2	102
Women		
Father dead	20.0	11
Mother dead	17.9	17
Both parents alive	19.4	131

No child had lost both parents before marriage. In the French village of Dornach, the father's death made virtually no difference for sons' marriages and the mother's death delayed them slightly; for daughters, either the father's or the mother's death delayed marriage about a year. When both parents had died, the delay was still longer for both sons and daughters (again, all these results exclude marriages where parents died after the child reached twenty). Lynch, "Marriage Age," p. 423.

44. In early Andover, Massachusetts, first sons married three years younger than second sons and two years younger than last sons. Greven, *Four Generations*, p. 37. In colonial Hingham, first sons married brides from wealthier families than did later sons. Smith, "Parental Power," p. 424.

45. Theodore Hershberg and Robert Dockhorn, "Occupational Classification," *Historical Methods Newsletter* 9 (1976): 59–98. Fathers not present in St. George in 1870 were assigned their 1880 occupation instead.

46. See Dean L. May, "The Making of Saints: The Mormon Town as a Setting for the Study of Cultural Change," *Utah Historical Quarterly* 45 (1977): 75–92.

47. In 1894, concerned about the decline of the self-sufficient Mormon farming village, church president Wilford Woodruff sang the praises of "My Twenty-Acre Farm." Woodruff maintained that twenty irrigated acres near Salt Lake City had supported his family for decades, producing forty or more bushels of wheat to the acre. But Woodruff's was not the usual case: Washington County's farms produced only fourteen bushels of wheat per acre in 1880 and the yield was just twenty bushels in 1900. Woodruff's speech in Utah Irrigation Commission, *Irrigation in Utah* (Salt Lake City, 1895), pp. 65–68. See also Leonard J. Arrington and Dean May, "'A Different Mode of Life': Irrigation and Society in Nineteenth-Century Utah," *Agricultural History* 49 (1975): 3–20.

48. This estimate of potential farmland per farmer is a modified version of a calculation made by Dean May in "Making of Saints," p. 85. Using an estimate of landowners and the 1880 federal census of agriculture, May estimated 14.5 acres of improved land and three acres unimproved per landowner in Kane County. The St. George estimate uses farmers only, who were less than one-fourth of household heads, instead of May's two-thirds estimate which includes all owners of farms and small household parcels. Computed by May's method, unimproved acreage in Washington County would have been 4.5 instead of 11.2.

49. The best discussion of the safety valve and its dynamics is Darrett B. Rutman, "People in Process: The New Hampshire Towns of the Eighteenth Century," *Journal of Urban History* 1 (1975): 268–92.

50. This more recent view of communities' evolution is in Rutman, "Assessing the Little Communities of Early America," *William and Mary Quarterly*, 3d ser., 43 (1986): 163–78.

51. On other Utah towns' overcrowding, see Leonard J. Arrington, *Great Basin Kingdom: An Economic History of the Latter-day Saints, 1830–1900* (Cambridge: Harvard University Press, 1958), p. 354. On conditions in the Arizona settlements, see Charles S. Peterson, *Take Up Your Mission: Mormon Colonizing along the Little Colorado River, 1870–1900* (Tucson: University of Arizona Press, 1973).

52. Life Sketch of George Frederick Jarvis, Brigham Young University Library, p. 5. See also Memories of George W. Fawcett, Library-Archives, Historical Department of the Church of Jesus Christ of Latter-day Saints (hereafter cited as LDS Church Archives).

53. Dean L. May, "Towards a Dependent Commonwealth," in Poll et al., eds., *Utah's History*, pp. 217–41.

54. Sketch of Mary Ann Bentley, p. 16. She was living on a small farm on the outskirts of St. George while her husband hauled goods for his father's store.

55. There were in fact more women in their twenties in St. George than men in 1870; the ratio evened in 1880. Looking at the prime marriage ages, there were likewise more women aged sixteen to twenty than men twenty-one to twenty-five in both censuses.

56. Autobiography of Francis Moody, entry for 1882. Moody had recently moved from St. George to Arizona with his father.

57. Oct. 25, 1866, in Diary of Charles Smith, LDS Church Archives, pp. 29–30; Biographical Record of Martha Cox, p. 27.

58. Quoted in Mary Ann Hafen, *Recollections of a Handcart Pioneer of 1860: A Woman's Life on the Mormon Frontier* (Lincoln: University of Nebraska Press, 1983), p. 91.

59. Autobiography of Hannah Romney, p. 4.

60. Autobiography of Ann Prior Jarvis, Brigham Young University Library, p. 22.

61. Utah's sex ratio in the twenties was 100 in 1870 and 109 in 1880 (counting non-Mormons as well as Mormons). Smith and Kunz, "Polygyny and Fertility," p. 469. On St. George's sex ratio, see note 55 above.

62. Hafen, *Recollections*, pp. 49–50; History of Margaret Jarvis, Huntington Library, p. 3.

63. On the nature and effects of a marriage squeeze, see Robert Schoen, "Measuring the Tightness of a Marriage Squeeze," *Demography* 20 (1983): 61–78.

64. See Foster, *Religion and Sexuality;* Muncy, *Sex and Marriage;* Louis J. Kern, *An Ordered Love: Sex Roles and Sexuality in Victorian Utopias* (Chapel Hill: University of North Carolina Press, 1981).

65. Biographical Record of Martha Cox, p. 27.

4

Tabernacles for Waiting Spirits

Once they were married, whether for the first or the third time, Mormons were expected to "fulfill the measure of their creation" by producing children. As we have observed, the Latter-day Saints believe that spirits wait in heaven for their chance at earthly self-improvement. The church insisted that the primary purpose of marriage was the embodiment of spirits. The *Doctrine and Covenants* made it clear that the earth was to be "filled with the measure of man, according to his creation before the world was made."[1] A Mormon theologian proclaimed: "Let the waiting spirits come! Let the children be born unto the earth! Let fatherhood and motherhood be the most honored of all the professions on earth."[2] Brigham Young declared that "it is the duty of every righteous man and woman to prepare tabernacles for all the spirits they can," and implied that couples could hurry the millennium by having children, since the resurrection would not start until the last waiting spirit came to earth.[3] In St. George, a sermon reminded residents that God "required the regeneration of the Human family," and another described marriages as "the channels which God had appointed for the bringing forth of the children of Men."[4] Charles Walker wrote a wedding poem in 1883 which reminded a couple of their duty:

> And may you twain thrice happy be,
> Enjoying life's short lease;
> The word to you is multiply,
> Replenish and increase.[5]

The Latter-day Saints were not unique in making childbearing the principal goal of marriage; other nineteenth-century Christian churches likewise insisted on the importance of marital procreation. But other churches kept reproductive issues largely out of public view, preferring "to say as little as possible" about procreation and birth control.[6] Mormonism, on the other hand, made fertility into the explicit system of obligations and rewards that one analyst has called the "quantum theory of salvation."[7] As related before, having their marriages sealed for eternity by the priesthood was a minimum requirement for devout Mormons to qualify for heaven's highest kingdom. Within that kingdom, however, there were degrees of glory, and parents' exaltation was proportional to their progeny: "Our children are considered stars in a mother's crown, and the more there are, if righteous, the more glory they will add to her and their father's eternal kingdom, for their parents on earth, if they continue righteous, will eventually become as Gods to reign in glory."[8] On the other hand, a couple without a large family "was bound to end up in a lesser social sphere both here and in the hereafter," because childbearing was "the *sine qua non* of the obligation and the glory which parents anticipate both in this world and the next."[9] Mormonism thus transcended conventional Christian pronatalism to promise that righteous parents could directly enhance their heavenly prospects by embodying waiting spirits. Plural marriage, of course, further raised a husband's status by dramatically increasing his progeny.

Mormons are well known for responding to their church with high fertility, keeping their birthrate well above the national level.[10] Yet St. George was among the most forbidding places in the Mormon region; raising children, like most activities in the southwestern desert, took exceptional stamina and determination. Polygamy complicated the task, adding more spouses for child care but also multiplying the mouths for one husband to feed.

Monogamous Fertility

Table 9 shows age-specific fertility rates and natural fertility measures for St. George monogamous marriages.[11] The seven age-specific rates are the number of births per thousand married woman-years in St. George in each five-year age range. The total fertility rate is the number of births each woman would have had if she had married at twenty and experienced the rates listed until age fifty (the fifteen-to-nineteen group is excluded from the rate because its fertility is heavily weighted toward the last year or two).

The measures of natural fertility test the conformity of observed fertility rates to a set of rates defined as "natural," that is, which show no evidence of deliberate fertility limitation.[12] The test compares the rates in question with both the natural fertility rates and the typical age pattern of fertility control. M, the comparative level of fertility, shows the overall level of fertility compared to the natural rates. The index of fertility control, *m*, shows whether the age structure of fertility is more like the natural fertility rates or like the typical pattern of family

Table 9: Age-Specific Fertility and Natural Fertility Measures, St. George Monogamous Marriages, 1861–80

	Births per 1,000 Woman-Years							
	15–19	20–24	25–29	30–34	35–39	40–44	45–49	TFR[a]
St. George	445	415	371	407	339	169	19	8.6
"Natural" Fertility	——	460	431	395	322	167	24	9.0

Natural Fertility Measures	M	m	MSE
St. George	.89	−.12	.002

[a]TFR = Total Fertility Rate (rates above age twenty expressed as a decimal, then summed, then multiplied by 5); M = level of fertility compared to natural rates; m = index of fertility control; MSE = Mean Square Error. See Ansley J. Coale and T. James Trussell, "Technical Note: Finding the Two Parameters That Specify a Model Schedule of Marital Fertility," *Population Index* 44 (1978): 203–13.

limitation. An m value of zero shows that the rates being analyzed conform precisely to the gradual decline of childbearing with age that happens under natural fertility. Negative values show natural fertility that falls more gradually with age than do the standard natural rates. Positive values of m above .20, on the other hand, suggest that family limitation, with its telltale drop in fertility after the wife reaches thirty, is being practiced.

Table 9 clearly illustrates that St. George monogamous couples had natural fertility. The negative value of m shows that childbearing declined even more slowly with age than it did in the standard natural groups.[13] The mean square error (MSE in the table) is another measure of natural fertility. An MSE of 0 shows a perfect fit to the natural fertility rates, .005 is a "mediocre" fit, and .01 is a "terrible" fit.[14] For St. George couples the MSE is below .005, again indicating natural fertility.

Table 10 shows fertility rates and natural fertility measures for two other American populations and an average for thirty-eight West European groups. The Mormon Demographic History (MDH) sample is of particular interest since its 1860 through 1879 rates (combined in the table) show the fertility of several thousand contemporaries of the St. George sample. The MDH group's total fertility rate of 9.2 births per woman is higher than St. George's, but there are subtle differences in sample construction that account for much of the fertility difference.

To have gotten into the MDH sample, a couple must have a family group sheet in the Latter-day Saints' archives and must have had a vital event on the Mormon trail or in Utah.[15] Couples who were married elsewhere and came to Utah during the wife's reproductive period, but

Table 10: Fertility Measures for Selected Populations

Population	Births per 1,000 Woman-Years							
	15–19	20–24	25–29	30–34	35–39	40–44	45–49	TFR
MDH Sample, 1860–79	455	464	426	386	332	196	30	9.2
Philadelphia Gentry,								
1700–1800	NA	521	484	423	341	212	33	10.1
1801–75	NA	448	411	332	248	80	12	7.7
38 West European Populations,								
17th-19th cent.	NA	475	450	398	316	158	NA	9.0[a]

Natural Fertility Measures	M	m	MSE
MDH Sample	.97	−.09	.002
Phila. Gentry,			
1700–1800	1.09	−.06	.004
1801–75	1.07	.46	.012
West Europ. Groups	1.05	.07	.000

[a]Assumes that 45–49 rate is zero.

Sources: Calculated from G. P. Mineau, L. L. Bean, and M. Skolnick, "Mormon Demographic History II: The Family Life Cycle and Natural Fertility," *Population Studies* 33 (1979): 432 (average of 1860–64 through 1875–79 rates); Louise Kantrow, "Philadelphia Gentry: Fertility and Family Limitation among an American Aristocracy," ibid., 34 (1980): 25; Daniel Scott Smith, "A Homeostatic Demographic Regime: Patterns in West European Family Reconstruction Studies," in Ronald Demos Lee, ed., *Population Patterns in the Past* (New York: Academic Press, 1977), p. 23.

whose sheet lists no vital events in Utah, would thus have escaped the MDH sample; a few families in St. George fit this description. A more important discrepancy between the St. George and MDH samples involves couples who simply have no family group sheet. A number of such marriages were reconstructed from published genealogies when their presence in St. George was known but no family records were found in the LDS archives (see Appendix B). Both these types of exclusions from the MDH sample primarily involve childless marriages, since births were among the qualifying vital events for the MDH sample on the one hand, and since births increase the chance that a descendant has filed a family sheet on the other. Omission of childless couples produces understated woman-years at risk and overstated fertility rates. Indeed, if childless couples (that is, without births from 1861 to 1880) who have no records in the LDS archives are excluded from the St. George fertility calculations, the total fertility rate for monogamous marriages rises from 8.6 to 8.9. The relationship of St. George's fertility to that of the entire Mormon region will not be truly known until the effects of sample design are disentangled from genuine differences in childbearing.

The eighteenth-century Philadelphia gentry, with more than ten births per woman, had higher fertility than either of the Utah samples, which underscores the drop in the gentry's rate to less than eight births in the nineteenth century. The west European rate of nine births represents populations whose total fertility rate varied from six births to eleven but who nonetheless did not control their fertility. The nineteenth-century Philadelphia data, on the other hand, reveal a group that was evidently limiting its family size. This population's childbearing dropped rapidly after the wife's early twenties, producing fertility measures that indicate deliberate contraception. St. George's monogamous couples clearly resemble the other natural-fertility populations more than they do this group.

Polygamous Fertility

Although one of the underpinnings for Mormon polygamy was that it would produce more children for God's kingdom, historians of Mormonism have been nearly unanimous in arguing that it had just the opposite effect.[16] The most influential of the fertility comparisons examined more than 6,000 marriages and found that monogamous wives averaged eight births per wife, compared to just under six for plural wives.[17] Another study, focusing on Mormon bishops, reported that monogamous wives bore about nine children on average, whereas polygamous wives had fewer than eight births each.[18] An analysis of Utah pioneers found that monogamous marriages averaged 7.8 children versus 7.5 births in plural marriages.[19] Most other historians have accepted these findings, attributing them to causes ranging from "older and hence less virile" husbands to deliberate family limitation.[20]

Table 11 shows fertility measures for polygamous marriages in St. George. The results are startling: the total fertility rate in these marriages is 8.7 children per woman, slightly *higher* than the monogamous fertility shown in Table 9. This clearly contradicts the prevailing wisdom about polygamous fertility. While other studies have found significantly lower fertility in plural marriages, St. George polygamous marriages show natural fertility at the same overall level as in monogamy. St. George could, of course, be a special case, a deviation from the usual Mormon pattern of fertility. But there are fundamental problems with the previous studies which have affected their findings.

The first two studies cited above use as their measure children ever born, which under natural fertility is directly related to marriage du-

Table 11: Age-Specific Fertility and Natural Fertility Measures, St. George
Polygamous Marriages, 1861–80

| | Births per 1,000 Woman-Years | | | | | | | |
	15–19	20–24	25–29	30–34	35–39	40–44	45–49	TFR
St. George	482	435	399	361	326	198	29	8.7
"Natural" fertility	——	460	431	395	322	167	24	9.0

Natural Fertility Measures	M	m	MSE
St. George	.89	−.15	.003

ration. We have seen in chapter 3 that husbands in Mormon plural marriages were typically at least ten years older when they married than were monogamists.[21]

This means that polygamous husbands stood a greater risk of dying before the end of the wife's fertile years, thus truncating the marriage. One expects to find fewer children born in shorter marriages, and the studies of Mormon polygamy confirm it. Indeed, the study of Mormon bishops shows that there was about the same shortfall in polygamous marriage length as there was in fertility.[22] Table 11, on the other hand, eliminates this truncation effect by adjusting each woman's contribution for her length of exposure to childbearing: if either spouse died, the couple was removed from the calculation. Recall that the total fertility rate is a composite estimate of children who would have been born *if* the marriage had begun when the wife was twenty and had lasted until she was fifty.

The study of Mormon pioneers cited above also allows for differences in marriage duration by reporting children ever born to "completed" marriages, that is, those in which the marriage was intact when the wife reached forty-five. Eliminating the truncation effect reduced the monogamous-polygamous difference in the sample, but polygamous marriages nonetheless had lower fertility. However, that study analyzed childbearing over the whole reproductive span of women married from 1850 to the 1880s, covering in effect the entire latter half of the nineteenth century and part of the twentieth. Women married to monogamists in the 1850s, for example, were compared to plural wives married in the late 1870s. Yet the fertility of the latter group, and indeed the fertility of all plural wives married after the 1860s, was unquestionably affected by the anti-polygamy campaign of the 1880s. As discussed in chapter 1, the "Raid" jailed some polygamists and sent others into hiding through much of the decade. This disruption of daily life clearly interrupted childbearing in plural families. In turn, it undoubtedly lowered the ultimate family size of plural wives in the sample of pioneers and so contributed to the finding of lower polygamous fertility. The data for St. George, on the other hand, focus on the experience of women before the upheavals of the 1880s. The uniqueness of St. George's polygamous fertility will be unknown until other Mormons' childbearing is measured with allowances made for both marriage duration and the effects of history.[23]

Polygamous fertility in St. George raises questions about how wives who shared husbands could have had as many children as monogamous wives. Robert Gardner's three plural wives, for example, lived as much as forty miles apart at times, yet they still had eight, eight, and nine children. Few of Gardner's fellow polygamists kept households in more than one town, but sharing a husband nonetheless means, in principle, reduced intercourse and thus reduced chances of conception for each wife. Although historical sources are particularly reticent about sexual customs, it is possible to get an idea, however indirect, of sexual activity from intervals between births. Table 12 shows average birth intervals for St. George and two other Mormon populations. St. George's monogamous intervals were slightly longer than the MDH sample's, but once again the difference may be partly due to smaller families escaping the MDH sample (families, for example, with only two widely spaced births outside Utah and no other vital events in the Mormon region). The data for St. George and the third Mormon sample agree in showing little difference between monogamous and polyga-

Table 12: Birth Intervals in St. George and Other Mormon Studies

	Average Interval in Months between Births
St. George	
Monogamous marriages	28.4
Polygamous marriages	29.6
MDH Sample	
Once-married women born 1850–59	27.5
"Polygyny and Fertility" Sample	
Wives of permanent monogamists	30.1
Wives of ever-polygamous men	28.7

Sources: Mineau et al., "Mormon Demographic History," p. 436; calculated from James E. Smith and Phillip R. Kunz, "Polygyny and Fertility in Nineteenth-Century America," *Population Studies* 30 (1976): 476.

mous marriages; indeed, polygamous intervals were shorter than monogamous ones among the last sample. Polygamous intervals were longer in St. George, but the margin over monogamous intervals is not statistically significant. In neither of these samples does it appear that polygamy had the assumed effect of significantly reducing the odds of conception in a marriage.

Yet the St. George data do suggest another kind of difference in sexual activity. Table 13 shows monogamous and polygamous intervals for the first five births (or four intervals) and for all later births. There are clear differences within and between marriage types. Intervals before the fifth birth in monogamous marriages were short and relatively uniform, as the standard deviation indicates. After the fifth birth, the intervals became both longer and more variable. These later intervals were products of the complex interaction of changing sexual activity and declining fecundity with age; one would expect them to be more variable than earlier intervals.

But polygamous intervals did not follow this course. There was little increase in average length from earlier to later births, and the later intervals were actually less variable than the earlier ones. This pattern shows that, insofar as birth intervals hint at sexual activity, frequency of intercourse early in polygamous marriages resembled what happened later in monogamy. Since an age-related fecundity decline was not involved in the early polygamous intervals, sexual behavior undoubtedly was more important in causing them to be longer and more variable than early monogamous ones. This variability suggests that there was no characteristic pattern of intercourse in polygamy. Some marriages did show the effect of a shared husband, where less frequent intercourse with each wife lengthened the time between births. Other plural marriages were like Robert Gardner's: his two wives in St. George had intervals that averaged only twenty-three months among their first five births. Husbands in such marriages may have had frequent inter-

Table 13: Earlier and Later Birth Intervals in St. George

	Number of Intervals	Mean	Standard Deviation
Monogamous Marriages			
First 5 births	233	26.4	9.8
All later births	191	30.9	13.9
Polygamous marriages			
First 5 births	197	29.2	12.6
All later births	176	30.0	11.0

course with all wives, or perhaps they had intercourse with only non-pregnant (and still fertile) spouses.[24] Later in the wives' reproductive years, as the biological factors that affect all marriages became more important, monogamous and polygamous intervals became more alike. There was thus a variety of sexual response to polygamy in St. George, helping to offset the effect on childbearing of sharing a husband. Too little is known about Mormons' sexual attitudes and behavior to go beyond these speculations. The church seldom gave sexual directions to members, and Mormons themselves were equally silent about their sexual behavior.[25] It is evident, however, that polygamous couples in St. George improvised adaptations to the changed relationships of polygamy and kept their fertility at monogamous levels.

The Determinants of Fertility

The absence of a monogamous-polygamous fertility differential in St. George does not rule out other influences on childbearing. Food shortages, the result of the area's unsuitability to farming, might have disproportionately affected poorer families, lowering their fertility through miscarriages and stillbirths caused by poor nutrition. On the other hand, wealthier parents may have begun deliberately to limit their families, with their behavior undetected in the overall pattern of natural fertility. Fertility may also have been significantly affected by the Mormon practice of sending men on foreign missions, or by the economic value of children in the town's families.

To assess the impact of parents' social status on fertility, Table 14 shows total fertility rates for wealthier versus poorer families and for those whose husbands had a higher-status versus a lower-status occupation. Wealth (that is, total wealth shown in the 1870 census) and occupation (for husbands present in both the 1870 and 1880 censuses, the "higher" of the occupations listed) were divided into higher and lower groups roughly equal in size.[26]

Woman-years would become too small if the groups were further divided into monogamous and polygamous, so marriage types are combined in the table. Wealth made little difference in fertility: the total fertility rates for the wealth groups are almost the same. The occupational groups, on the other hand, show a larger disparity in fertility rates than in any of the St. George data shown so far. To test the importance of this difference, general fertility rates are shown in the bottom section of the table. Each rate is simply the sum of all the births used in the age-specific rates, divided by the total number of married woman-years lived from fifteen to fifty. The resulting rate is in a sense

Table 14: Fertility for Wealth and Occupational Groups

	Total Fertility Rate
A. Total Wealth in 1870	
$1,150 or more	8.8
Under $1,150	8.9
B. Occupation	
Professionals and farmers	8.5
All others	8.9

General Fertility Rates	Births per 1,000 Woman-Years 15–50
$1,150 or more	286
Under $1,150	320
Significance of difference	p > .05
Professionals and farmers	305
All others	322
Significance of difference	p > .05

an aggregate total fertility rate, showing the number of births for each thousand woman-years in the childbearing period. Differences in general fertility rates can be tested for significance, and the table shows that neither economic-group difference in fertility is significant. Social and economic standing, insofar as they can be measured, made no appreciable difference in the fertility of St. George families.

The striking feature of foreign missionary work among St. George residents, another possible influence on fertility, is how few missionaries were actually called. Traveling from home in search of converts, now a standard part of Mormon males' training as young adults, was not so routinized nor confined to unmarried men at a time when many Mormons were themselves converts. With the perceived urgent need for immigrants to Utah, men were pressed into service as they were needed. But foreign missions were not the only type of service that nineteenth-century Mormons were asked to provide. Indeed, pulling up stakes and moving to towns like St. George was itself a kind of mission (hence the term "cotton mission" for Utah's Dixie). Only a relative handful of married St. George residents went on missions outside Utah. A history of St. George's pioneers lists thirty-three missionaries, seventeen of whom were married at the time.[27] Three of these men went with their wives, leaving only fourteen married men whose records show extended absences on missions. Mormon authorities also appointed "home missionaries," who traveled locally to conduct church business, but there were few of them, and their time away from home was usually short. Unless large numbers of missionaries went unnoticed by local historians, husbands' extended absences on church business were at most minor disturbances to fertility in St. George. Indeed, an examination of records for Utah points to the same conclusion, noting that less than 1 percent of men were on missions at any given time.[28]

A final potential influence on fertility in St. George was the economic value of large families. Children could indeed be useful on the town's small farms. Mary Ann Bentley described a flood that washed away most of her father's topsoil and noted that in spite of this setback, "father still had his sons Mathew and Johnie to help him and so the farming went on." She and her sister were also helpful, picking berries, gleaning wheat, and carding cotton, "for there was always so much to do in this new country that everyone was needed to help."[29] Most diaries and journals from St. George likewise mention sons' and daughters' help with a variety of chores.

This points to the theory of fertility which stresses the economic rationality of large families in pre-industrial societies. Historical and third-world families have used their fertility potential sensibly, the theory argues, because they have known that large families were "an investment in the real sense of the term."[30] For most of their lives, children in these societies have helped their parents, first with chores and later with support in the parents' old age. This model would explain St. George's consistently high fertility as a conscious effort by the townspeople to ensure a flow of support from offspring to parents.

Yet the economic fertility model does not finally explain large families in St. George, for two reasons. First, the actual benefit of large families is doubtful. Some children were clearly useful workers at certain times: in the harvest, for example, wives, children, and temporary hired hands all pitched in. But chores were more sporadic during the rest of the year, and harvest help was of little use when crops withered in a drought or washed away in a flood. Repairing and improving the irrigation system, perhaps the most important part of farming, was heavy work that required grown sons. Older sons were also the most likely contributors to the majority of St. George households that were not farms, because they could supply the casual labor that a frontier town sometimes needed.

But grown sons, and indeed all children, fared badly in St. George's labor market. The town's high fertility contributed to a labor surplus, and the public works projects to build the temple and the tabernacle could barely keep household heads employed. Children's lack of success in helping their families is underscored by federal census data on occupations. Census-takers were to list an occupation for all children who were "contributing to the family support."[31] This proviso could be problematical when sons were indispensable laborers within the family while earning no pay, but such cases were probably rare. Francis Moody, for example, who found it necessary to restrict his courting because "I had to assist in helping to support a large family," was listed as a farm laborer in the 1880 census.[32] One of the brothers Mary Ann Bentley named as an essential helper was likewise identified as a laborer. Charles Smith often acknowledged help from his sons in the farming that supplemented his watchmaking income, and two sons were given occupations in the 1880 census.[33] The census-taker usually recognized children as workers when they made significant contributions, either within the family or through outside jobs.

However, only 8 percent of boys age ten through fourteen had jobs, compared to 25 percent in rural areas throughout the United States in 1900 (occupation listings for females of all ages were all but nonexistent in St. George and so only males will be considered here).[34] In the later teens, when employment should have been crucial for St. George teenagers, 42 percent still lacked a job. Sons were also economically marginal when viewed in their families: three-quarters of the households in St. George had no employed sons. This datum ignores differences between new and older households, but sons were only relatively brief contributors in any case. Counting all unmarried males of whatever age, sons were first employed on average between their sixteenth and seventeenth birthdays.[35] We have seen that sons of St. George families married before age twenty-four, so parents could expect little more than seven years' return after a sixteen-year investment in each son. This accounting had additional debits: each family that did have one or more employed sons (one was the norm) had, on average, four nonworking siblings to feed and clothe. And there was a good chance that a son would simply not be around to provide help when he reached the productive years. As observed in chapter 3, out-migration substantially shrank the young-adult population in St. George.

Nor was support in old age, the second keystone of the economic fertility model, widespread in St. George. Elderly parents typically continued to run their own households: 60 percent of household heads sixty years or older had no employed offspring living with them. Virtually all elderly household heads also reported occupations. How many of these occupations were current and how many were former jobs is unknown, but it is clear that most aged parents did not depend on a co-resident son or daughter. On the other hand, residents' diaries indicate that married children who lived in the town did occasionally look after their aged parents' needs. As noted previously, however, half of St. George's children who had not already left the town out-migrated at their marriage, and more left in the following years. The Female Relief Society's aid to the poor undoubtedly lessened parents' need to count solely on help from children in old age, as did networks of friends and relatives.[36]

But this economic accounting does not itself disprove the economic fertility model in St. George. If residents *perceived* large families as beneficial, this perception could have ruled their childbearing whatever the actual costs and benefits of children. Indeed, Dixie resident Allen Stout, whose children were often too sick to work and thus were "so destitute of clothes that we dont go to meeting," was nonetheless thankful that God "has rewarded me with a large family who are now a great help to me."[37] Yet Stout stands virtually alone in expressing this attitude. Mormon doctrine made it clear that responsibility flowed from older to younger generations, not vice versa. Parents were expected to spend their lives in self-improvement; if they were successful, they would always be in advance of their children. There was ideally a permanent dependent relationship between parents and children as they all worked for heavenly glory. Parents' role was to guide "those of tender age, to mansions of eternal life and salvation"; in heaven, "children will be [their parents'] subjects."[38] Mormon doctrine encouraged parents to see children as primarily an obligation, as dependents to be perfected under a patriarchal system. Even Allen Stout acknowledged this view of his children when he prayed that "I may live to see my little ones all men and women and able to do for themselves."[39]

For other residents this sense of obligation was a sobering economic reality as well as a spiritual necessity. While their families were still growing, parents saw numerous children as a burden rather than an investment. Robert Gardner, who found his plural families rapidly expanding in the 1870s, "began to realize that I was to raise a large family and maintain them in a hard country" and so had to redouble his efforts to do this duty.[40] Charles Walker caught neatly the dilemma of growing families in another verse of the above-quoted wedding poem:

> The Darlings may come thick and fast
> And make you scratch your head;
> Dont fret. The Lord He will provide
> You with your daily Bread.[41]

Childbearing brought a very different kind of trouble for women. As related in the next chapter, repeated pregnancies weakened women and made them vulnerable to other causes of death even when they survived childbirth itself. The toll of childbearing is clear in Mary Ann Hafen's recollection of her first three confinements. The first birth caused a nearly fatal hemorrhage, but Hafen arose after ten days, "the prescribed time when a woman should resume her housework after childbirth." Hafen developed an infection and fever after the second birth, but she again got up on the tenth day and promptly experienced a relapse that once more almost killed her. After the third birth, Hafen was "troubled with sinking spells, nearly suffocating at times."[42] Mary Nelson likewise had complications following several of her deliveries, and her trauma was even deeper. After her recovery from her eighth birth had dragged on for months, Nelson twice tried to kill herself, once by beating her head against a child's bed. Her husband was puzzled by her despair, but he nonetheless managed to revive her spirits.[43] Nelson and Hafen recovered physically and indeed each had several more children.

These accounts give rare glimpses into Mormon women's discontent with a culture which demanded that they have repeated brushes with death. No less than other American women, Mormon wives knew well the physical and mental price of perhaps nine pregnancies in little more than twenty years. They made their risks tolerable in much the same way as other women, controlling most of their resentment through mutual support at childbirth. When they report births, Mormon diaries often tell of comfort given by friends and relatives to prevent the kind of despair that overwhelmed Mary Nelson.[44]

In spite of such undercurrents of dissatisfaction by both men and women over their unrestrained fertility, most eventually surveyed their large families with pride and pleasure. But Allen Stout notwithstanding, it was not the pleasure of economic security but rather that of responsibility fulfilled and spiritual progress insured. Mary Ann Hafen, for example, thanked God "for my dear children that He has blessed me with and for the wisdom and light they have to become useful in His hands to help carry on His work on the earth." To insure that usefulness, "the Lord has been good to care for us all in time of need and protect us from danger."[45] John Woodbury maintained that "the sacrifices [his children] made necessary only strengthened our love for them," and echoed Hafen's gratitude that "our children have grown to man's and woman's estate."[46] What mattered to these residents was the incarnation and guidance of new spirits. Parents were pleased with their sacrifices, confident that they had met their obligation to release waiting souls, and hopeful of the heavenly glory the church offered them in return.

Large families were therefore not the sound economic investment that the economic fertility model implies, either in fact or in perception. A more sensible economic strategy in St. George, given the absence of work for teenagers and the rapid increase of mouths to feed, was fertility perhaps half as high as the actual rate. But there is little reason to believe that any kind of economic strategy guided fertility in St. George. It is just as likely that children were put to work because families were large, as Francis Moody's above-cited remark suggests, as it is that families were large since children were useful. The advice "Dont fret" about their growing families was clearly more relevant to residents' lives than the adage that "more hands grow more food."

Conclusion: Insuring the Future

The chief feature that emerges from the St. George fertility data is a uniform pattern of unrestrained childbearing. Couples in the town bore children at a rate that would result in nearly nine births over a woman's reproductive span; this rate held firm up and down the social scale. Moderately high natural fertility was the rule for St. George marriages, and the small subgroup deviations that did occur were submerged by this rule.

A more unexpected finding is that polygamous marriages conformed to the same rule. The total fertility rate in plural marriages was about the same as in monogamous ones. Against theories on the lowering of fertility through reduced intercourse, the St. George data show the invariability of childbearing even when wives' access to their husbands was restricted. However it was managed, polygamous residents kept their fertility comparable to that of monogamous couples.

Polygamy thus did not affect the *rate* of childbearing, but did plural marriage serve its avowed purpose and embody more souls for God's kingdom? Recall that studies of Mormon fertility have consistently found that fewer children were ultimately born in plural marriages because childbearing was more often cut short by the husband's death. Yet it does not necessarily follow that, had there been no polygamy, these women would have had more children as monogamous wives. On the one hand, polygamy insured virtually universal marriage for women and thus ruled out any significant loss of fertility through celibacy.[47] But more important was polygamy's effect on women's age at marriage. We have seen that Mormon women married young in spite of a sex ratio that resembled ratios where women married later. The spiritual obligation to marry was partly responsible for these youthful Mormon marriages, but plural marriage undeniably reinforced the church's urgings by raising the demand for brides. Competition for brides lowered the marriage age for *all* women, not just plural wives, and when there is unchecked fertility, age at marriage is the pivotal influence on family size.[48] The sooner marriages began the more children were born, and polygamy's impact on marriage age may well have offset the truncation of individual plural marriages and raised the fertility of the Mormon people.

High fertility among St. George's families was not dictated by economic necessity. On the contrary, in a community that had too many workers to begin with and where parents were expected to remain permanently, indeed eternally, superior to their children, the incentive to count on offspring for security was slight. The ability of sons to contribute was overwhelmed by a shortage of jobs for teenagers and by large numbers of siblings to support. There was a good chance that a given son would be unable to contribute significantly to his family, either because he out-migrated in his late teens or, like many of his peers who stayed in town, because he did not have enough work to do to justify calling it a job when the census-taker came.

The real determinant of fertility in St. George was the church's prescription for large families. Just as they did when they married, members both fulfilled a sacred obligation and benefited themselves by bearing as many children as possible. Fertile marriages met the duty of Mormons to embody spirits waiting for their mortal experience and at the same time accumulated treasure for the parents' own afterlife, since heavenly exaltation depended in part on a large progeny.

Even if they were not an economic investment, children were clearly an investment of another kind. St. George parents believed that economic difficulties in the present were an acceptable price for a chance at a better position in the eternal kingdom. That they maintained unchecked fertility, in spite of economic realities and in spite of steadily falling fertility elsewhere in America, testifies to residents' determination to succeed in the afterlife. Looked at in this way, fertility that otherwise appears to show a lack of initiative turns out to be part of the effort by each family to shape its eternal destiny.

NOTES

1. 49:17
2. John A. Widtsoe, *Rational Theology* (Salt Lake City: Deseret News Press, 1915), p. 147.

3. Widtsoe, comp., *Discourses of Brigham Young* (Salt Lake City: Deseret Book Co., 1925), p. 305; sermon reported in A. Karl Larson and Katharine M. Larson, eds., *Diary of Charles Lowell Walker*, 2 vols. (Logan: Utah State University Press, 1980), Mar. 3, 1861, 1: 168.

4. Sermons by George Q. Cannon and Charles Walker, reported in Larson and Larson, eds., *Diary of Charles Walker*, Apr. 27, Dec. 4, 1884, 2: 630, 639.

5. Ibid., Nov. 1, 1883, 2: 620. See similar poems in Charles Lowell Walker, Book of Verse, Mormon Biographies File, Bancroft Library, University of California, Berkeley, pp. 49, 65–66, 99. This file is a copy of originals in the Library of Congress.

6. Flann Campbell, "Birth Control and the Christian Churches," *Population Studies* 14 (1960): 132.

7. Kimball Young, *Isn't One Wife Enough?* (New York: Henry Holt, 1954), chap. 5.

8. Helen Mar Kimball Whitney, quoted in ibid., p. 53.

9. Ibid., pp. 140, 113.

10. See Lester E. Bush, Jr., "Birth Control among the Mormons: Introduction to an Insistent Question," *Dialogue* 10 (Autumn, 1976): 12–44; Judith C. Spicer and Susan O. Gustavus, "Mormon Fertility through Half a Century: Another Test of the Americanization Hypothesis," *Social Biology* 21 (1974): 70–76; Dean L. May, "A Demographic Portrait of the Mormons, 1830–1980," in Thomas G. Alexander and Jessie L. Embry, eds., *After 150 Years: The Latter-day Saints in Sesquicentennial Perspective* (Provo: Charles Redd Center for Western Studies, 1983), pp. 39–69.

11. There are two ways of defining monogamy for fertility analysis. One is to include only those marriages where the husband never took a plural wife, assigning the fertility of first wives to polygamy. However, Mormons who became polygamists typically waited until their late thirties to make a second marriage (see chapter 3); they were therefore monogamists for well over a decade before changing status. This chapter assigns the pre-polygamous fertility of first wives to the *monogamous* category, changing their status only when the husband took a plural wife. In any case, this procedure makes little difference in the results. For example, the total fertility rate for permanent monogamists, as compared to the current monogamists shown in Table 9, is also 8.6.

12. Ansley J. Coale and T. James Trussell, "Model Fertility Schedules: Variations in the Age Structure of Childbearing in Human Populations," *Population Index* 40 (1974): 185–258; Coale and Trussell, "Technical Note: Finding the Two Parameters That Specify a Model Schedule of Marital Fertility," ibid. 44 (1978): 203–13.

13. The rates for women age forty-five to forty-nine were excluded from the calculation of m because of their small values and high variability.

14. Coale and Trussell, "Technical Note," p. 204.

15. M. Skolnick, L. Bean, D. May, V. Arbon, K. de Nevers, and P. Cartwright, "Mormon Demographic History I: Nuptiality and Fertility of Once-Married Couples," *Population Studies* 32 (1978): 6–8.

16. "This is the reason why the doctrine of plurality of wives was revealed that the noble spirits which are waiting for tabernacles might be brought forth." Widtsoe, comp., *Discourses*, p. 305. See also Gustive O. Larson, *The "Americanization" of Utah for Statehood* (San Marino, Calif.: Huntington Library, 1971), p. 40; Young, *Isn't One Wife Enough?*, p. 103; Stanley P. Hirshson, *The Lion of the Lord: A Biography of Brigham Young* (New York: Knopf, 1969), p. 121.

17. Stanley S. Ivins, "Notes on Mormon Polygamy," *Western Humanities Review* 10 (1956): 236.

18. D. Gene Pace, "Wives of Nineteenth-Century Mormon Bishops: A Quantitative Analysis," *Journal of the West* 21 (Apr., 1982): 53.

19. James E. Smith and Phillip R. Kunz, "Polygyny and Fertility in Nineteenth-Century America," *Population Studies* 30 (1976): 471. This relatively small fertility difference masks a more substantial difference between first wives (including first polygamous plural ones) and later ones. In Smith and Kunz's study, for example, plural wives (that is, second and third wives in plural marriages and excluding marriages with more than three wives) had an average of 6.7 children. The study cited in note 18 shows a similar drop in family size when only later wives are considered.

20. Klaus J. Hansen, *Mormonism and the American Experience* (Chicago: University of Chicago Press, 1981), p. 160; Louis J. Kern, *An Ordered Love: Sex Roles and Sexuality in Victorian Utopias* (Chapel Hill: University of North Carolina Press, 1981), p. 182. See also Thomas F. O'Dea, *The Mormons* (Chicago: University of Chicago Press, 1957), p. 246; Leonard J. Arrington and Davis Bitton, *The Mormon Experience: A History of the Latter-day Saints* (New York: Knopf, 1979), p. 199.

21. See Table 5 and Pace, "Wives of Bishops," p. 52.

22. Pace, "Wives of Bishops," pp. 53–54, reports that monogamous first wives averaged 9.13 children, 15 percent more than the 7.92 born to polygamous wives; however, childbearing in the monogamous marriages lasted an average of 19.5 years, 14 percent longer than the 17.04 years reported for polygamous marriages.

23. L. L. Bean and G. P. Mineau, "The Polygyny-Fertility Hypothesis: A Re-evaluation," *Population Studies* 40 (1986): 67–81, came to my attention as this book went to press. The central finding confirms that of Smith and Kunz, "Polygyny and Fertility": plural wives had lower fertility than monogamous wives or first wives of polygamists. Yet the article does not disconfirm the arguments presented here. First, time periods, which are among the variables controlled, are measured as *husbands'* birth cohorts. Taking cases within one standard deviation of the mean, the second of the three cohorts, for example, includes second marriages that began anywhere from 1847 to 1879; polygamy's tenuous early years as well as later persecution probably affected such broad cohorts. Moreover, the article's focus on first wives of polygamists is an analytical distinction and not a historical one. First wives in St. George, for example, typically spent three-quarters of their reproductive years as monogamous spouses.

24. The latter possibility is suggested in Smith and Kunz, "Polygyny and Fertility," p. 475. When Robert Gardner married for the third time, his first wife was in her late thirties, and she reached the end of her childbearing years soon after Gardner married his fourth wife.

25. Church leaders overcame their reticence primarily to give advice on intercourse during pregnancy, and even then they gave mixed signals. Brigham Young once announced that couples "could suit themselves" about sex during pregnancy, but Erastus Snow later endorsed folklore on the subject by advising men to have intercourse "where it was right and consistent that they might not entail on their offspring unholy desires and appetites"; he also encouraged husbands to curb their sexual demands while their wives were nursing an infant. Young quoted in Bush, "Birth Control," p. 18; Snow's pronouncements reported in Larson and Larson, eds., *Diary of Charles Walker*, Nov. 3, 1883, 2: 620–21.

26. Occupations were classified by the scheme reported in Theodore Hershberg and Robert Dockhorn, "Occupational Classification," *Historical Methods Newsletter* 9 (1976): 59–98.

27. A. K. Hafen, *Devoted Empire Builders (Pioneers of St. George)* (St. George: privately published, 1969).

28. May, "Demographic Portrait," p. 56.

29. Life Sketch of Mary Ann Mansfield Bentley, Brigham Young University Library, p. 12.

30. John C. Caldwell, *Theory of Fertility Decline* (New York: Academic Press, 1982), p. 108. The passage quoted here refers specifically to societies where the hope is that one child will find success in the city, but it reflects a more general assumption among adherents to the economic model of fertility.

31. Carroll D. Wright, *The History and Growth of the United States Census* (Washington: U.S. Government Printing Office, 1900), p. 172.

32. Autobiography of Francis W. Moody, in Family Record of John Monroe Moody, Huntington Library, San Marino, Calif., entry for 1880. All items from the Huntington Library cited by permission.

33. Diary of Charles Smith, Library-Archives, Historical Department of the Church of Jesus Christ of Latter-day Saints.

34. Avery M. Guest and Stewart Tolnay, "Children's Roles and Fertility: Late Nineteenth-Century United States," *Social Science History* 7 (1983): 375. Employment figures for St. George are for 1870 and 1880 combined.

35. Average age at first employment was estimated by applying the formula for the singulate mean age of marriage to the proportion of males unemployed in each age group. The result is a "singulate mean age of employment," which unfortunately is a cruder estimate than the marriage-age one because the census does not distinguish between unemployed and never-employed. For the marriage formula, see Henry S. Shryock and Jacob S. Siegel, *The Methods and Materials of Demography*, 2 vols. (Washington: U.S. Government Printing Office, 1975), 1: 295.

36. Henry Bigler's journal gives a partial accounting of aid received from friends and relatives. Of a dozen reported donations, Bigler's sons sent him

two contributions totaling $25; most aid came from Bigler's siblings, in-laws, and friends. Autobiography and Journal of Henry William Bigler, Huntington Library, passim. See also Diary of Mary G. Whitehead, in Sketch of the Life of Adolphus Rennie Whitehead and Diary of Mary G. Whitehead, Brigham Young University Library, passim, for indications of the crucial role of friends and neighbors as well as children in supporting widowed residents.

37. Journal of Allen Joseph Stout, Huntington Library, Sept. 20, Dec. 5, 1863.

38. Parley P. Pratt, *Key to the Science of Theology* (Liverpool: F. D. Richards, 1855), p. 166; Joseph Smith, quoted in Julie Roy Jeffrey, *Frontier Women: The Trans-Mississippi West, 1840–1880* (New York: Hill and Wang, 1979), p. 163. Wandle Mace copied into his journal Parley Pratt's promise that each father "will hold lawful jurisdiction over his own children, and over all the families which spring of them to all generations." Autobiography of Wandle Mace, Huntington Library, p. 200.

39. Journal of Allen Stout, pp. 56–57.

40. "Journal and Diary of Robert Gardner," in Kate B. Carter, comp., *Heart Throbs of the West* 10 (1949): 319.

41. Larson and Larson, eds., *Diary of Charles Walker*, Nov. 1, 1883, 2: 620.

42. Mary Ann Hafen, *Recollections of a Handcart Pioneer of 1860: A Woman's Life on the Mormon Frontier* (Lincoln: University of Nebraska Press, 1983), pp. 56–61. The tenth-day rule may have been a central European custom (Hafen was born in Switzerland) because to my knowledge it does not appear elsewhere in diaries from Utah's Dixie. Its implication of women's tendency to malinger, however, undoubtedly reflects a more prevalent attitude.

43. Journal of William Nelson, Washington County Library, St. George, Aug. 13–31, 1885.

44. Mary Whitehead wrote of visiting a neighbor who was "in a crittical condition having been delivered of a dead baby, after a great deal of suffering was doing as nicely as could be expected [but] her Mother, and others were nearly worn out." Diary of Mary Whitehead, June 17, 1895. Charles Walker remarked that "the Sisters in this neighborhood have visited [my wife] and showed great kindness to her and the little one." Larson and Larson, eds., *Diary of Charles Walker*, Oct. 17, 1866, 1: 270. On the ways in which American women coped with the risks of childbirth, see Judith Walzer Leavitt, "Under the Shadow of Maternity: American Women's Responses to Death and Debility Fears in Nineteenth-Century Childbirth," *Feminist Studies* 12 (1986): 129–54.

45. Hafen, *Recollections*, p. 98.

46. John Taylor Woodbury, *Vermilion Cliffs: Reminiscences of Utah's Dixie* (St. George: privately published, 1933), pp. 70, 72.

47. May, "Demographic Portrait," p. 56. This effect of polygamy should not be overestimated, however, because marriage was nearly universal in nineteenth-century America. See Daniel Scott Smith, "Family Limitation, Sexual Control, and Domestic Feminism in Victorian America," in Mary S. Hartman

and Lois Banner, eds., *Clio's Consciousness Raised: New Perspectives on the History of Women* (New York: Harper & Row, 1974), pp. 120–21.

48. John Bongaarts, "Why High Birth Rates Are So Low," *Population and Development Review* 1 (1975): 292; G. P. Mineau, L. L. Bean, and M. Skolnick, "Mormon Demographic History II: The Family Life Cycle and Natural Fertility," *Population Studies* 33 (1979): 440–42.

5

Mortality

Marriage and fertility could be controlled, but death for most nineteenth-century people was a matter for reaction rather than regulation. As observed earlier, St. George residents reacted by acknowledging God's hand in death's timing and seeing death as a "short nap" until the resurrection. But death was, on the other hand, the demographic event with perhaps the longest history of *attempted* control. Long before societies tried to influence other aspects of their fate, they were trying to stave off death with superstition, religion, and science. Until the dramatic medical improvements of the twentieth century, however, illness and death were dominant facts of daily life. Although people remained largely powerless to cure sickness in the nineteenth century, they could at least avoid some deadly diseases. Public health campaigns to purify water and dispose of sewage began to improve life-chances in a number of nineteenth-century American cities. If death was still capricious, at least it did not threaten as often as it had.[1]

The desert frontier, however, was an unlikely place for municipal sanitation, and so St. George was without even this means of resisting death. Nonetheless, there were ways in which the townspeople influenced their mortality, some conscious and others unintentional.

St. George Life Tables

Genealogies, censuses, and other records give the vital events of just under 2,400 residents of St. George in its first two decades. Over 90 percent contain complete birth and death records and reliable information on when they came to town and left; almost all the rest can be estimated to form a reasonably complete mortality record for the townspeople.[2]

Life table measures for the St. George sample are shown in Table 15. These are "period" measures, illustrating what would happen to a hypothetical cohort born between 1861 and 1880 and throughout

A Sermon in the Desert

Table 15: Selected Life Table Measures, St. George, 1861–80

Age(x)[a]	Males				Females			
	PY	l_x	$_nq_x$	e_x	PY	l_x	$_nq_x$	e_x
0	459	1000	.143	47.5	428	1000	.147	45.6
1	1466	857	.172	54.4	1440	852	.152	52.4
5	1606	710	.033	61.4	1620	723	.036	57.6
10	2528	686	.031	58.5	2389	696	.037	54.7
20	1088	665	.018	50.2	1238	671	.078	46.6
30	645	653	.075	41.1	1171	618	.066	40.0
40	801	604	.061	34.0	902	577	.115	32.5
50	740	567	.115	25.8	534	511	.173	26.1
60	330	502	.114	18.5	214	422	.086	20.4
70	77	444	.388	10.2	43	386	.201	12.2
80	10	272	1.000	4.4	3	308	1.000	4.4

[a]PY = Person-years lived in age interval; l_x = number living at age x of 1000 births; $_nq_x$ = probability of dying from age x to next age in table (next age is thus age x + n years); e_x = life expectancy at age x (i.e., additional years to live).

life facing the death rates of those decades (see Appendix B for more details). Since the number of person-years at older ages becomes too small with standard five-year age groups, the table is abridged to ten-year groups after age ten.

Childhood Mortality

Taking first the top three rows of Table 15, which describe the experience of children, it is clear that St. George was a hostile place for the very young. Nearly 150 of each 1,000 newborns died before their first birthday, and mortality worsened in the next four years. Only 710 boys and 723 girls of each original 1,000 would live to age five. The severity of this mortality is underscored by Table 16, which shows comparison data on infant and child death rates. Death records for over 60,000 Utah Mormons (the MDH sample) show a much lower first-year mortality than in St. George.[3] The other places in the table had equal or higher infant death rates than St. George, but the town's mortality caught up after the first birthday. Only in Italy, where disease and famine took a devastating toll, were fewer children left at age five than in St. George.

St. George's first-year mortality compared with the rest of Utah points to the town's special dangers to children. To be sure, St. George was not alone in its lack of public sanitation. Most towns in Utah had stables

Table 16: Infant and Child Mortality in St. George Compared with Other Populations

	Probability of Dying before Age 1	Probability of Dying from 1 to 5	Survivors to Age 5 of 1,000 Births
Males			
St. George, 1861–80	.143	.172	710
Mormon Demographic History Sample, Born 1860–80	.112	——	——
U.S. Whites, 1870	.185	.081	749
England and Wales, 1871	.180	.126	717
Italy, 1881	.246	.214	592
Females			
St. George, 1861–80	.147	.152	723
Mormon Demographic History Sample, Born 1860–80	.096	——	——
U.S. Whites, 1870	.166	.078	769
England and Wales, 1871	.148	.123	747
Italy, 1881	.220	.215	612
La Hulpe, Belg., 1847–66	.152	.099	764

Sources: Calculated from Katherine A. Lynch, Geraldine P. Mineau, and Douglas L. Anderton, "Estimates of Infant Mortality on the Western Frontier: The Use of Genealogical Data," *Historical Methods* 18 (1985): 159 (weighted average of 1860–69 and 1870–79 cohorts); Michael R. Haines, "The Use of Model Life Tables to Estimate Mortality for the United States in the Late Nineteenth Century," *Demography* 16 (1979): 307; Samuel H. Preston, Nathan Keyfitz, and Robert Schoen, *Causes of Death: Life Tables for National Populations* (New York: Seminar Press, 1972), pp. 228, 230, 384, 386; Susan Cotts Watkins and James McCarthy, "The Female Life Cycle in a Belgian Commune: La Hulpe, 1847–1866," *Journal of Family History* 5 (1980): 170.

near houses and no protection against the insects that went from stable to house and back. Moreover, household water in most towns came from ditches that ran past stables and behind privies. But the effect of all this was worse in southwestern Utah. The territory's warmest area was the ideal environment for parasites, bacteria, and insects. Water-borne organisms flourished in the summer, when air and water were always warm and there was little rainwater to supplement the ditches' supply. Infants died of intestinal diseases in these months, but they were still not safe in other seasons. A variety of bacteria thrived most of the year, causing scarlet fever, typhoid, and other infectious diseases that struck harder in St. George than elsewhere in Utah.[4]

Yet infant mortality was actually lower in St. George and in all of Utah than in other places shown in Table 16. The study analyzing Utah's infant death rates has suggested that physicians and midwives were important in keeping mortality from being higher; in fact, St. George had both physicians and midwives during most of the settlement period.[5] Although midwives undoubtedly prevented some neonatal deaths, they could do little about the diseases of later infancy. As in many nineteenth-century places, over half of infant deaths in St. George happened after the first month.[6] Midwives' main concern was a safe delivery, and as will be seen, they experienced enough problems in seeing to the mother's health. In addition, it has been noted that physicians made only modest headway against the townspeople's reliance on faith-healing.

A more likely reason for Mormons' healthier infants was the mothers' tendency to breast-feed their infants. Breast-feeding transmits immunities to infants, and places where breast-feeding was common had lower infant mortality than where artificial feeding was the rule.[7] There is little direct evidence on breast-feeding among Mormons, but custom seems to have specified about a year of nursing. Bottle-feeding was probably uncommon outside Salt Lake City, not least because of problems with feeding cattle and preserving milk in places like St. George.[8] Moreover, birth intervals in St. George show the apparent effects of breast-feeding. Nursing suppresses a woman's ovulation and thus delays her next conception, and all else being equal there should be a longer birth interval the longer an infant nurses. This in fact happened in St. George: each month of an infant's survival (and presumably of breast-feeding) delayed the next birth by half a month. Put another way, the average interval after an infant's death (and the end of the mother's lactation) was more than nine months shorter than when the infant survived.[9] Because they could not join in the movement toward artificial feeding, most Mormon families had healthier infants.

There are no data for deaths after infancy in the MDH sample, but mortality estimates for the central Utah town of Manti show the typical drop in mortality after age one.[10] Indeed, death rates in most populations fall after the first birthday even when infant mortality is high, but not in St. George. A child's chance of dying actually rose after the first year, which further confirms the prevalence of breast-feeding. Immunities from breast milk fade later in infancy, and in any case children in St. George were probably weaned around the first birthday. The town's cemetery records grimly note the weanlings' vulnerability. The second leading cause of death (nearly equal to typhoid) was "teething," a name for the intestinal diseases that seemed to coincide with weaning and were made worse by St. George's climate. If they had escaped the town's diseases while they were nursing, children were attacked with double force once they were weaned. Now they had to depend on polluted water and other sources of disease, and they also relied on food that occasionally ran short. The town's recurring food shortages clearly did not improve children's health. It is not known exactly how malnutrition affects death rates, especially when nutrition varied as it did in St. George, where modest harvests followed crop failures.[11] But young children especially needed good nutrition, and periods of subsistence on carrot greens or cane-seed bread undoubtedly lowered resistance to childhood diseases. Breast-feeding postponed the toll of the desert frontier on newborns, but it could not ultimately keep disease from claiming nearly three of ten children before their fifth birthday.

Death in Adulthood

It is clear that something different happened after early childhood in St. George, at least to males. Table 15 shows that residents who reached age five could expect to live well past sixty. In contrast, five-year-olds in England and Wales could count only on living to their mid-fifties, as could girls in the Belgian village of La Hulpe, despite their better health in the early years.[12] Ten-year-olds in St. George had a similar advantage over their peers elsewhere in the United States, again despite worse mortality among the town's children.[13]

This is remarkable longevity given what we know of the nineteenth century, but life expectancies understate the extent to which this was a male phenomenon. Relatively few adults over age sixty in the St. George sample died in the period studied here; low mortality in old age adds to life expectancy at all ages. However, life-chances in early and middle adulthood clearly favored men. Table 17 underscores men's advantage by focusing on the likelihood of dying from age twenty to sixty in St. George and contemporary populations. Men in St. George stood only a one-in-four chance of dying before old age, while the odds in England and Italy approached fifty-fifty. But women did not have this advantage: one in three St. George women would not survive the middle years, worse mortality than among La Hulpe's women and much closer to England's and Italy's death rates than was their hus-

Table 17: Comparative Young- and Middle-Adult Mortality

	Probability of Dying between Ages 20 and 60	
	Men	Women
St. George, 1861–80	.245	.370
England and Wales, 1871	.477	.418
Italy, 1881	.426	.412
La Hulpe, 1847–66	——	.360

Sources: See Table 16.

bands' mortality.[14] Indeed, "model" life tables, which are adapted from actual populations to illustrate mortality trends and relationships, show that women's young- and middle-age mortality in St. George was worse than we would expect based on what happened to younger residents. The closest model table to St. George's childhood mortality (that is, before age twenty) has a 34 percent chance of death for women before age sixty, whereas Table 17 shows that women in St. George had a 37 percent chance of dying. The corresponding model table for men, on the other hand, suggests that they should have a 38 percent chance of dying before sixty, but St. George men actually had only a 24 percent chance of death.[15] Women in the town had mortality that fit their circumstances, but their husbands enjoyed remarkably good life-chances.

This is all the more surprising because in most populations women live longer than men, especially when adults' health is generally good.[16] One would thus expect, given the high male life expectancy at twenty, that women in St. George would live even longer. Indeed, looking again at model life tables, a male life expectancy of fifty years at age twenty should be accompanied by a female expectancy of more than fifty-three years.[17] But Table 15 shows that women could expect less than forty-seven more years when they reached adulthood. There is thus more than a six-year difference between the model tables' prediction and St. George women's actual mortality.

Table 17 and other historical data likewise indicate that nineteenth-century women generally had lower mortality than men. In the United States and England, females had longer life expectancies than males throughout their lives. Even in Italy, though their probabilities of dying were higher at some ages, women had a slightly higher life expectancy at birth.[18] Rural Massachusetts, on the other hand, was one place with mortality data that show women at a disadvantage in the early adult

years. Like women in St. George, they had four years less to live than
men at twenty, though in both places women began to catch up thereafter.[19]

The cause of women's relatively high mortality in Massachusetts
was tuberculosis, which was that state's principal cause of death year
after year. One in five deaths in 1860 resulted from this disease, and
it was so dominant that the second and third leading causes together
accounted for only half as many deaths.[20] More important, tuberculosis
was particularly selective of young women. The crude death rate for
tuberculosis was virtually identical for both sexes at ages below fifteen
and over forty in Massachusetts. However, not only was the tubercular
death rate nearly one-third higher for women than men between fifteen
and forty, but the female rate itself, fifty deaths per 10,000 adults, far
exceeded rates in England and Italy, places for which we have data.[21]
The divergence of male and female tuberculosis death rates in Massachusetts roughly parallels the divergence in life expectancies;[22] there
is thus every reason to believe that, given the importance of tuberculosis, its sex-specificity explains the mortality difference between males
and females in rural Massachusetts.

Tuberculosis was also the leading cause of death among women in
St. George, and it likewise affected them far more than men. But St.
George had no long indoor seasons that helped the disease spread,
and tuberculosis did not dominate as it did in Massachusetts. Less than
a third of women's deaths resulted from tuberculosis, while it caused
nearly half of women's middle-adult deaths in contemporary Massachusetts.[23] Nearly as many women in St. George died in childbirth as
from tuberculosis, and it is this maternal mortality that sets St. George
apart from the other populations that have been examined. In contemporary England, Italy, and Massachusetts, childbed deaths accounted
for only 5 to 7 percent of women's deaths before age fifty, but one-
fourth of St. George women's deaths occurred in childbirth.[24] Maternal
deaths were apparently even more common in Manti, suggesting that
childbirth was especially dangerous on the Mormon frontier.[25]

Of course some of this danger was due to Mormon women having
more babies. The birthrate in St. George's first two decades was fifty
per thousand population, versus about thirty-five in England and Italy
and twenty-nine in Massachusetts.[26] Women in St. George clearly ran
a greater risk of dying in childbirth simply because each woman had
more pregnancies; chapter 4 gave a hint of the physical and psychic
toll of this risk. But it is not likely that a birthrate about half again as
high as other places could by itself produce maternal mortality more
than three times as high. Imprecise death reporting and primitive med-

ical care could obviously have contributed to Mormon childbed mortality rates, but these problems affected other populations as well. Complications surely intervened to make each pregnancy especially risky for the women of St. George.

Two complications of childbirth correspond to what we know of St. George's conditions. We usually associate malaria with the tropics, but it is an occasional problem in deserts as well. There is an anopheline mosquito that lives in the American West, breeding, among other places, in irrigation ditches and thriving on sunshine. Historians of St. George mention mosquitos, noting that they lived in marshes near the Virgin River and that malaria occurred in Dixie.[27] St. George's cemetery records also list a few deaths from "intermittent fever," "chills and fever," and "bilious fever," which were terms for malaria. But malaria has a chronic effect much more widespread than its usually modest death rate. Even if its sufferers do not die from malaria, it reactivates latent infections, strains the body's systems, and "so debilitate[s] patients that new infectious agents have found hosts who offer little resistance."[28] The demands of pregnancy on women's health worsened malaria's effect and increased a woman's risk of dying from any number of diseases. Indeed, a study of a colonial Virginia county has cited malaria and its consequent diseases as the cause of dramatically higher female than male mortality at reproductive ages.[29]

St. George's recurring food crises probably further worsened the risks that went with pregnancy. Experiments have shown that allocation of protein within a pregnant woman's system favors the fetus at the expense of maternal tissue.[30] When pregnancy followed a poor harvest, a woman was ill prepared to survive delivery or withstand infectious disease.

Malaria and malnutrition undoubtedly reinforced each other, combining with repeated pregnancies to lower the life-chances of women in the reproductive years. But it was not only in giving birth that women were at risk. Even if all the women who died in childbirth are assumed instead to have survived to age fifty, women's mortality in St. George is still worse than men's. Indeed, there is no reason why malaria and poor nutrition would not have continued to lower the resistance of women who survived all their births. The continued high mortality of women (compared to men) in their fifties shown in Table 15 points to the lingering effects of debilities from the reproductive years.[31]

Yet men seem surprisingly unaffected by St. George's conditions. They were bitten by mosquitos and subjected to food shortages as well, but they enjoyed remarkable health. Of course, they were not exposed to the risks of childbirth, but neither were men in England or Italy or elsewhere in the United States, where they had worse mortality than women. Even in Manti, where maternal mortality was at least as high as in St. George, men's overall life-chances were apparently worse than women's.[32] Women's mortality in St. George suggests a nineteenth-century population which, though it no longer had the ruinous mortality of the early Chesapeake, was still occasionally victimized by chronic disease and malnutrition.[33] Men's death rates, on the other hand, resemble those of the twentieth century.[34]

Indeed, men's causes of death in St. George sound comparatively modern.[35] Men died in accidents as young adults and from causes such as heart disease, asthma, and paralysis in later life. Unlike places such as England, where men generally died from the same diseases as women and often at higher rates, men in St. George seem to have escaped the malaria-malnutrition weakening cycle.[36]

Once again, what is known about the Mormons of St. George gives important clues to this paradox of unexpectedly different mortality patterns for the sexes. The Word of Wisdom, the church's proscription of alcohol, tobacco, and caffeine, was not primarily a health measure, but it clearly had the potential to neutralize some of the members' most destructive habits.[37] The church did know of this doctrine's health benefits, and leaders occasionally pointed to its advantages.[38] Men had the most to gain by not smoking and drinking, but the ultimate effects of the Word of Wisdom in St. George were probably marginal. Widespread cigarette use is largely a twentieth-century phenomenon; diseases from cigars, pipes, and chewing tobacco probably had little to do with male mortality in the comparison populations we have noted.[39] On the other hand, Utah's Dixie produced nearly all the territory's wine, and there was drunkenness around St. George. Indeed, much of the High Council's activity consisted of rebuking drinkers, occasionally including its own members.[40] Yet any effort to link abstinence with God's will was bound to have an effect in a religious community. Although the Word of Wisdom remained advice rather than commandment until the turn of the century, diaries and disciplinary reports nonetheless suggest that drunkenness was isolated rather than endemic.[41] In turn, any restraint in drinking meant fewer deaths from cirrhosis and heart disease, fewer accidental deaths, and fewer alcohol-related murders than in non-Mormon populations.[42] It is unlikely that the Word of Wisdom accounted for all of the difference between men's and women's mortality, but it probably did forestall some men's deaths in St. George.

If the church was not ready to canonize the Word of Wisdom, it had long spelled out precisely the role of men in their families. There was no mistaking the patriarchy of the Latter-day Saints. The theologian Parley Pratt wrote that a husband "is designed to be the head of a woman . . . a guide of the weaker sex . . . to mansions of eternal life and salvation. . . . A woman . . . is designed to be the glory of some man in the Lord; to be led and governed by him, as her head in all things, even as Christ is the head of the man; to honour, obey, love, serve, comfort, and help him in all things; to be a happy wife . . . devoting her life to the joys, cares and duties of her domestic sphere."[43] Husbands were wives' means of salvation; families would remain together in the afterlife, where husbands would "lead their wives into [God's] presence."[44] Wives were expected to devote their efforts to this joint salvation. "The order of heaven places man in the first rank," Orson Hyde insisted. "[A wife's] desire should be unto her husband, and he should rule over her."[45] Daniel Wells, another early church leader, instructed women that "[your husbands'] feelings should not be concentrated in you, but your feelings should be in them, and their's should be in those who lead them in the Priesthood. As they progress and lead on, you will feel to travel in the same road."[46] At the end of this road was an eternal reward for the wives of men who fulfilled their mortal potential. A Mormon author promised that "to all that man attains, in celestial exaltation and glory, woman attains. She is his partner in estate and office."[47]

Yet this was a complex patriarchy, one that required women's participation in addition to their obedience to authority. Joseph F. Smith declared that a woman "is responsible for her acts, and must answer for them. She is adorned with intelligence and judgment, and will stand upon her own merits as much so as the man."[48] The church reconciled self-reliance and obedience for women by casting around them the net of nineteenth-century domesticity. As with all True Women, the center of a Mormon woman's efforts was the home. "The married woman is the husband's domestic faith," wrote a contributor to the *Juvenile Instructor.* "His well-being is in her hand."[49] A wife was required to be an expert home manager, making do with what she had and doing without when she must. Brigham Young told the women of St. George that "I want the sisters to take the lead in custom and fashions. . . . I want to see the sisters practice prudent economy."[50] Women were to be continually on guard against self-indulgence, because if they were "the means of plunging this whole people into debt so as to distress them, will there be anything required of you? I think there will, for you will be judged according to your works."[51] Women were saved through their husbands, but they could either contribute to that salvation by selflessly keeping a well-managed home or else endanger their family's fate by what church leaders considered wastefulness.

In St. George, celebrations of female nobility underscored women's special role in doing without. A Pioneers' Day poem, written by Charles Walker and "applauded by the vast assembly especially by the Sisters" when he read it, celebrated among other virtues the ability of the "self sacraficeing sisters" to endure hunger in early Utah:

> Who mid these vales in days of yore,
> To help eke out their scanty store,
> Ate rawhide, roots, and patient bore
>   Pangs of starvation?
>
> Who was it when Starvation reigned
> Distresed and weak with hunger pained,
> Who bore it all, and ne'er complained?
>   Those gritty Sisters.[52]

Years later, another poem by Walker again commemorated the pioneers' ability to withstand hunger and once more singled out women:

> With faces pinched by hunger
> They trod the desert wild,
> The famished mother failing,
> To nurse her new born child;
> Yet 'Midst these dire privations,
> God looked on them and smile[d];
> As they came marching to Utah.[53]

Mormon pioneer folklore had thus enshrined female self-denial. By retelling, on the anniversary of the westward journey's end, the story of women's role in founding God's kingdom, poems like these showed which of their acts were considered significant and exemplary. Withstanding hunger was clearly one such act.

It was thus fully consistent with church doctrine and Mormon folklore for women to ignore their own nutrition so that their husbands had more food when there were shortages. Famine was not constant in St. George: when there was just enough rain to keep irrigation ditches flowing without washing out the dams that supplied the ditches, crops grew well and households had enough food. In 1874, for example, Charles Walker's family had "plenty to eat," though his mention suggests that this was not a typical year.[54] The crop reports cited in chapter 1, on the other hand, underscore the food shortages that residents faced in other years. Orvilla Empey's recollection of her childhood in St. George illustrates what such shortages meant for wives.

Trying to buy meat, she and her mother "would have to stand for hours at a time . . . to see if [the meat] went around to all. Often it did not & we went home with our hands empty & how about dinner for hungry men it meant hard work."[55] Knowing their power to sustain their men and their obligation of self-denial, it probably also meant going hungry so that the men had a better share of what food there was. When food remained scarce for months on end, malnutrition would thus make women vulnerable to disease and the risks of childbirth while men survived malaria and other illnesses.

If women in St. George did periodically neglect their own nutrition, they were not alone. Wives of nineteenth-century English farm laborers often underfed themselves to insure their husbands' nutrition. A government report noted that the differential diet "is not only acquiesced in by the wife, but felt by her to be right, and even necessary for the maintenance of the family."[56] Unusually high female mortality in nineteenth-century Ireland and Germany has also been linked to a pervasive culture of male dominance.[57] Preferential feeding in non-western traditional societies likewise produces higher mortality among women.[58] Elsewhere in nineteenth-century America, on the other hand, food distribution was seldom a problem, though not because of any absence of American patriarchy. As discussed previously, Mormonism's view of female subordination drew heavily on attitudes elsewhere. Indeed, in the midwestern society where many Mormons were born, one analyst has found that "systematic oppression of women" was the rule. Like Mormon doctrine, midwestern culture encouraged "self-denial . . . passivity and endurance" among women.[59] Yet such inequalities did not affect nutrition and thus mortality, because rural Americans seldom faced chronic food shortages. In the Midwest, for example, "food was abundant" and "three heavy meals a day was the rule."[60] There was usually ample food in rural America, and unequal food distribution was probably rare.

But droughts and floods often insured that there was not enough food in St. George, and women could not have the usual health advantage over men. Their husbands showed how healthy nineteenth-century men could be when they were reasonably well fed, made some effort to control their drinking, and avoided the unhealthful confinements of long winters. Women benefited from the climate as well, but malaria and poor nutrition combined with recurring childbirth brought their health closer to nineteenth-century levels.

Yet it is an oversimplification to conclude that Mormon women were oppressed literally to death. When they endured repeated pregnancies or denied themselves food, women did not necessarily see themselves as victims. The last chapter implied some women's resentment of unrestrained childbearing, but the same women continued to have children. The Mormon doctrine of accountability made obedience to authority a privilege as well as an obligation. Eternal rewards would come to faithful followers of the church, but there were ways out for those who could not tolerate submission. Church-sanctioned divorce, for example, was available when the Mormon patriarchy became unbearable.[61] Getting divorced and leaving the church were clearly no trivial steps for Mormon women, but the trauma was undoubtedly softened by the continuing shortage of women in the non-Mormon West. Rejecting the Mormon regimen did not mean rejecting marriage; a divorced woman in the nineteenth-century West could reasonably expect a new marriage outside the church.

For women who stayed married, Mormonism offered a positive view of self-denial and endurance. If wives helped their husbands in every way they could, both spouses would be rewarded with eternal glory. Embodying waiting spirits and keeping husbands healthy so they could earn heavenly credit by building God's kingdom were essential and obvious ways of providing such help.

It is easy for modern readers to see in this doctrine a subjugation of women that was rigid even for the nineteenth century. By insisting on high fertility as well as domesticity, the church prevented wives from controlling their sexuality in the way that non-Mormon women apparently did.[62] To a large extent, men held center stage in a culture they determined, and the role they defined for women was an especially restrictive bondage.[63]

But strict patriarchy was not the whole of Mormon domestic culture. As long as most Mormons kept God's kingdom and their own eternal fate uppermost in their minds, the church accommodated a surprising amount of nineteenth-century feminism. Prominent Mormon women used the Female Relief Society and the *Woman's Exponent* as instruments for activism in much the same way as non-Mormons used urban benevolent societies and feminist publications.[64] Emmeline Wells, an editor of the *Exponent*, wrote in her diary that she was "determined to train my girls to habits of independence . . . [and to] have sufficient energy of purpose to carry out plans for their own welfare and happiness."[65] The church established university classes for women's business education, sponsored women's training in the professions, and encouraged their work outside the home.[66] The understood qualifier to all such endorsements of female autonomy was women's fundamental commitment to the church and their family's salvation. The Female Relief Society, for example, saw its mission as working for "such accomplishments as might make [its members] 'examples to the world,' " but only if "the home and the family were given their rightful establishment in the very center of the circle."[67]

The modern reader's analytical dilemma is the unclear relationship between this public feminism and most women's private lives. The tangible significance of women physicians and editors was minor for the majority of women who were fully occupied with their family's welfare. But all women were urged to take cues from the purposefulness of eminent women's autonomy. The church took pains to characterize women's achievements primarily as contributions to God's kingdom and their family's salvation. Eliza R. Snow, wife to both Joseph Smith and Brigham Young and perhaps the most influential Mormon woman of the nineteenth century, explicitly linked the religious and domestic priorities of successful women. Female activists, Snow declared, were "women of God—women filling high and responsible positions—performing sacred duties—women who stand not as dictators, but as counselors to their husbands, and who, in purest, noblest sense of refined womanhood, [are] truly their helpmates."[68] Few women could expect to lead an organization or advise the church's president, but all were encouraged to use their abilities to improve their family and community. St. George women's testimony suggests that they did indeed see their sacrifices as crucial contributions to the people who depended on them. Their own view of their role allowed them, like non-Mormon women in the West, "to transcend the Cult of True Womanhood" and to judge themselves achievers rather than victims.[69] A Mormon woman's essay on pioneer life caught the feeling of St. George wives about the effectiveness of their lives. The pioneer woman, we are told, "takes hold of the conditions, determined to shape them for the best good of all."[70] Heavenly glory was the greatest good imaginable, and so Mormon women did what they thought necessary, even jeopardizing their own health, to shape conditions for the best chance at that glory.

Conclusion: Death Redirected

Death was first and foremost a part of childhood in St. George. Newborns were partly protected from the town's diseases by breast-feeding, but they still had worse mortality than infants elsewhere in Utah. And when breast-feeding's protection was gone, children in St. George were even more likely to die than in their first year, leaving fewer survivors at age five than in the rest of the United States and western Europe.

Modern sanitation and effective medicine were far in the future, and parents saw more than a fourth of their children die.

Yet death was surprisingly rare in adult life, especially for men. They largely escaped death from tuberculosis, pneumonia, and the other diseases that killed men elsewhere. St. George's climate hindered infectious diseases among survivors of nineteenth-century childhood, the Word of Wisdom forestalled some deaths from alcohol-related diseases while keeping accidents from being more common than they were, and men seemed immune from the town's food shortages. Ill-fed men could not have resisted nearly so well the combined effects of malaria and other diseases.

Women, on the other hand, were not immune from the town's dangers. Their death rates were even worse than one would expect given the town's childhood mortality. Women died from infectious diseases and childbirth and other maladies, all made more deadly by malaria. And they were also surely weakened by poor nutrition, because preferentially feeding their husbands fits both Mormon culture and the town's mortality rates.

The people of St. George can hardly be said to have gained control of their mortality. Their children died at rates that would shock us today, and nearly four of ten women who turned twenty would not reach sixty; the grief that these deaths caused has been chronicled in chapter 2. Yet the townspeople did manage somewhat to redirect death's claims. A vigorous male priesthood was the key to building God's kingdom, and cooperative wives were the key to a vigorous priesthood. Having large families and doing everything in their power to help their husbands' work were women's vital contributions to church and family. Even if it threatened their own health, wives continued to bear children and saw to their husbands' nutrition because faithful attention to duty helped to insure the whole family's salvation. Moderation with alcohol, though it was only dimly perceived as healthful, brought the townspeople even closer to their goal. Husbands and wives together produced a healthy priesthood actively working for eternal glory.

NOTES

1. Edward Meeker, "The Improving Health of the United States, 1850–1915," *Explorations in Economic History* 9 (1972): 353–73; Robert Higgs, "Mortality in Rural America, 1870–1920: Estimates and Conjectures," ibid. 10 (1973): 177–95.

2. The proportion of the sample that has complete dates is 91 percent. The remaining individuals were estimated for mortality analysis as follows: 5.2

percent have a missing month or day in a date, which was assigned the mid-point of that year or month; 2.1 percent were assigned an entry or exit date as the midpoint of two other dates at which their status could be ascertained; 1 percent were "probable deaths," infants with nothing but a birthdate who were assumed to have died shortly after birth plus a few adults who similarly vanished from the records and were assumed to have lived five years after their last listed date; and less than 1 percent consisting of true unknowns, those with such vague information (usually nothing but a name) that they must be dropped altogether from mortality calculations. See also Appendix B.

3. The mortality rate shown for the MDH sample is the "medium" estimate preferred by the authors. The "high" rate, assuming that all of the 4.4 percent of children with only birthdates died, is 136 deaths per 1,000 male births and 116 per 1,000 females, still lower than St. George's mortality. Katherine A. Lynch, Geraldine P. Mineau, and Douglas L. Anderton, "Estimates of Infant Mortality on the Western Frontier: The Use of Genealogical Data," *Historical Methods* 18 (1985): 159. The same assumption was in fact made for similar cases in St. George, but there were fewer of them to affect mortality rates. The southern Utah town of Kanab also had a lower infant-mortality rate than St. George—10 percent of infants born to Kanab's families (whether or not they stayed in the town after 1874) died before age one. Dean L. May, "People on the Mormon Frontier: Kanab's Families of 1874," *Journal of Family History* 1 (1976): 183.

4. Causes of death are listed in the St. George City Cemetery Records, St. George Branch Genealogical Library. Almost 22 percent of all attributed deaths in St. George were from the summertime digestive diseases of infancy; this is twice the proportion of such deaths in contemporary Salt Lake City and Manti, Utah. Figures for Salt Lake City are in Ralph T. Richards, *Of Medicine, Hospitals, and Doctors* (Salt Lake City: University of Utah Press, 1953), pp. 142–43; for Manti, calculated from Catherine Hofer Levison, Donald W. Hastings, and Jerry N. Harrison, "The Epidemiologic Transition in a Frontier Town—Manti, Utah: 1849–1977," *American Journal of Physical Anthropology* 56 (1981): 90. Other diseases of infancy such as pneumonia and whooping cough, however, caused enough deaths at other times to rule out for St. George the kind of infant death seasonality found in the MDH sample outside the Salt Lake area. See Lynch et al., "Infant Mortality," p. 162.

5. Lynch et al., "Infant Mortality," p. 161. On midwives in St. George, see Albert E. Miller, *The Immortal Pioneers: Founders of City of St. George, Utah* (St. George: privately published, 1946), pp. 219–20.

6. Nearly 58 percent of infant deaths in the MDH sample occurred after the first month (among children born in the 1870s); in early Manti, the proportion was 48 percent, and in rural death-registration areas of the United States in 1901 it was 67 percent. Lynch et al., "Infant Mortality," p. 161; calculated from Levison et al., "Epidemiologic Transition," p. 90; James W. Glover, *United States Life Tables: 1890, 1901, 1910, and 1901–1910* (1921; reprint ed., New York: Arno Press, 1976), p. 52. In five of six German districts from 1875 to 1877, deaths after the first month were over 60 percent of all infant deaths. John

Knodel, "Natural Fertility in Pre-industrial Germany," *Population Studies* 32 (1978): 486. See Appendix B for the distribution of infant deaths by age in St. George.

7. See Hallie J. Kintner, "Trends and Regional Differences in Breastfeeding in Germany from 1871 to 1937," *Journal of Family History* 10 (1985): 163–82; John Knodel and Hallie Kintner, "The Impact of Breast Feeding Patterns on the Biometric Analysis of Infant Mortality," *Demography* 14 (1977): 391–409.

8. For evidence of artificial feeding in Utah and Salt Lake City in particular, see Lester E. Bush, Jr., "Birth Control among the Mormons: Introduction to an Insistent Question," *Dialogue* 10 (Autumn, 1976): 38n. On the apparent Mormon custom of a year of breast-feeding, see Kimball Young, *Isn't One Wife Enough?* (New York: Henry Holt, 1954), p. 243. Infant mortality in the nineteenth century was in fact generally lower outside the Salt Lake City area, which further suggests more breast-feeding in outlying areas. Lynch et al., "Infant Mortality," p. 160.

9. The correlation between survival (in months) of a child and the interval (in months) to the next birth is .29; survival is measured only to twenty-four months because infants were almost certainly weaned by then. This correlation's squared value indicates that survival accounts for only 8 percent of the variation in birth intervals, but the relationship is weakened by, among other things, varied frequency of intercourse and the probable variety of weaning ages.

10. Levison et al., "Epidemiologic Transition," p. 89. Mortality in Manti is not given in Table 16 because, instead of using the population at risk from the manuscript censuses when it was available, the authors made an estimated age distribution based on Utah's population. An estimated population at risk by age group is less reliable than the real one, and the reliability of the mortality rates is likewise uncertain. Unless the age distribution is grossly in error, however, childhood death rates in Manti were about one-sixth of those in St. George. Among Kanab's families, on the other hand, 23 percent of children died by age eighteen, with less than half of these dying in infancy; like children in St. George, those in Kanab had a greater risk of dying after than before the first birthday. May, "Mormon Frontier," p. 183.

11. Susan Cotts Watkins and Etienne van de Walle, "Nutrition, Mortality, and Population Size: Malthus' Court of Last Resort," *Journal of Interdisciplinary History* 14 (1983): 205–26.

12. On life expectancies, see Samuel H. Preston, Nathan Keyfitz, and Robert Schoen, *Causes of Death: Life Tables for National Populations* (New York: Seminar Press, 1972), pp. 228, 230; Susan Cotts Watkins and James McCarthy, "The Female Life Cycle in a Belgian Commune: La Hulpe, 1847–1866," *Journal of Family History* 5 (1980): 170. On childhood mortality in St. George, see Table 16.

13. Life expectancies for U.S. whites in 1870 have been estimated at 48.5 years for ten-year-old males and 49.7 years for females, about ten and five years less than in St. George. For survivors to age five in both populations, see Table 16 (survivors to ten are unavailable for U.S. whites). U.S. data from

Michael R. Haines, "The Use of Model Life Tables to Estimate Mortality for the United States in the Late Nineteenth Century," *Demography* 16 (1979): 307.

14. Mortality rates are not reported for men in La Hulpe, but the authors state that men's life expectancy was "slightly higher" than women's; this difference would probably not translate into the gap between male and female mortality we see in St. George in Table 17. Watkins and McCarthy, "Female Life Cycle," 177.

15. Ansley J. Coale and Paul Demeny, *Regional Model Life Tables and Stable Populations* (Princeton: Princeton University Press, 1966), pp. 665–66. This is the "South" group of model tables, based on mortality in nineteenth- and twentieth-century Portugal, Spain, Sicily, and southern Italy, places whose climates resemble St. George's.

16. Henry S. Shryock and Jacob S. Siegel, *The Methods and Materials of Demography*, 2 vols. (Washington, D.C.: U.S. Government Printing Office, 1975), 2: 401; George J. Stolnitz, "A Century of International Mortality Trends: II," *Population Studies* 10 (1956): 17–42; Lewis I. Dublin, Alfred J. Lotka, and Mortimer Spiegelman, *Length of Life: A Study of the Life Table*, rev. ed. (New York: Ronald Press, 1949), p. 61. On the biological basis of women's mortality advantage, see Francis J. Madigan, "Are Sex Mortality Differentials Biologically Caused?" *Milbank Memorial Fund Quarterly* 35 (1957): 202–23.

17. Coale and Demeny, *Model Life Tables*, p. 674.

18. On the United States, see Haines, "Mortality for the United States," p. 307. On England and Italy, see Preston et al., *Causes of Death*, pp. 228, 230, 384, 386.

19. In towns under 1,000 population in 1860, men had a life expectancy at age 20 of 46 years and women's expectancy was 42.3 years. Maris A. Vinovskis, "Mortality Rates and Trends in Massachusetts before 1860," *Journal of Economic History* 32 (1972): 211.

20. The second and third diseases were cholera infantum and scarlet fever. See Massachusetts Secretary of the Commonwealth, *Twentieth Report . . . of Births, Marriages, and Deaths in the Commonwealth* (Boston, 1863).

21. The tuberculosis death rate in England in 1871 was 28 per 10,000 women age 15 to 40; in Italy in 1881 the rate was 30. Calculated from Preston et al., *Causes of Death*, pp. 230, 386.

22. That is, the difference in life expectancies between the sexes rises steadily until the twenties and drops thereafter, which is roughly what happens to the difference in tuberculosis death rates. See Vinovskis, "Mortality Rates," p. 211. Tuberculosis death rates calculated from Secretary of the Commonwealth, *Twentieth Report.*

23. However, one-third of death causes in St. George were not reported in the cemetery records. It is assumed here that unknown deaths were distributed among causes the same as knowns were, except that childbed deaths were assigned by proximity to a birth (see note 24 below). The tuberculosis death rate, after unreported causes are thus distributed, is 36 per 10,000 women 15 to 60, still below Massachusetts' rate of 50.

24. Expressed another way, England's childbed death rate was 7 per 10,000 women 15 to 50, Italy's was 8, Massachusetts' was 6, and St. George's was 27. Childbed deaths that were not identified in St. George's cemetery records were estimated by using the generally accepted assumption that a woman's death within forty-two days of giving birth was a childbed death. Comparison rates calculated from Preston et al., *Causes of Death*, pp. 230, 386; Secretary of the Commonwealth, *Twentieth Report.*

25. Childbed deaths were about 5 percent of all attributed deaths in early Manti, regardless of age; the corresponding figure in St. George is 4 percent. About 20 percent of all death causes in Manti were unknown. Levison et al., "Epidemiologic Transition," pp. 87, 90. Maternal mortality this high was not unknown in the nineteenth century. St. George's childbed mortality translates to 91 maternal deaths per 10,000 births; in New York in 1880 the rate was 130 and in four German communities it was 81. Judith Walzer Leavitt, "Under the Shadow of Maternity: American Women's Responses to Death and Debility Fears in Nineteenth-Century Childbirth," *Feminist Studies* 12 (1986): 135; Arthur E. Imhof, "Women, Family and Death: Excess Mortality of Women in Child-Bearing Age in Four Communities in Nineteenth-Century Germany," in Richard J. Evans and W. R. Lee, eds., *The German Family: Essays on the Social History of the Family in Nineteenth- and Twentieth-Century Germany* (New York: Barnes & Noble, 1981), p. 164.

26. The birthrate was 35 per 1,000 in England in 1871 and 37 per 1,000 in Italy from 1862 to 1881. B. R. Mitchell, *European Historical Statistics, 1750–1970* (New York: Columbia University Press, 1975), p. 113; Massimo Livi-Bacci, *A History of Italian Fertility during the Last Two Centuries* (Princeton: Princeton University Press, 1977), p. 53. Massachusetts rate calculated from Secretary of the Commonwealth, *Twentieth Report.*

27. Miller, *Immortal Pioneers*, pp. 28, 222; John Taylor Woodbury, *Vermilion Cliffs: Reminiscences of Utah's Dixie* (St. George: privately published, 1933), p. 76.

28. S. F. Kitchen, "Symptomology: General Considerations," in Mark F. Boyd, ed., *Malariology: A Comprehensive Survey . . . from a Global Standpoint* (Philadelphia: W. B. Saunders, 1949), p. 988.

29. Darrett B. Rutman and Anita H. Rutman, "Of Agues and Fevers: Malaria in the Early Chesapeake," *William and Mary Quarterly*, 3d ser., 33 (1976): 31–60.

30. D. J. Naismith, "The Foetus as a Parasite," *Proceedings of the Nutrition Society* 28 (1969): 25–31.

31. These lingering effects are a general phenomenon. In many populations, "high rates of maternal mortality are significantly associated with high death rates in the postmaternal age interval of 40 to 59," and both rates are signs of poor living conditions for women. Samuel H. Preston, *Mortality Patterns in National Populations* (New York: Academic Press, 1976), p. 134.

32. Men in Manti had a slightly lower life expectancy at birth in most nineteenth-century decades, though women had higher death rates in the reproductive years. These findings must be viewed with caution, however, be-

cause of probable inaccuracies in the population at risk (see note 10 above). Levison et al., "Epidemiologic Transition," p. 89.

33. Life expectancy at twenty in the seventeenth-century Chesapeake was less than thirty years for both sexes. See Darrett B. and Anita H. Rutman, "'Now-Wives and Sons-in-Law': Parental Death in a Seventeenth-Century Virginia County," in Thad W. Tate and David L. Ammerman, eds., *The Chesapeake in the Seventeenth Century: Essays on Anglo-American Society* (Chapel Hill: University of North Carolina Press, 1979), p. 172.

34. Life expectancy at twenty for men in the United States caught up with that of St. George's men (shown in Table 15) in 1950. See Preston et al., *Causes of Death,* p. 752.

35. Again, unattributed deaths are distributed by cause in the same way as known deaths.

36. Men in England and Wales in 1871 had higher death rates than women at most ages for most diseases. See Preston et al., *Causes of Death,* pp. 228, 230.

37. On motivations behind the Word of Wisdom, see Leonard J. Arrington, "An Economic Interpretation of the 'Word of Wisdom'," *Brigham Young University Studies* 1 (1959): 37–49.

38. Lester E. Bush, Jr., "The Word of Wisdom in Early Nineteenth-Century Perspective," *Dialogue* 14 (Autumn, 1981): 47–65. In an address in 1883, George Q. Cannon insisted that adherents to the Word of Wisdom had suffered fewer deaths in a recent epidemic. *Journal of Discourses by Brigham Young . . . and Others,* 26 vols. (1854–86; reprint ed., Los Angeles: Gartner, 1956), 24: 147.

39. Bush, "Word of Wisdom," p. 59.

40. Nels Anderson, *Desert Saints: The Mormon Frontier in Utah* (Chicago: University of Chicago Press, 1942), pp. 435–37; Andrew Karl Larson, *Erastus Snow: The Life of a Missionary and Pioneer for the Early Mormon Church* (Salt Lake City: University of Utah Press, 1971), pp. 571–75; Diary of Charles Smith, Library-Archives, Historical Department of the Church of Jesus Christ of Latter-day Saints (hereafter cited as LDS Church Archives), entry for summer of 1881.

41. Robert J. McCue, "Did the Word of Wisdom Become a Commandment in 1851?" *Dialogue* 14 (Autumn, 1981): 66–77; Thomas G. Alexander, "The Word of Wisdom: From Principle to Requirement," ibid., 78–88. Charles Walker noted a Christmas in St. George when there was "nobody drunk nor no disturbence." A. Karl Larson and Katharine M. Larson, eds., *Diary of Charles Lowell Walker,* 2 vols. (Logan: Utah State University Press, 1980), Dec. 25, 1869, 1: 303.

42. Reports of drunkenness in St. George pale beside the descriptions in Roger D. McGrath, *Gunfighters, Highwaymen, & Vigilantes: Violence on the Frontier* (Berkeley: University of California Press, 1984), chap. 4. There were, however, occasional alcohol-related homicides and accidents in and around St. George; see, for example, Larson and Larson, eds., *Diary of Charles Walker,* Mar. 31, Apr. 2, 1881, 2: 547–48. But there is no non-Mormon standard of comparison for accidents in western towns, and standards for homicides depend on where one looks. Western cattle and mining towns had murder rates

several times those of modern American cities, but Oakland, California, had only two homicides from 1870 to 1875. See McGrath, *Gunfighters*, pp. 254–55, 261–71.

43. Parley P. Pratt, *Key to the Science of Theology* (Liverpool: F. D. Richards, 1855), p. 166.

44. Address by Brigham Young, in *Journal of Discourses*, 9: 308. See also Newell G. Bringhurst, *Brigham Young and the Expanding American Frontier* (Boston: Little, Brown, 1986), p. 192.

45. *Journal of Discourses*, 4: 258.

46. Ibid., p. 256.

47. Edward W. Tullidge, *The Women of Mormondom* (New York: Tullidge & Crandall, 1877), p. 486.

48. *Journal of Discourses*, 16: 347.

49. Jan. 1, 1892. Cf. John Demos, "Images of the American Family, Then and Now," in Virginia Tufte and Barbara Myerhoff, eds., *Changing Images of the Family* (New Haven: Yale University Press, 1979), pp. 53–54.

50. Quoted in James G. Bleak, "Annals of the Southern Utah Mission," 2 vols., Brigham Young University Library, 2: 242.

51. *Journal of Discourses*, 14: 105.

52. Larson and Larson, eds., *Diary of Charles Walker*, July 24, 1880, 2: 497.

53. Ibid., July 24, 1897, 2: 848.

54. Ibid., 1: June 15, 1874, 1: 388.

55. Biography of Elizabeth Reeves Liston, in Diary of Commodore P. Liston, Huntington Library, San Marino, Calif. Used by permission. The Listons' dilemma was made worse by boarders in their household, but empty larders plagued many families in St. George, with or without boarders.

56. Privy Council report on laborers' diets, quoted in John Burnett, *Plenty and Want: A Social History of Diet in England from 1815 to the Present Day*, rev. ed. (London: Scolar Press, 1979), p. 161.

57. Robert E. Kennedy, Jr., *The Irish: Emigration, Marriage, and Fertility* (Berkeley: University of California Press, 1973), chap. 3; Imhof, "Women and Death," p. 153.

58. See, for example, Lincoln C. Chen, Emdadul Huq, and Stan D'Souza, "Sex Bias in the Family Allocation of Food and Health Care in Rural Bangladesh," *Population and Development Review* 7 (1981): 55–70; M. A. El-Badry, "Higher Female Than Male Mortality in Some Countries of South Asia: A Digest," *Journal of the American Statistical Association* 64 (1969): 1234–44; Stolnitz, "Mortality Trends," p. 31.

59. John Mack Faragher, *Women and Men on the Overland Trail* (New Haven: Yale University Press, 1979), p. 178.

60. R. Carlyle Buley, *The Old Northwest: Pioneer Period, 1815–1840*, 2 vols. (Bloomington: Indiana University Press, 1950), 1: 221. See also Evadene A. Burris, "Frontier Food," *Minnesota History* 14 (1933): 378–92. Diets in nineteenth-century New England likewise consisted of "ample, diversified fare." Sarah F. McMahon, "A Comfortable Subsistence: The Changing Composition

of Diet in Rural New England, 1620–1840," *William and Mary Quarterly*, 3d ser., 42 (1985): 29.

61. Henry Eyring and his wife ended their marriage in 1860 partly because, in his words, she had "no disposition to be subject to good teachings." A church official "felt to fully justify me in my separation." Eyring soon remarried, but there is no further record of his former wife. Journal of Henry Eyring, LDS Church Archives, Apr. 4, 1860.

62. Daniel Scott Smith, "Family Limitation, Sexual Control, and Domestic Feminism in Victorian America," in Mary S. Hartman and Lois Banner, eds., *Clio's Consciousness Raised: New Perspectives on the History of Women* (New York: Harper & Row, 1974), pp. 119–36.

63. For a fictionalized protest against this bondage written by a descendant of St. George's settlers, see Maurine Whipple, *The Giant Joshua* (Boston: Houghton Mifflin, 1942). Polygamy is the apparent cause of the main character's despair, but her anguish runs as deep as Mormonism's male-determined culture.

64. On feminism in the Female Relief Society and the *Woman's Exponent*, see Carol Lynn Pearson, *The Flight and the Nest* (Salt Lake City: Bookcraft, 1975), chaps. 1, 2. See also Sherilyn Cox Bennion, "The *Woman's Exponent*: Forty-two Years of Speaking for Women," *Utah Historical Quarterly* 44 (1976): 222–39. On expressions of American urban feminism, see Barbara J. Berg, *The Remembered Gate: Origins of American Feminism* (New York: Oxford University Press, 1978).

65. Quoted in Leonard J. Arrington, "Persons for All Seasons: Women in Mormon History," *Brigham Young University Studies* 20 (1979): 54.

66. Ibid., p. 50; Chris Rigby Arrington, "Pioneer Midwives," in Claudia L. Bushman, ed., *Mormon Sisters: Women in Early Utah* (Cambridge, Mass.: Emmeline Press, 1976), pp. 43–65; Pearson, *Flight and Nest*, chap. 8; Ann Vest Lobb and Jill Mulvay Derr, "Women in Early Utah," in Richard D. Poll, Thomas G. Alexander, Eugene E. Campbell, and David E. Miller, eds., *Utah's History* (Provo: Brigham Young University Press, 1978), pp. 344–46.

67. Quoted in Pearson, *Flight and Nest*, p. 8.

68. Quoted in Leonard J. Arrington, *Brigham Young: American Moses* (New York: Knopf, 1985), p. 364.

69. Elizabeth Jameson, "Women as Workers, Women as Civilizers: True Womanhood in the American West," *Frontiers* 7:3 (1984): 7.

70. Quoted in Pearson, *Flight and Nest*, p. 46.

EPILOGUE

The Mormon Identity in St. George

The apostle Matthias F. Cowley offered his opinion about why Mormons remained Mormons. He believed that the Latter-day Saints had a "real and tangible" knowledge of the resurrection and eternal life, "as contrasted with the poor, rambling, uncertain theories of uninspired men." Cowley described the sustaining power of this knowledge: "Glorious thought! The righteous rewarded for all their trials and tribulations! . . . This reward is well worth all the hardships incidental to preaching the Gospel and living the life of a Saint."[1]

Less prominent Mormons echoed Cowley's statement. A northern Utah woman explained her acceptance of polygamy by pointing out that "we do not count the trials of this present life worthy to be compared with the glory which will be given to us, if we will faithfully discharge our duties."[2] In Utah's Dixie, Allen Stout wrote of his eagerness to "see the Lord's kingdom triumph and enemies of righteousness brought low in the dust. . . . for this cause I labor and toil in pain and sickness, and esteem my affliction light when I contemplate the glory that will be given those who endure to the end."[3]

Some of those trials and afflictions have been woven throughout this book. Coping with plural marriage, raising large families in the desert, and living with ever-present death were among the hardest of the circumstances that tried the souls of St. George's residents. In a sense, of course, the Latter-day Saints brought their trials on themselves. Polygamy caused friction in households and encouraged anti-Mormonism, and families complying with the church's insistence on high fertility grew faster than the means to support them. Yet both polygamy and unrestrained fertility made perfect sense for the Latter-day Saints as a separatist population. There was undeniably strength in numbers for a group trying to hold a vast territory; growth through high fertility was necessary even with continuing immigration. And as has been seen, polygamy bolstered this natural growth by creating a shortage of single women, keeping the marriage age young for all women and thus insuring high fertility. The anti-Mormon furor that polygamy caused, as long as it stayed at a distance, further strengthened the church by drawing its members together.

But for ordinary Mormons none of these issues outweighed the desire to master their own fate. These were nineteenth-century individuals who understood as well as their non-Mormon peers that men and women were not receptacles of grace, that they could instead influence the course of their lives and their place in the afterlife. Yet they were also people who were reluctant to cut all their ties to tradition and so resisted setting their own agenda for self-determination. Many nineteenth-century Americans could consider themselves self-made men (and occasionally women) on various and fluid criteria—notoriety, political power, possessions—and could as never before decide for themselves, without much oversight from a professional clergy, if they were to be saved. Mormons, on the other hand, wanted a program by which to engineer their fate. They too insisted on being self-made, but not in what they considered to be a formless and chaotic society. The Latter-day Saints wanted a clear-cut path to tangible goals, with a paternal clergy to urge the faithful along the path.

The church's program for self-determination clearly appealed to St. George's residents. They married early and then entered polygamy in surprising numbers, they maintained unchecked fertility, and they apparently took extraordinary steps to ensure a healthy priesthood, all of which conformed to central church tenets and helped ensure members' salvation. But the townspeople did not hesitate to reshape doctrine and policy when they felt it necessary. As described in chapter 2, they resisted the church's seeming denigration of the individual under the United Order, and they only partially adopted the church's concept of spirits' activity between death and the resurrection.

The people of St. George had found, and struggled to maintain, a balance between what we know as "modern" society and the traditional existence that preceded it. Believers in choice and accountability for everyone, they were nonetheless uncomfortable with the hurly-burly of nineteenth-century life. They had therefore decided to express their modern sentiments in a decidedly unmodern way, by working for self-improvement within a system of hierarchical authority. St. George residents' remarkable conformity to church teachings on marriage, fertility, and the primacy of the male priesthood suggests that the church's balance between modernity and tradition served its purpose in their eyes. Residents followed their leaders, but only because they saw in their obedience the way to exaltation as individuals.

St. George grew from a precarious settlement in the early 1860s into the center of southern Utah in the 1880s, but Mormon culture in the same period remained essentially seamless. The United Order did focus special attention on the family as a metaphor for Mormon society in the 1870s, and concern with the outside world ebbed and flowed with the Civil War and anti-polygamy legislation, but the outlines of Mormon identity were largely the same until the Raid of the 1880s. The Raid sent shock waves through Mormons' lives that did not subside until the Latter-day Saints had given up the attempt to be a separatist culture. The invasion by federal authorities caused obvious disruptions—a few residents, including Erastus Snow, went to Mexico, some polygamists went to jail, and those who avoided prison had to play cat-and-mouse with the lawmen—but the Raid's aftermath in the 1890s was a more subtle cultural crisis. The church ended the struggle with Washington by renouncing polygamy, but in doing so it removed a cornerstone of Mormon culture. Plural marriage had been among the holiest of obligations for dedicated Latter-day Saints, a requirement for distinction in this life and glory in the next. Now, in 1890, the church partly reversed itself: without explicitly retracting any of its praise for polygamy as a sacred institution, the leadership simply announced that it would perform no more plural marriages.

Monogamists and polygamists alike, though they undoubtedly understood the need to end the federal government's siege of their church, were nonetheless confused about their future. Charles Walker described the Latter-day Saints' bewilderment in 1891: "[The repudiation of polygamy] has caused an uneasy feeling among the People, and some think [the church's president] has gone back on the Revealation on Plural Marriage and its covenants and obligations. . . . Some are wavering, and seem to doubt the Power of God to overrule all things for the onward progress of his glorious work."[4] Four years later, Walker wrote that "some of the Leaders of the Church had not the entire confidence of the People as in days past," and Francis Moody described a St. George priesthood meeting in 1896 in which "there was considerable coment on the Manifesto [that ended polygamy] and the nesisity of being obediant to the priesthood."[5] But Utah was now a state and the kingdom of God was becoming a distant ideal rather than an imminent reality; the basis of church leadership and priesthood government had permanently changed.

Twentieth-century Mormonism has shed much of its subversive image. Non-Mormons undoubtedly still mistrust the church's control over its members and their considerable political and economic leverage.[6] But it should be remembered that this is a group whose practices were once vilified along with slavery as "relics of barbarism," and which responded in kind; Americans' suspicion is now mixed with admiration for the Latter-day Saints' familial values and patriotism.[7] Both the Mormon and the larger American societies have changed on the way to this rapprochement, and whether the change in Mormonism was determined by inescapable currents originating in non-Mormon America is a central question of Mormon history.

If early Mormons brought to Utah the nineteenth century's commitment to individual agency, it makes sense for some historians to suppose that the church's own emphasis on self-determination fostered a modern, individualistic personality that eventually outgrew Mormon antimodernism. In this view, the crisis of faith in the 1890s and the evolution of a Mormon middle-class culture were inevitable results of an earlier rise of modern behavior that paralleled the same development elsewhere in America. Polygamy, the preeminent difference between Mormons and nineteenth-century Americans, was apparently "doomed from the start precisely because Mormons had always been too 'American' at heart"; the demise of plural marriage was thus an acknowledgment of the Latter-day Saints' modern American attitudes rather than the *cause* of those attitudes.[8]

This modernity should have been evident in Mormons' behavior well before the Raid, and indeed the seemingly low incidence of polygamy has been cited as resistance to this most antimodern of the church's doctrines. An apparent decline in plural marriages after 1860 is seen as a "backlash" against polygamy, demonstrating the emergence of modern social attitudes in spite of the leadership's wishes.[9] But neither plural marriage nor other forms of behavior in St. George suggest a groundswell of modern attitudes that overwhelmed traditional tendencies and ended Mormon separatism. Instead, polygamy was unexpectedly common in St. George and has probably been underestimated in other Mormon communities as well; indeed, a shortage of single women undoubtedly limited plural marriage as much as the reluctance of men and women to enter polygamy. Nor was there a dramatic decline over time in polygamy: of the plural marriages made before 1880 by the St. George residents studied here, 37 percent took place in the 1850s, 32 percent in the 1860s, and 29 percent in the 1870s. In raw numbers, there were just ten fewer plural marriages in the 1870s, a time of supposed resistance, than in the 1850s, a "peak" period for polygamy.[10] The threat of arrest, enforced by federal marshals' surveillance of the St. George temple, finally curtailed plural marriage in the 1880s.

Moreover, control of fertility, a hallmark of the modern personality, did not appear in nineteenth-century St. George. As detailed in chapter 4, natural fertility was the rule before 1880, and indeed unchecked childbearing continued thereafter. Couples married in the 1870s, whose childbearing years extended into the 1890s, continued to have about nine births when their marriages stayed intact throughout the reproductive years. Other Utah Mormons had the same unrestrained fertility through the rest of the nineteenth century; by the second decade of the present century, however, the Latter-day Saints had begun to practice family limitation.[11]

Nor did St. George parents see their children in a modern light, which would likewise indicate a weakening of Mormon separatism. Families in several nineteenth-century American communities apparently signaled a modern, child-centered domestic culture by abandoning the practice of passing on parents' and grandparents' names; the first settlers of St. George did likewise. But later residents, those born and raised as Mormons, reversed this trend: these parents named more than three-quarters of first sons for their father, a 50 percent increase over the previous generation's paternal naming. The townspeople did not similarly increase maternal naming of daughters, which underscores the church's success in advocating a pervasive patriarchy.[12]

Instead of looking increasingly like modern Americans, the people of St. George exhibited all the signs of a group traveling an increasingly divergent path to a separate future. Yet the Latter-day Saints never reached that future. The behavioral data and cultural evidence from St. George suggest the outlines of the Mormons' evolution from nineteenth-century separatists to twentieth-century Americans.

Plural marriage played a critical role in this transformation. Polygamy was deeply woven into the fabric of the community: as previously examined, it involved over one-third of married men and the majority of women and children before the Raid. The people of St. George used polygamy not only to enhance their status now and in the afterlife, but also to hasten the millennium. Diarists charted anti-polygamy campaigns along with non-Mormons' other sins, aware that their own individual decisions to enter polygamy added up to a continual provocation of the outside world. They interpreted the world's rising fury as the approach of Armageddon and the thousand-year reign.

But the end of polygamy fundamentally changed ordinary Mormons' ability to influence events. Latter-day Saints could no longer "magnify their calling" by fully participating in what their church had for decades called celestial marriage; nor could they provoke non-Mormons' rage with the church's blessing. Though residents like Charles Walker could still speak of the impending millennium after the Manifesto, Mormons' best method to help bring on the apocalypse had disappeared, and the belief in the millennium itself eventually faded.

Since they could no longer ensure heavenly glory by forming multiple families and since the millennium was becoming less certain, end-of-the-century Mormons turned their attention to this world instead. They were aided by the church itself, which was faced with an undeniable this-worldly crisis of its own. The confiscatory anti-Mormon legislation of the 1880s had left the church deeply in debt, and leaders responded with several financing schemes plus an appeal to the membership.[13] Tithing, always stressed by the church, now became a crucial test of commitment. An official announced in 1900 that "by this principle it shall be known who is for the kingdom of God and who is against it."[14] The tithing crusade had in fact begun in St. George a year earlier, when the church's president promised an end to a drought if tithers paid up; accounts were settled, the rains came, and the tithing "reform" caught on.[15] Payment of tithing in commodities was forbidden a year later, the final signal of "a more acceptable adjustment between spiritual and secular interests."[16]

Through all its trials and accommodations, Mormonism is a religion that survives. It survived the crisis of the 1890s and became a belief system suited to the twentieth century. The church's new stress on economic security coincided with a surge in Utah's industry and commerce, and church members who found places in the new economy could still take comfort in their religion. Mormon doctrine now provided direction for economic achievement. Even if God's kingdom and the millennium were becoming abstractions, members now earned heavenly rewards and strengthened God's special people by combining financial success with commitment to their church. Indeed, church leaders assured members that nothing fundamental had changed, that twentieth-century Mormons could continue the mission of Joseph Smith and Brigham Young.[17] But a number of Mormons surely had trouble seeing continuity in their society. Not everyone was successful in the modernizing Utah economy, especially in southern Utah. Commercial farming was a mainstay of Utah's development, but farms in Washington County remained small at the turn of the century in spite of long-awaited irrigation improvements that supported more farmers. The nearest mines still operating were in Nevada, and railroads and factories were even farther away. St. George remained a modest commercial center for southwestern Utah, but these were nonetheless hard times for some Dixie residents caught in the transition from a largely communal to a mostly commercial economy. These were the Mormons who felt abandoned by a leadership that seemed to have repealed much of the heavenly promise and the basis for building God's earthly kingdom.

Yet Mormonism persevered and continues to grow today. It has turned out to be as adaptable to modern middle-class concerns as it was to the new array of choices that confronted individuals in the nineteenth century. But the transition to modernity was not inevitable, except in the sense that in defying the U.S. government the Mormons were playing with a fire that was bound to engulf them. In other respects, nineteenth-century Mormonism was on a course toward a separate commonwealth in which modernization and accommodation to American middle-class life might have taken unprecedented forms or not happened at all. But Americans' wrath triumphed: Mormons were wrenched out of their course and set on a new one more in step with the larger society. The type of Mormonism which once thrived in St. George could never again support a thoroughgoing scheme of marriage, childbearing, and health, aimed at heavenly more than earthly rewards. Where that scheme would have led on its own will never be known.

NOTES

1. M. F. Cowley, *Cowley's Talks on Doctrine* (Chattanooga, Tenn.: Ben E. Rich, 1902), pp. 168, 164. Though these remarks were published after the renunciation of plural marriage, they are the views of a steadfast polygamist: Cowley was removed from the church's leadership and disfellowshipped when he continued to perform plural marriages long after the Manifesto. His view of the afterlife had been shared by Brigham Young, who declared that "some people talked about suffering, and making a sacrifice for the Kingdom of Heaven; but we really sacrificed nothing, but were preparing ourselves for an exaltation." Quoted in James G. Bleak, "Annals of the Southern Utah Mission," 2 vols., Brigham Young University Library, 2: 157.
2. Letter to the Editor, *Woman's Exponent*, Oct. 15, 1872.
3. Journal of Allen Joseph Stout, Huntington Library, San Marino, Calif., p. 97. All items from Huntington Library quoted by permission.
4. A. Karl Larson and Katharine M. Larson, eds., *Diary of Charles Lowell Walker*, 2 vols. (Logan: Utah State University Press, 1980), Oct. 20, 1891, 2: 728.
5. Ibid., Oct. 20, 1895, 2: 802; Autobiography and Journal of Francis W. Moody, in Family Record of John Monroe Moody, Huntington Library, Apr. 22, 1896.
6. This suspicion informs studies such as Robert Gottlieb and Peter Wiley, *America's Saints: The Rise of Mormon Power* (New York: G. P. Putnam's Sons,

1984) and John Heinerman and Anson Shupe, *The Mormon Corporate Empire* (Boston: Beacon, 1986). Such investigations make it equally clear that this suspicion is to an extent mutual.

7. On the course of Americans' attitude change, see Jan Shipps, "From Satyr to Saint: American Attitudes Toward the Mormons, 1860–1960," paper presented at the annual meeting of the Organization of American Historians, Chicago, 1973.

8. Grant Underwood, "Re-visioning Mormon History," *Pacific Historical Review* 55 (1986): 412. This essay argues that both Mormons' separatism and their later accommodation have been overemphasized. See also Klaus J. Hansen, *Mormonism and the American Experience* (Chicago: University of Chicago Press, 1981), p. 206.

9. Hansen, *Mormon Experience*, pp. 175–76. See also Stanley S. Ivins, "Notes on Mormon Polygamy," *Western Humanities Review* 10 (1956): 239; Julie Roy Jeffrey, *Frontier Women: The Trans-Mississippi West, 1840–1880* (New York: Hill and Wang, 1979), p. 164.

10. On the "peaks" in plural marriage, see Thomas F. O'Dea, *The Mormons* (Chicago: University of Chicago Press, 1957), pp. 245–46; Leonard J. Arrington, *Great Basin Kingdom: An Economic History of the Latter-day Saints, 1830–1900* (Cambridge, Mass.: Harvard University Press, 1958), p. 238; Ivins, "Notes," pp. 231–32.

11. The index of fertility control (m) confirms Mormons' natural fertility through 1895. See G. P. Mineau, L. L. Bean, and M. Skolnick, "Mormon Demographic History II: The Family Life Cycle and Natural Fertility," *Population Studies* 33 (1979): 435. The value of m for fertility from 1911 to 1920, however, is .21, which indicates the onset of family limitation not long after the end of Mormon separatism. Calculated from M. Skolnick, L. Bean, D. May, V. Arbon, K. de Nevers, and P. Cartwright, "Mormon Demographic History I: Nuptiality and Fertility of Once-Married Couples," ibid. 32 (1978): 15. See chap. 4 for a discussion of the fertility index.

12. Larry M. Logue, "Modernization Arrested: Child-Naming and the Family in a Utah Town," *Journal of American History* 74 (1987): 131–38.

13. Arrington, *Great Basin Kingdom*, pp. 403–9.

14. Joseph F. Smith, quoted in O'Dea, *Mormons*, p. 197.

15. James B. Allen and Glen M. Leonard, *The Story of the Latter-day Saints* (Salt Lake City: Deseret Book Co., 1976), p. 450.

16. Arrington, *Great Basin Kingdom*, p. 409.

17. Jan Shipps, *Mormonism: The Story of a New Religious Tradition* (Urbana: University of Illinois Press, 1985), chap. 7.

1876 panoramic view of St. George. Utah State Historical Society.

Main Street in early St. George. Lynne Clark Collection.

Tabernacle Street housed several early St. George businesses, including the town's first post office (far l.) and Booth Photography (far r.).

Erastus Snow (1818–88) served as both a Brigadier General Missionary and as a colonizer for the LDS Church. He was largely responsible for the successful colonization of southern Utah. Utah State Historical Society.

Charles Walker (1832–1904) was considered the poet laureate of Dixie. He wrote many songs that helped people laugh at their troubles. Utah State Historical Society.

Workmen whitewashing the newly constructed St. George Temple, mid-1870s.
Lynne Clark Collection.

Tabernacle choir of early St. George. Singing was another diversion the settlers
enjoyed. Lynne Clark Collection.

1888 photo showing several St. George men serving time for polygamy in the Salt Lake Prison. Pictured (l. to r.): Jacob Bastian, Casper Bryner, Bp. Granger, George Q. Cannon, Bro. Carter, and Bro. Hardy. Lynne Clark Collection.

Interior of a St. George classroom, c. 1890. Lynne Clark Collection.

A reminder of the hardships faced by St. George pioneers. Standing with the shovel is Aaron Nelson, sexton, and seated on the hearse are George Woodard, owner of the hearse, and Alf Larson. Utah State Historical Society.

APPENDIX A

Mormon Diaries and Sample Validity

The Latter-day Saints are irrepressible record-keepers, as a visit to the church archives in Salt Lake City will demonstrate. Not only do Mormons record the vital events of their ancestors for posthumous baptism and preserve the discourses of their leaders; they also keep accounts of their own lives in diaries and journals. Latter-day Saints believe that self-knowledge is a key to self-improvement, and their leaders have long encouraged the habit of regular introspection. Echoing Joseph Smith's instructions, the leadership especially promoted diary-keeping among missionaries, but it also assured all priesthood members that a diary could be a lifelong "silent monitor, a guide, a friend to succor and to save."[1]

Mormons have always taken this advice seriously. If they did not keep a diary while they were young, there was a chance they would compensate for it by writing an autobiography and, failing that, they might still be a biographer's subject. St. George residents were no exception, and a search through various collections has uncovered over forty published and unpublished diaries, autobiographies, biographies, and brief life sketches. The majority are retrospective life histories and biographies; they are used in this study chiefly for their evidence of impressions that last over time, such as the remembered first response to Mormonism and the reaction to the call to St. George. Eighteen other documents are actual diaries that report on life in early St. George.[2] Because the advice to keep diaries was given primarily to the male priesthood, all but one of these diaries were written by men. This obvious bias is partly offset by women's retrospective accounts, which are about one-third of the non-diary material; women's recollections are thus an important part of the town's cultural evidence.

But the diaries remain the best guide to life and attitudes in St. George, though they have problems of their own. The first problem is that historical diaries tend to come from a subgroup of the literate elite who felt their daily lives were worth recording. Generalizing from such individuals to any larger population is clearly risky. Are St. George's diarists such a group?

Comparisons with the whole town suggest that the diarists are less elite than would be expected. They could obviously read and write, but so could almost every adult in St. George: nearly 98 percent of residents over age twenty satisfied the census-taker in 1870 that they could read and write. But we nonetheless expect diarists to be a social and economic elite. Twelve of the diarists were in St. George at the 1870 census, and their median wealth (real and personal property combined) was $1,650, whereas the median for the whole town was $1,000.[3] However, the diarists included individuals with as little as $200 as well as those with as much as $12,000; over one-fourth of all St. George households had more than the diarists' median of $1,650, which makes the diarists' apparent wealth less impressive.

Occupations can be determined for sixteen of the diarists by using both the 1870 and 1880 censuses. All major job categories are represented by the diarists (professional and merchant, farmer and white-collar, artisan, and laborer), and farmers and artisans are the two largest groups (six and five diarists) just as they are in the entire town. The diarists, though they were relatively comfortable, were too diverse to be called an economic elite.

Their church status likewise suggests a group that was above average but not quite a privileged class. The typical diarist was a Seventy, a member of the Melchizedek or higher Mormon priesthood charged with being an emissary for the Gospel; the woman diarist likewise held a responsible position in the Female Relief Society. Seventies, a small proportion of church members today, were more common in the nineteenth century.[4] Many of the diarists, indeed many of the household heads of St. George, joined the church when its survival depended on attracting converts and they were quickly placed into the traveling priesthood as Seventies. In selecting settlers for St. George, as they did when calling residents for any new settlement, Mormon leaders chose people whose service had proved their reliability. Elevated church rank was not uncommon either among all adults in St. George or among diarists.

Their economic and social characteristics put St. George's diarists somewhere above the average of the town's residents, but they are not the privileged coterie that might be expected in dealing with preserved diaries. Mormonism did (and does) have a ruling elite, generally wealthy men interlocked by kinship and marriage who have directed the church's affairs.[5]

However, the diarists in this study were neither notably wealthy nor particularly interlocked: eight of the diarists were related by blood ties or marriage, but such linkages were just as common among the town's whole population. The social biases in this group of diarists are surprisingly modest when seen against the background of St. George's residents.

But there is a second problem apart from the social characteristics of the diary-keepers. Any sample of diaries will show wide variability of subject matter and detail. Some journals are one-line summaries of each day's activities, others are extensive daily barometers of the writer's inner state, and still others mix features of each extreme. Since almost no diary mentions all the pivotal issues analysts want to explore, how should a reader interpret many diarists' failure to write about a key topic? Are such omissions missing data that pare an already small sample down to a negligible one?

Missing data in present-day surveys signal people who undoubtedly differ from respondents. Confronted with a uniform stimulus (a question on a form or asked by an interviewer), some people decline to respond where others answer. Non-respondents' motivations, if they were known, might well indicate fundamental differences from respondents, and it would be a mistake to infer their views from respondents' data.

But we have no way of knowing whether different diarists in the past, even ones who were in the same place on the same day, faced stimuli that would have prompted similar entries.[6] Two St. George residents at the same Sunday worship meeting might have recorded different details in their journals, because a sermon that addressed a vital concern of one might have found the other asleep. Diarists faced conditions so subtle and complex that we seldom compare them to the uniformly administered questions in a survey.

Something about stimulus and response in St. George's diaries can be determined, however, by simply tabulating mentions of important questions in this study, "polling" each diary on whether it ever speaks of the nature of non-Mormons, the fate of the soul after death, faith-healing of the sick, and so on. It could happen that four of the diaries mention every issue and the other fourteen never speak of any of these topics. A reader could then conclude that, since stimuli must overlap at some times among people living together, the four are a unique subsample on these issues and their authors are essentially different from their fellow diary-keepers. Put another way, personal idiosyncrasy in such a case would undoubtedly have outweighed circumstances in producing diary entries. On the other hand, if mentions and non-mentions are scattered randomly among diarists and issues, it is safe to determine that stimulus dominated personality; that no matter who the diarist was, he or she had to face some combination of circumstances to produce an entry on a given topic.

A test recently proposed by Murray Murphey can indicate which of these cases an actual set of diaries most resembles.[7] Figure 1 shows a tabulation of the eighteen St. George diarists on seven key issues in this study. There is a range of responses from no issues mentioned to reports on six of the seven issues. To interpret this distribution of mentions, computer-generated random numbers were used to "scramble" the entries in each row of Figure 1. The result is Figure 2, which shows how a different set of diaries might appear, responding not to the conditions in St. George but to random stimuli.[8] A test of our real diarists' mentions against those of the hypothetical "diarists" indicates that the two distributions are not significantly different.[9] Diarists are not especially associated with issues, which suggests that if diarists who were silent on a topic had faced the same circumstances as others, they would have written about it as well. In other words, there is no compelling reason to suppose that some diarists differed fundamentally from others in their views on central issues.

The findings here should not be taken as a dismissal of the importance of diarists' peculiarities as individuals. The analyst's judgment is always crucial in sorting out personal and social reasons behind conflicting views reported in diaries. This appendix should instead dem-

Figure 1: Mentions of Key Issues by St. George Diarists[a]

Topics	Diarists[b]																	
	1	2	3	4	5	6	7	8	9	10	11	12	13	14	15	16	17	18
Gentiles		x					x						x	x	x	x		
Satan	x						x							x		x		
Faith-healing	x					x				x	x		x	x	x	x	x	
Settling quarrels						x	x							x		x		
Fate of soul	x				x		x					x		x	x	x		
Help by children	x	x	x	x			x		x		x		x	x				x
Food shortages							x						x	x		x		

[a]X = topic mentioned in diary.

[b]Key: 1, William Bigler; 2, Lorenzo Brown; 3, Anthony Ivins; 4, Charles Johnson; 5, Joseph Johnson; 6, William Lang; 7, George Laub; 8, Commodore Liston; 9, Daniel McAllister; 10, John McAllister;11, William Nelson; 12, John Oakley; 13, Charles Smith; 14, Allen Stout; 15, Henry Sudweeks; 16, Charles Walker; 17, Augustus Whitehead; 18, Mary Whitehead.

Figure 2: Random Mentions of Key Issues

Topics[a]	Diarists																	
	1	2	3	4	5	6	7	8	9	10	11	12	13	14	15	16	17	18
Gentiles	x	x	x		x					x	x							
Satan		x	x		x											x	x	
Faith-healing		x		x	x	x				x	x	x	x	x	x			
Settling quarrels					x					x						x		
Fate of soul				x							x			x	x	x		
Help by children	x	x	x		x		x	x		x		x	x	x				
Food shortages	x		x			x					x	x				x	x	

[a] "Entry" generation was based on row totals in Figure 1. That is, the first row of Figure 1 has six entries, so each cell has a .33 probability of containing an entry. Eighteen random numbers were selected for the first row of Figure 2; if a number was less than .33 an "entry" was recorded for that cell of the row.

onstrate that bias in a collection of diaries needs to be tested rather than assumed, and that such tests can produce encouraging results. St. George's diarists are reasonably representative of much of the town's population, and the issues raised in their diaries reasonably reflect the unexpressed sentiments of their neighbors.

NOTES

1. "Keeping Journals," *The Contributor*, Apr. 1883.

2. For this purpose, diaries are defined as sources that consist primarily of daily entries.

3. Father's occupations were used for two individuals who lived with their parents in 1870.

4. James B. Allen and Glen M. Leonard, *The Story of the Latter-day Saints* (Salt Lake City: Deseret Book Co., 1976), p. 508.

5. D. Michael Quinn, "The Mormon Hierarchy, 1832–1932: An American Elite" (Ph.D. diss., Yale University, 1976).

6. Murray G. Murphey, "Nonresponse in Samples from Historical Populations: Observations on the Problem," *Social Science History* 8 (1984): 455–67.

7. Ibid.

8. The number of entries in corresponding rows of Figures 1 and 2 does not always match, because random generation of entries produced occasional deviations from the original row totals. I am grateful to Murray Murphey for sharing with me some refinements to the source-testing technique presented in his "Nonresponse in Samples."

9. Mann-Whitney's U is 113.5 and $p > .05$. Whether a group of diaries can *ever* be considered a truly random sample of some larger population, an issue

on which the applicability of statistical tests partly depends, is one of the many unresolved (and essentially unexamined) topics in historical methods. The assumption here is that the diaries from St. George are not so biased on the variables that are known that they rule out an exploratory test of other variables.

APPENDIX B

Assessment of the Demographic Data

Reconstructing the sequence of vital events for groups of families offers unique access to important forms of past behavior. Whether the method is family reconstitution or another technique, historical demographers can follow ordinary as well as elite individuals through the life cycle. The vital records that offer these benefits, however, come with a potentially serious problem. Any study whose raw material is names and dates is obviously handicapped if a substantial part of that material is inaccurate or missing. As a result, data quality has been a closely examined issue in historical demography. Since outright omission in vital records is especially troublesome, it has led to some ingenious methodology.[1] Historians analyzing vital records with suspected omissions typically use known data to set a likely range for the knowns plus the unknowns. In this way, for example, mortality estimates can be made from cases with known death ages plus those whose age at death can be approximated from a birthdate and a last date known alive. Analysts who could make such adjustments and do not, find their studies cited as examples of the damage poor data can do.[2]

Knowing the pitfalls that threaten historical demography, this appendix will assess the extent to which analysis of family data from St. George can avoid them. A description of the research design underlying this book's demographic data is first, followed by an evaluation of the quality of the data that were collected, and by a discussion of the data set's representativeness of St. George's population.

Sources and Method

In any demographic community study, the concept of a community must be translated into a data set. In most studies the data set is determined by the source, typically a parish record or other register of vital events. A family enters such a data set by having had vital events recorded in the place being examined. This kind of research design allows for "cohort" or "generational" analysis, in which specific groups are observed over their lifetimes. For example, a life table for a New England town's males born from 1700 to 1725 would show the actual mortality rates of these men until all were dead.

Mormon data, on the other hand, present different requirements and opportunities. Mormon genealogies are not generally grouped by towns like New England records, for example, so there must be another way to get families into a sample.[3] The obvious answer is a census, a resource usually unavailable to analysts of early America. Combining censuses with reconstructed families for cohort analysis, however, causes its own set of problems, as a study of the Mormon town of Kanab in 1874 has shown.[4] A census artificially "freezes" a community that is actually in flux, and although the genealogies for Kanab do contain longitudinal information for the families that comprised the town in 1874, these families ceased being a "population" almost at once.

This study of St. George has taken a different approach to collecting and analyzing its data. Two U.S. manuscript censuses, for 1870 and 1880, plus the original settlers' lists, framed the St. George community and the period of analysis. All families that lived in the town at any of these enumerations were eligible for the data set, and they have been observed only for the time they were residents of St. George. This is a form of "period" analysis, which pretends that the vital events being studied happened to an actual birth cohort. For example, Table 15 reports mortality and survival for persons in age groups from birth to eighty *as if* they had all been born between 1861 and 1880 and were followed through their lives; in fact, of course, their births were scattered throughout the nineteenth century and earlier. Period analysis constructs a hypothetical life history from pieces of lives that intersected for a time, while cohort analysis constructs an actual life history from lifelong data on all of its subjects.

Data collection for this study began with a list of all household heads who were named as settlers in St. George and environs in 1862 or who appeared in the 1870 or 1880 censuses of the town.[5] "Family group sheets," the genealogies of uniform format which the Latter-day Saints use for posthumous sacraments, were sought for each head in the Mormon archives.[6] The objective was to find records of all marriages for each household head (including polygamous marriages) in order to reconstruct the experience of each family for the time it spent in St. George. This clearly does not include every family that lived in the town in the period; a family that arrived in 1863 and left in 1868, for example, would be excluded. Yet there is no actual bias against transient families, for the settlers' lists and the censuses captured transients as well as long-term residents. Since this is a study of families, the data set also excludes "non-family" individuals—single boarders without relatives elsewhere in the town, similarly independent servants, and widows and widowers without evidence of resident children; such individuals were less than 10 percent of St. George's population.

Although the principal source was the family group sheets, they were supplemented when necessary by a collection of genealogies for St. George pioneers compiled by Arthur K. Hafen and by the federal censuses.[7] Census data were used only for filling minor gaps in vital events, not as the primary source for reconstructing families. Though an attempt could have been made to reconstruct families not found in other sources (hereafter called "unfound" families) solely from the censuses, the problem of unlisted deceased children and the absence of marriage dates would have made the effort questionable at best. But in some cases the census list of children's ages complemented the Hafen collection's data on marriage dates and children ever born, and these families were reconstructed and removed from the unfound category.

In all, the St. George data set consists of the records of 446 marriages, 370 of which were found in the Mormon archives and 76 reconstructed according to the rules described above. The data set covers the demographic experience of 2,406 individuals for the time they were in St. George before the 1880 census. Each person has a date of entry and an exit date (except for nineteen "unknowns"—see below). In addition to entering by registering a vital event, the usual way in family reconstitution studies, individuals could also enter the St. George sample by in-migration. Dates for arrival in St. George are frequently given in the Hafen book; if an in-migration date had to be established in another way, the midpoint between a person's last vital event outside St. George (family group sheets include such locations) and his or her first in the town became the entry date. When this information was unavailable, the entry date was the midpoint between two other dates when the person could be located, such as censuses. Exit dates were assigned in the same way; all individuals listed in the 1880 census were given an exit date of June 1, the day the count began. Fifteen individuals had to be "exited" on June 1, 1870, since there was no evidence of their fate afterward.

Quality of the Data

Determining the quality of a set of reconstructed families requires two different kinds of assessment—judging the accuracy of information included in the set, and estimating the amount of information omitted altogether. For this section the estimates of omissions will concern missing data *within* "found" families only; the situation of entire families whose vital events could not be found at all is discussed in the next section.

In any analysis based on genealogies, the completeness of listed dates is one indicator of the sources' reliability. If a large number of events are identified by the year alone, genealogists may have been relying on less precise dating sources such as censuses, or worse still they may have been simply guessing. Table 18 gives the proportions of year-only dates in St. George compared to a group of births taken from the Mormon Demographic History (MDH) sample. In no case in either sample does the year-only proportion exceed 5 percent of all dates. The largest category of year-only dates in St. George is birthdates, reflecting the use of reported age in the censuses to replace missing dates.

Another and potentially more serious data problem occurs when an individual's existence and perhaps some of his or her vital events are known, but other dates are missing entirely. Year-only dates can be estimated at the year's midpoint as long as they are used with caution in some forms of analysis, but missing dates, if they are numerous and there is no reasonable way of making estimates, can be crippling. Table 19 lists the various kinds of date omissions in the St. George data set, along with comparison proportions from the MDH sample and several French and German studies; European demographic studies are thought to have especially good data.[8] Birthdates are seldom missing in either St. George or the MDH sample, while roughly one-third of all wives' birthdates are unknown in the French and German studies. Most birthdates missing for St. George can be estimated as the midpoint between two known births that have a long interval between them; this is jus-

Table 18: Accuracy of Dates, St. George and Mormon Demographic History (MDH) Samples

Type of Date	St. George		MDH Sample, Males Born 1880–89
	Number of Dates	Percent Year Only	Percent Year Only
Birthdates	2,406	4.3	1.1
Marriage dates	594	3.4	——
Death dates	357	0.8	1.5

Source: Calculated from Katherine A. Lynch, Geraldine P. Mineau, and Douglas L. Anderton, "Estimates of Infant Mortality on the Western Frontier: The Use of Genealogical Data," *Historical Methods* 18 (1985): 157.

Table 19: Missing Dates, St. George and Other Historical Samples

Type of Date	Number of Cases	Percent with Date Missing
St. George:		
Birthdates	2,406	1.0
Marriage dates	594	9.7
Death dates	2,406[a]	1.4
Entry and exit dates	2,406	0.8
MDH Sample:		
Birthdates for males born 1880–89	28,411	0.5
Death dates for males born 1880–89	28,411	15.2
Marriage dates for wives born 1800–1869	17,124	13.6
4 French Populations, 17th and 18th Centuries:		
Birthdates for wives	3,430	36.1
6 German Populations, 17th and 18th Centuries:		
Birthdates for wives	951	30.0

[a]Entire population used as the denominator because all individuals in the St. George data set were at risk of dying in the period studied.
Sources: Calculated from G. P. Mineau, L. L. Bean, and M. Skolnick, "Mormon Demographic History II: The Family Life Cycle and Natural Fertility," *Population Studies* 33 (1979): 431; Lynch et al., "Infant Mortality," p. 157; J. Knodel and E. Shorter, "The Reliability of Reconstitution Data in German Village[s]," *Annales de Démographie Historique,* 1976: 129.

tifiable when fertility was not controlled, and the estimated dates can be used in age-specific fertility rates (though obviously not for computing birth intervals).

Marriage dates, on the other hand, appear to be a significant problem in both Mormon samples—one in ten dates is missing in each population. But marriage dates for Mormons can be estimated with reasonable accuracy by using the endowment date or the date of the first child's birth. The endowment date is recorded in family group sheets; in over half the cases where both endowment and marriage dates are given, they match within a year. Though endowment was generally meant to precede marriage, Mormons in remote areas had to travel to Salt Lake City to receive this ordinance (until 1877, when the St. George temple was opened), and they often combined it with the marriage ceremony. The endowment date is thus a reasonable substitute for a missing marriage date. Omissions can be further reduced by backdating a marriage thirteen months from the first birth, which is the interval found in the rest of the sample. These estimates reduce the proportion of missing marriage dates in St. George to under 2 percent.

Death date omissions in St. George consist primarily of children for whom there is some evidence of birth but also an indication of not having lived to age eight, the Mormon age of baptism. Such evidence, in families where baptism recording was good, is a notation of "child" in the baptism space on the family group sheet. Again, the omission rate in St. George is lower than the rate in the MDH sample.

There are nineteen other cases where not even the baptism or endowment information was available to supplement missing vital dates. These are persons of "unknown fate," reported as the final category of St. George data in Table 19. The date of entry or exit, or both, could not be ascertained for these individuals. As observed previously, many entry and exit dates for the sample are estimates to some degree, though the large majority are dates from the Hafen collection or from sequential locations of vital events in the family group sheets; just over 5 percent of all individuals had to be "exited" at the 1870 census or halfway to the next census for lack of other information. For some of the unknowns, however, it was impossible to tell when (or if) they came to St. George and for others an exit date could not be estimated. This category includes some of the omissions listed in previous rows of Table 19, because missing birth and death dates are major reasons for not knowing an individual's fate. That these unknowns are so small a proportion of the sample is an especially encouraging feature of this data set.

In this hierarchy of inaccuracies, the next level is persons who should be within "found" families but who have been utterly lost to history. These were most likely children who entirely escaped the notice of a genealogist, not leaving so much as the mention of a name. Such cases are clearly important because they are detectable only indirectly and since overlooking them will distort demographic measures. There are several methods of estimating the incidence of lost cases, the simplest of which is to calculate sex ratios. Genealogies are, in principle, likely to underrepresent females, because most societies focus on males' activities. A sex ratio at birth that is significantly different from the biological standard of about 105 males to 100 females indicates that females have been lost. For St. George, the sex ratio for the 986 live births from 1861 to June of 1880 is 104.8, which gives no reason to suspect disproportionate loss of females. These births, however, are less than two-thirds of children in the St. George data set, so an extension of the sex ratio test to children who had been born elsewhere adds to its usefulness. Just over 700 children under age fifteen came to the town before 1880; after that age, sex ratios become affected by differential home-leaving patterns, so the 86 individuals over age fifteen who came with their parents are ignored. The sex ratio among the under-fifteen in-migrants is 110.1, which is not significantly different from 105.[9] Even if we allow for higher mortality among boys by comparing with a sex ratio of just under 104, the difference between the in-migrants' sex ratio and the hypothetical one is still probably due to chance.[10] Disproportionate omission of females in the St. George data set is thus a negligible problem.

But the sex-ratio test can only indicate gender-based omissions, and other tests are needed for other omissions. One such test is based on analysis of birth intervals.[11] The test assumes that "normal" birth intervals (that is, those not shortened by the early resumption of a woman's ovulation after an infant's death) will vary over a fairly narrow range *within* any family, provided there is no contraception. If widely fluctuating intervals appear under these circumstances, the longest intervals are almost surely the sum of *two* intervals between which there was an unrecorded birth. Louis Henry has supplied guidelines for the "tolerable" amount of birth interval variation within families before one should suspect omissions. Working with data from Geneva families that he felt were essentially free of omissions, Henry estimated the acceptable variance of intervals within a family. Using families with four or more live births and in which the wife married before age thirty, Henry paired the normal intervals among the first four births within each family. For illustration, consider two hypothetical families in St. George:

	Family 1	Family 2
First child's birth	January 1, 1870	July 1, 1873
First interval	24 months	24 months
Second child's birth	January 1, 1872	July 1, 1875[a]
Second interval	27 months	18 months[a]
Third child's birth	April 1, 1874	January 1, 1877
Third interval	30 months	27 months
Fourth child's birth	October 1, 1876	April 1, 1879

[a]Child dies within one year.

Family 1 has three normal intervals that can be made into two pairs (that is, the first and second intervals as one pair and the second and third intervals as the other); the datum used in the test is the difference in months between the members of each pair. In Family 2, the death of the second child before age one makes the second interval unusable, so the pairing here includes the first and third intervals and the family would have only one difference, three months (27 months minus 24). If the third child had also died, no pairings would be possible in this family and it would be ineligible for the test. The estimate of intrafamily variance is made by squaring all the differences in the population, summing them, and dividing the sum by the total number of pairs minus one. If the illustration were an entire population, its variance would be 13.5.[12]

Essentially the same steps were taken to apply this test to St. George. Families were selected where the wife married before thirty, and where the first four births occurred in St. George before mid-1880. Polygamous families, defined for the test as those in which any of the first four children were born to a father with plural wives, were split off for separate analysis if they otherwise qualified.[13] Plural marriage, with its variety of cohabitation patterns, may subtly disturb the presumption of natural fertility that underlies the birth-interval test.[14] Results for polygamous families are given largely for comparison, with the proviso that it is not known how closely these families *should* conform to Henry's guidelines. Another departure from Henry's practice is the elimination of births whose month and day are unknown; this rule affects only a few cases. Table 20 shows the results of Henry's test for monogamous and polygamous families in St. George, compared with Henry's own results for Geneva. Within St. George monogamous fam-

Table 20: Analysis of Birth Intervals for Omissions

	St. George Monogamous	St. George Polygamous	Geneva 1600–1649
No. of Paired Normal Intervals			
First and second	24	14	33
Second and third	24	22	34
First and third	4	0	10
Total (N)	52	36	77
Sum of Squared Differences within Pairs			
First and second	1488	2909	4280
Second and third	2423	3340	2967
First and third	583	0	478
Total (TSS)	4494	6249	7725
Variance (TSS/N-1)	88.1	178.5	101.5

Source: Louis Henry, *Anciennes Familles Genovoises: Etude Démographique, XVIᵉ–XXᵉ Siècle* (Paris: Presses Universitaires de France, 1956), p. 41.

ilies that qualify for the test, the variation of intervals is even less than in Henry's "model" group. The test clearly gives no cause to suspect missing births in the monogamous group. The polygamous variance suggests an omission rate of perhaps 3 percent of all births, but again it cannot be assumed that variations in polygamous intervals are due to missing births.[15]

The birth-interval test thus provides additional encouragement about the quality of the St. George data, but there is one more type of test for reconstructed families. Since missing cases were most likely infants who died, infant mortality must be examined separately for hints of omissions.

The fundamental components of first-year mortality are deaths from "endogenous" causes (congenital or obstetrical problems) and "exogenous" ones (post-partum environmental problems such as disease and malnutrition). The bulk of endogenous mortality occurs in the first month, so the distribution of deaths by attained age in the first year suggests the endogenous-exogenous relationship.

Table 21 shows the distribution of known infant deaths in St. George. The first-month proportion and the deaths per 1,000 births are both fairly low for historical populations; indeed, historical demographers begin to suspect missing cases when the first-month proportion is below 50 percent.[16]

Before making conclusions about omitted deaths in the St. George data set, however, we must look at the distribution of infant deaths in light of Jean Bourgeois-Pichat's biometric theory of newborns' mortality.[17] Bourgeois-Pichat has found that in most populations the cumulative number of deaths from the first month onward takes a linear form when age at death is transformed by $[\log(n+1)]^3$, n being age in days. An estimate of actual endogenous mortality is found where a graphed line fitting the cumulative monthly death rates, when extrapolated, intersects the vertical axis on which the death rate is scaled.

Table 21: Age Distribution of Known Infant Deaths among Children Born in St. George, 1861–80

Age at Death in Months	N	Percent
0–1	44	33.8
1–3	14	10.8
3–6	16	12.3
6–12	56	43.1
Total	130	
Total live births	986	
Infant deaths per 1000 live births	131.8	

Cumulative deaths conform quite closely to the line posited by Bourgeois-Pichat's theory in some populations, but in other groups they do
not. St. George clearly is one such nonconforming case, as Figure 3
reveals. After a gradual climb over the first few months, the curve
bends sharply upward to the end of the year. Comparison of a line
that would fit cumulated deaths at one month and six months versus
one fitted at six and twelve months underscores the deviation of the
St. George data from the model. If there is truly a linear relationship
between infant mortality and age, the two lines should have the same
slope; the greater the difference in slopes, the greater the departure
from linearity. For St. George, the ratio of the late-year slope to the
earlier one is 2.8 to 1, while it is only 1.6 to 1 in a non-conforming
case noted by Bourgeois-Pichat.[18] Indeed, the late-year line for St.
George, if extrapolated to the vertical axis, would produce a *negative*
endogenous death estimate.[19]

These results, along with the low proportion of first-month deaths
and relatively low infant mortality rate, would suggest serious problems
in the St. George data if a powerful variable were not affecting infant
deaths. The prevalence of breast-feeding differentiates between a steep
rise in early-infant mortality in some populations versus the modest
early slope and concave overall curve that we see in St. George. The
late-year slope is usually less than the earlier slope for artificially fed

Figure 3: Biometric Plot of Infant Deaths in St. George

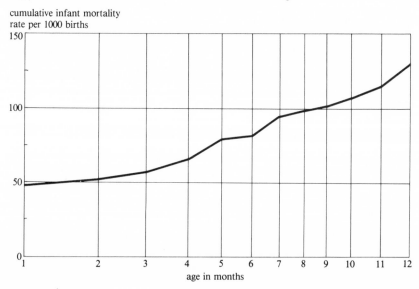

infants, while the later slope is nearly always *greater* than the early one when breast-feeding is common.[20] The cause of these different mortality patterns is the neonatal survival advantage given by breast milk.[21] Infants in pre-modern societies have enjoyed a remarkable survival advantage over their artificially fed counterparts, especially in the first months of life; thereafter, the difference begins to disappear.[22] The St. George curve in Figure 3 resembles a concave breast-fed pattern more than a convex artificial-feeding one. The sharp upturn in the St. George curve late in infancy may indeed have been exacerbated by seasonal diseases that struck as infants' immunities wore off. In regions bordering the Mediterranean, for example, deaths late in the first year produce a biometric curve similar to St. George's. These deaths are primarily from summertime gastrointestinal diseases; such diseases were also common in St. George.[23]

Without a significant imbalance in the sex ratio, suspiciously variable birth intervals, or unexplained timing of infant deaths, there is no compelling reason to suppose that the St. George data are not essentially omission-free. As far as can be determined, there are no missing individuals, and estimates can be made to fill gaps in most vital dates. Failing that, families still without marriage dates, for example, can simply be dropped from marriage-age calculations because they are too small a group to invalidate the results.

Coverage and Representativeness

The first enumerations of settlers in the St. George area, made in 1862, list the names of 275 men, but they include some who settled in nearby communities as well as the founders of St. George. St. George's residents were identified in two ways for the data set: first, family group sheets for all 275 men were sought in the Latter-day Saints' archives; next, names in the settlers' lists were checked against the Hafen collection of genealogies, which often mentions the brief presence of a family in the town even when there is not a full family record.

If a family group sheet had no evidence that the family ever resided in St. George, and if Hafen's collection makes no mention of it among the town's first settlers, it was presumed to have settled elsewhere and was excluded from the data set. Hafen's genealogies and the family group sheets thus served as checks on each other. Hafen's collection appears to be largely independent of the Mormon archives, since he included families not found in the archives and vice versa. Moreover, he was less obligated to file reasonably complete genealogies than are compilers of group sheets for church ordinances; Hafen included, for example, special sections for fragmentary evidence of a family's presence in the town. If Hafen's collection mentions a family, however briefly, it was counted as eligible for the data set, whether it was found in the archives or not. This applies only to first settlers, since the federal censuses counted individuals actually living in St. George. Conversely, when Hafen does not mention a family, chances are good that the archives will corroborate him. In only eight cases where Hafen's genealogies fail to mention a family's presence at settlement was there reason to include it in the data set based on evidence in the family group sheet. The chief problem with this method of confirming residence involves the forty settlers who were neither mentioned in Hafen's genealogies nor represented by a family group sheet. If Hafen missed any such settlers who were likewise absent from the church's archives, their families were wrongly excluded from the data set. Given the general agreement between Hafen and the family group sheets, however, it is unlikely that he missed many settlers. Moreover, any of these improperly discarded families that were still in the town in June of 1870 would have been eligible for the data set by being counted in the federal census. Any bias caused by this selection method for first settlers is surely negligible.

The roll of first settlers thus defined for the St. George data set comprises 152 families ("family" here actually means a family head—a husband, no matter how many wives may have been present, or the first-listed wife if the husband was absent or deceased). Of these, 119, or 78 percent, were reconstructed and included in the data set. The missing group is substantial, but it may be partly an artifact of the aim to be inclusive rather than exclusive in choosing the eligible population. For example, fifteen of the thirty-three missing families were counted as eligible for the data set solely because they were assigned lots in the town. But such families may never have occupied their lots, or they may have come to St. George well after the town's founding.[24] In either case, these families can reasonably be removed from the denominator for the reconstructed proportion of first settlers. If they are excluded, the proportion of families missing drops from 22 to 13 percent. A more realistic estimate of the data set's coverage of the first settlers is thus close to 87 percent.

Coverage statistics for the 1870 and 1880 censuses are less approximate, because the enumerations are for the town of St. George alone.[25] The 1870 census lists 179 households eligible for the data set (five more are ineligible as single-person households). One hundred fifty-six, or 87 percent, of these households are represented in the data set. Households increased to 242 in 1880, and the represented proportion also grows, to 89 percent. Comparing individuals, 93 percent of the 1,112 eligible persons in the 1870 census are in the data set; the corresponding statistics for 1880 are 1,264 eligible individuals with again 93 percent included in the data set (the reason for the higher representation of individuals than households will be discussed below). These coverage proportions contrast sharply with most west European and American family reconstitution studies, where the proportion of the total population included is two-thirds or less, and they indicate that the St. George data are comparable to the European studies that use presumably comprehensive civil registers or "village genealogies."[26]

The number of "unfound" families in St. George is small, but these families' characteristics compared to families in the data set must be considered. Genealogies are generally assumed to be biased in favor of large families, the wealthy, and the geographically stable.[27] Although little can be determined about unfound first settlers except for their out-migration, the censuses of 1870 and 1880 list enough data about subsequent unfound residents to allow several comparisons with those in the data set.

The first comparison regards the distribution of individuals by age. Since many demographic indicators are functions of the age structure of the population at risk as well as the ages of those experiencing vital events, biases in the overall age distribution could affect the demographic rates. The test done here uses the age distribution from the federal censuses compared to "censuses" of the data set. That is, everyone in the data set whose entry and exit dates indicate presence in the town at either of the two census dates was counted in an artificial census. The resulting age pyramids, combining 1870 and 1880, are shown in Figure 4. There are differences at some ages between the actual and the artificial censuses, the largest being under age five for both sexes. However, in no age group is the difference between the actual and the data-set censuses statistically significant.[28] It is thus reasonably certain that the age structure of the data set corresponds to the actual censuses.

The data-set "censuses" produce a remarkable statistic: only 93 percent of individuals in the federal censuses are in the data set, but the artificial censuses produce *higher* total population counts than do the actual censuses. This is due to the decision to treat the actual censuses as *minimum* population lists. For example, John Lund entered the St. George sample as a first settler in 1861 with his wife and two children. Lund's third through eighth children were born in the town, including births in July of 1867 and September of 1870, yet the family is missing from the 1870 census taken in June. The ninth birth to the Lunds

Figure 4: Population Distributions, St. George Data Set and Federal Censuses
(1870 and 1880 Combined)

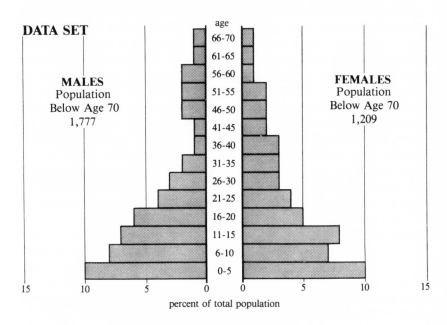

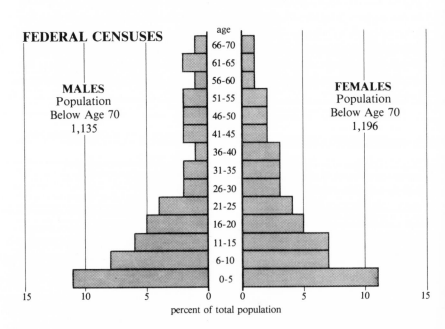

occurred in Nevada in 1879 and the family is again missing in the 1880 census. We can assume that the Lunds left St. George in the 1870s, but in June of 1870 it is more likely that they were simply out of town when the census-taker came. Moreover, there are individuals *within* families listed in the censuses whom the census-taker may have mistakenly excluded from the listing or who were temporarily out of town and should have been counted. This kind of judgment runs the risk of masking some true migration, but evidence from the family group sheets, plus additional indications that some residents were indeed temporarily absent and were not out-migrants, are reasons to believe that judiciously adding such cases improves the data set's representativeness of the "true" St. George population.[29]

To test for biases in wealth and family size, the found and unfound groups were compared using the variables available in the censuses. Wealth is given in 1870, listed as real estate and personal holdings. Comparisons are made here on a household basis, since the relationship of other wealth-holders to the household head was uncertain in unfound families. Table 22 reports this analysis of wealth for 1870 households. The top half of the table lists the proportion of households represented in the data set by wealth categories. It is clear that missing households are concentrated in the lower wealth groups. Descriptive statistics on wealth in the bottom half of the table further confirm the differences between the represented and unrepresented households. But the bias largely disappears when the found households are compared with the total population. The data set's median personal wealth is no higher than the town's median, and found families overstate the townspeople's average total wealth by about 10 percent. There are enough of the poorer households in the found group, and found households are a large enough percentage of all households, so that the wealth gap between found and unfound families shrinks in an overall comparison.

Wealth is not given in the 1880 census, but occupations are listed in both censuses, and they can be used to compare found and unfound families. Each household was given an occupation code for the highest-rated occupation of any of its members on the hierarchical scale developed for the Philadelphia Social History Project.[30] Unfound households have lower-rated occupations than found households in both censuses. But again, when the households represented in the data set are compared with all households, the occupational distributions nearly match. An analysis of household size shows much the same pattern. For Table 23, the two federal censuses were combined and apparent non-family members such as unmarried servants and boarders were

Table 22: Households Compared—Wealth in 1870 Census and Inclusion in St. George Data Set

Combined Household Wealth (Real + Personal)	Number of Households	Probability of Inclusion in St. George Data Set
Less than $200	11	.64
$200–399	18	.67
$400–599	10	.80
$600–799	33	.79
$800–999	19	.89
$1000–1199	13	.92
$1200–1399	16	1.00
$1400–1599	7	1.00
$1600 or more	52	.98
Total	179	.87

Wealth per Household		
Real Property		
	Found Households	Unfound Households	Total Population
N	156	23	179
Mean Wealth	$1067	$300	$969
Standard Deviation	1443	256	1374
Median	$ 650	$300	$600

Personal Wealth		
	Found Households	Unfound Households	Total Population
N	156	23	179
Mean Wealth	$ 665	$210	$607
Standard Deviation	915	155	869
Median	$400	$125	$400

excluded to make households as analogous to families as possible. The smallest households were the ones most likely to be missing from the data set; the means and medians for the found group are roughly twice those for the unfound group. This is why, as we saw earlier, the representation of individuals in the data set is 3 to 5 percent greater than representation of households. Once more, however, the mean for found households is not much larger than the mean for all households taken together.

Table 23: Households Compared—Size and Inclusion in St.
George Data Set, 1870 and 1880 Censuses Combined

Members per Household	Number of Households	Probability of Appearance in Data Set
1	10	.70
2	61	.70
3	71	.84
4	42	.81
5	45	.91
6	53	.94
7	36	.97
8	24	1.00
9	28	.96
10 or more	51	1.00
Total	421	.88

	Found Households	Unfound Households	Total Population
N	372	49	421
Mean Size	6.0	3.2	5.7
Standard Deviation	3.6	1.6	3.5
Median	6	3	5

A critical demographic variable in any study of families is age at marriage. If a data set contains individuals whose marriage-timing differs from that of the population it claims to represent, any analysis of marriage will be questionable. An assessment of marriage data for St. George can be done by computing the singulate mean age of marriage for individuals in the 1880 census (data on marital status were not collected in 1870). This statistic is an estimate of the average marriage age, using the proportion never married in each age group.[31] For the found individuals and St. George's total population in 1880, the singulate mean ages are 24.1 and 24.0 for men and 20.5 for both groups of women. The number of unfound individuals is too small to allow the singulate mean age to be separately calculated for them.

The final potential bias in genealogies that can be tested for St. George is over-representation of geographically stable families. The variable for comparing stability is continued residence in St. George from one enumeration to the next. Measuring stability with census persistence is a problematic technique, but it is the only indicator available for unfound families in St. George.[32] Persistence is measured here on a household basis: non-migration was assumed if a household was represented by either parent in a later census, minimizing the effect of male mortality. In addition, the fifteen families mentioned above whose presence in 1862 was doubtful were excluded altogether.

Table 24 shows the proportions of households in the data set, and of all households in St. George, that could be linked from one enumeration to the next. Again, the difference between the data set and all households is in the expected direction (that is, biased toward persisters), but the bias is modest. All the linkages show remarkably high stability for the nineteenth century. Nearly two-thirds of all families stayed in St. George through the 1870s, and over half the families counted in 1862 were still there nearly two decades later. Record-linkage studies have found that less than 40 percent of nineteenth-century residents stayed as long as a decade; even a study that avoided the problems involved in linkage showed no more than 55 percent persistence for ten years.[33] Moreover, only 39 percent of Kanab's families of 1874 were still living there in 1880.[34] It is clear that St. George families, in total as well as those in the data set, showed unusual geographic stability.

These comparisons indicate that there are indeed some distortions in this as in other data sets compiled from genealogies. Moreover, the biases are in the expected directions: small families, the poor, household heads with low-rated occupations, and the geographically mobile are more likely than others to be missing from the St. George data set. But the proportion of the total population included in the data set is so high that these omissions are ultimately unimportant. Unfound families do differ substantially, as far as can be determined, from those in the data set when the two groups are directly compared. Yet when the found group is compared with all households on a variable, which in effect allows the size difference between the found and unfound groups

Table 24: Households Compared—Persistence Rates

	1862	1870
Total Households Counted	137	179
Percent Traced to 1870		
All households	57.7	——
Households in data set	63.0	——
Percent Traced to 1880		
All households	51.8	63.1
Households in data set	54.6	66.7

to have its proper weight, the found group closely resembles the town as a whole.

All these comparisons rely on the accuracy of information in the manuscript censuses. If these data were collected carelessly, or worse, if inaccuracies are biased, the importance of the above comparisons diminishes. Indeed, for the data that can be found in both censuses and family group sheets, that is, age and presence of individuals, there are a few discrepancies, some of which are surely errors in the censuses.[35] But enumerator mistakes and misreporting by residents appear to be random, and in any case the census variables are the only ones that permit comparisons at all. The information gained from the comparisons is well worth risking the problems of census inaccuracies.

NOTES

1. See, for example, E. A. Wrigley, "Mortality in Pre-Industrial England: The Example of Colyton, Devon, over Three Centuries," *Daedalus* 97 (1968): 546–80; Daniel Scott Smith, "Population, Family and Society in Hingham, Massachusetts, 1635–1880" (Ph.D. diss., University of California, Berkeley, 1973), chap. 2; Lorena S. Walsh and Russell R. Menard, "Death in the Chesapeake: Two Life Tables for Men in Early Colonial Maryland," *Maryland Historical Magazine* 69 (1974): 211–27; Darrett B. and Anita H. Rutman, " 'Now-Wives and Sons-in-Law': Parental Death in a Seventeenth-Century Virginia County" in Thad W. Tate and David L. Ammerman, eds., *The Chesapeake in the Seventeenth Century: Essays on Anglo-American Society* (Chapel Hill: University of North Carolina Press, 1979), pp. 153–82; Rutman and Rutman, *A Place in Time: Explicatus* (New York: Norton, 1984), chap. 4; James M. Gallman, "Mortality among White Males: Colonial North Carolina," *Social Science History* 4 (1980): 295–316; Daniel Blake Smith, "Mortality and Family in the Colonial Chesapeake," *Journal of Interdisciplinary History* 8 (1978): 403–27; Katherine A. Lynch, Geraldine P. Mineau, and Douglas L. Anderton, "Estimates of Infant Mortality on the Western Frontier: The Use of Genealogical Data," *Historical Methods* 18 (1985): 155–64.

2. Such criticisms are in Daniel Scott Smith, "The Estimates of Early American Historical Demographers: Two Steps Forward, One Step Back, What Steps in the Future?" *Historical Methods* 12 (1979): 24–38; Maris A. Vinovskis, "Mortality Rates and Trends in Massachusetts before 1860," *Journal of Economic History* 32 (1972): 184–213; T. H. Hollingsworth, "The Importance of the Quality of the Data in Historical Demography," *Daedalus* 97 (1968): 415–32. See also a rebuttal of Hollingsworth's comments on the Colyton analysis in Wrigley, "Mortality in England," pp. 570–72.

3. As will be seen below, however, "unofficial" genealogies (as opposed to the church's family group sheets) have been published specifically for St. George.

4. Dean L. May, "People on the Mormon Frontier: Kanab's Families of 1874," *Journal of Family History* 1 (1976): 169–92.

5. The settlers' list is printed in Albert E. Miller, *The Immortal Pioneers: Founders of City of St. George, Utah* (St. George: privately published, 1946), pp. 17–21.

6. For descriptions of the church's holdings and of family group sheets as sources for demographic research, see Lee L. Bean, Geraldine P. Mineau, Katherine A. Lynch, and J. Dennis Willigan, "The Genealogical Society of Utah as a Data Resource for Historical Demography," *Population Index* 46 (1980): 6–19; M. Skolnick, L. Bean, D. May, V. Arbon, K. de Nevers, and P. Cartwright, "Mormon Demographic History I: Nuptiality and Fertility of Once-Married Couples," *Population Studies* 32 (1978): 5–19; Lee L. Bean, Dean L. May, and Mark Skolnick, "The Mormon Historical Demography Project," *Historical Methods* 11 (1978): 45–53.

7. St. George genealogies are in Arthur K. Hafen, *Devoted Empire Builders (Pioneers of St. George)* (St. George: privately published, 1969).

8. For a testimonial to the quality of French vital records, see D. V. Glass, preface to "The Demography of the British Peerage" by T. H. Hollingsworth, *Population Studies* supplement to 18 (1964): ii; on the German data, see J. Knodel and E. Shorter, "The Reliability of Reconstitution Data in German Village[s]," *Annales de Démographie Historique*, 1976, 115–54.

9. Significance is measured at the .05 level.

10. Roughly eight more boys than girls out of each 1,000 born would die before age fifteen, lowering the sex ratio at age fifteen to 103.8. See the survival rates at ages ten and twenty in Table 15.

11. Louis Henry, *Anciennes Familles Genovoises: Étude Démographique, XVIe-XXe Siecle* (Paris: Presses Universitaires de France, 1956), pp. 38–44.

12. $(24–27)^2 + (27–30)^2 + (24–27)^2 / (3–1)$

13. This includes children born to the first wife after the husband's plural marriage.

14. Age-specific fertility rates are indeed "natural" for polygamous families, but their birth intervals suggest patterns of sexual intercourse that differed from monogamous marriages. See chap. 4.

15. Omission estimate calculated by interpolation from Henry's table of variances and their corresponding omission rates. *Anciennes Familles*, p. 42.

16. Wrigley, "Mortality in England," pp. 564–70; David Levine, *Family Formation in an Age of Nascent Capitalism* (New York: Academic Press, 1977), pp. 171–73; Smith, "Population in Hingham," pp. 27–28. Hollingsworth, "Quality of the Data," pp. 423–25, is concerned with the proportion dying in the first three months. On the other hand, only 42 percent of infants who died in all of Utah in the 1870s were in their first month. See Lynch et al., "Infant Mortality," p. 161. In fact, first-month mortality that was less than 50 percent of infant deaths was common in the nineteenth century. See chap. 5, note 6.

17. J. Bourgeois-Pichat, "De la Mesure de la Mortalité Infantile," *Population* 1 (1946): 53–68.

18. Cited in John Knodel and Hallie Kintner, "The Impact of Breast Feeding Patterns on the Biometric Analysis of Infant Mortality," *Demography* 14 (1977): 393.

19. Another measure of linearity is the correlation coefficient. The correlation between infant mortality and age for Tuscany in 1951–53, for example, is nearly perfect at .999 (calculated from Louis Henry, *Population,* trans. Etienne van de Walle and Elise F. Jones [New York: Academic Press, 1976], pp. 149–50), whereas the fit for St. George, although still very good, drops to .967.

20. Knodel and Kintner, "Impact of Breast Feeding," pp. 396–406.

21. On breast-feeding in St. George, see chap. 5.

22. Knodel and Kintner, "Impact of Breast Feeding," p. 395.

23. Yves Blayo and Louis Henry, "Données Démographiques sur la Bretagne et l'Anjou de 1740 à 1829," *Annales de Démographie Historique,* 1967, pp. 137, 142.

24. The evidence of lot assignments used by Hafen was primarily a composite map showing lots assigned throughout the 1860s, not solely those occupied by the first settlers. The map is reproduced in Daughters of Utah Pioneers, Washington County Chapter, *Under Dixie Sun* (Salt Lake City: privately published, 1950).

25. The nearby settlement of Middletown, part of St. George's precinct in 1880, is also included in the data set.

26. See, for example, Knodel and Shorter, "Reliability of Reconstitution Data"; Etienne van de Walle, "Household Dynamics in a Belgian Village, 1847–1866," *Journal of Family History* 1 (1976): 80–94.

27. See T. H. Hollingsworth, "A Demographic Study of the British Ducal Families," in Michael Drake, ed., *Population in Industrialization* (London: Methuen, 1969), p. 74.

28. The distributions can also be compared on the Index of Dissimilarity. When the data set and actual censuses are compared for each sex, the result is about 5, indicating a very close match (100 is absolute dissimilarity).

29. Henry Riding, for example, who had come to St. George in 1862 with his father's family, and Elizabeth Blake, who had likewise arrived in 1861, went uncounted in the 1870 census of the town. They were instead in Salt Lake City, where they were married on June 6 while the census was underway. They returned, had five children in St. George in the following decade, and were counted in the 1880 census.

30. Theodore Hershberg and Robert Dockhorn, "Occupational Classification," *Historical Methods Newsletter* 9 (1976): 59–98.

31. For a description of the singulate mean age and its computation, see Henry S. Shryock and Jacob S. Siegel, *The Methods and Materials of Demography,* 2 vols. (Washington, D.C.: U.S. Government Printing Office, 1975), 1: 295.

32. For an overview of mobility studies of past communities, and especially their problems, see Donald H. Parkerson, "How Mobile Were Nineteenth-Century Americans?" *Historical Methods* 15 (1982): 99–109.

33. Ibid.

34. May, "Mormon Frontier," p. 181.

35. For an assessment of census inaccuracies and their generally minor importance, see Larry M. Logue, "Belief and Behavior in a Mormon Town: Nineteenth-Century St. George, Utah" (Ph.D. diss., University of Pennsylvania, 1984), Appendix B.

Bibliography of Works Cited

ABBREVIATIONS

Bancroft—Mormon Biographies File, Bancroft Library, University of California, Berkeley (copy of originals in Library of Congress).

BYU—Manuscripts Collection, Harold B. Lee Library, Brigham Young University, Provo.

Huntington—Mormon File, Huntington Library, San Marino, Calif.

LDS Church Archives—Library-Archives, Historical Department of the Church of Jesus Christ of Latter-day Saints, Salt Lake City.

Utah—Manuscripts Collection, Marriott Library, University of Utah, Salt Lake City.

Washington County—WPA Pioneer Diary Collection, Washington County Library, St. George.

PRIMARY SOURCES

Andrus, Milo. Autobiography. Huntington.

Atkin, William. Biography. Bancroft.

"Autobiography of Hosea Stout." *Utah Historical Quarterly* 30 (1962): 53–75, 149–74, 237–61.

Bentley, Mary Ann Mansfield. Life Sketch. BYU.

Bigler, Henry William. Autobiography and Journal. Huntington.

Bleak, James G. "Annals of the Southern Utah Mission." 2 vols. BYU.

The Book of Mormon.

Brown, Lorenzo. Journal. Huntington.

The Contributor, Salt Lake City. "Keeping Journals," Apr. 1883.

Cowley, M. F. *Cowley's Talks on Doctrine*. Chattanooga: Ben E. Rich, 1902.

Cox, Martha. Biographical Record. Washington County.

Crocheron, Augusta Joyce. *The Children's Book . . . a Mormon Book for Mormon Children*. Bountiful, Utah: privately published, 1890.

Deseret News, Salt Lake City:

Erastus Snow to Editor, Apr. 5, 1865.

[Martha Cragun]. "Lines Written by a Lady of St. George," Aug. 21, 1867.

"Diary of Cotton Mather, 1681–1708." *Massachusetts Historical Society Collections*, 7th ser., 7 (1911).

Doctrine and Covenants of the Church of Jesus Christ of Latter-day Saints.

Eyring, Henry. Journal. LDS Church Archives.

Family Record and Journal of John Monroe Moody. Huntington.

Fawcett, George W. Memories. LDS Church Archives.

Hafen, A. K. *Devoted Empire Builders (Pioneers of St. George).* St. George: privately published, 1969.

Hafen, Mary Ann. *Recollections of a Handcart Pioneer of 1860: A Woman's Life on the Mormon Frontier.* Lincoln: University of Nebraska Press, 1983.

Hancock, Mosiah Lyman. Life Story. LDS Church Archives.

Hubbard, Lester A. *Ballads and Songs from Utah.* Salt Lake City: University of Utah Press, 1961.

Ivins, Anthony W. Journal. Utah.

Jarvis, Ann Prior. Autobiography. BYU.

Jarvis, George Frederick. Life Sketch. BYU.

Jarvis, Margaret. History. Huntington.

Jenson, Andrew. "St. George Ward." LDS Church Archives.

"Journal and Diary of Robert Gardner." In Kate B. Carter, comp., *Heart Throbs of the West* 10 (1949): 269–324.

Journal of Discourses by Brigham Young . . . and Others. 26 vols. 1854–86. Reprint, Los Angeles: Gartner, 1956.

Juvenile Instructor, Salt Lake City:

Francis S. Smith, "Spoil the Rod and Spare the Child," Apr. 1, 1889.

Editorial, June 1, 1889.

"Called and Chosen," Oct. 15, 1889.

Editorial, Jan. 1, 1892.

Editorial, Oct. 1, 1892.

Kelsey, Easton. Life Synopsis. Bancroft.

Lang, William. Autobiography and Journal. LDS Church Archives.

Larson, A. Karl, and Katharine M. Larson, eds. *Diary of Charles Lowell Walker.* 2 vols. Logan: Utah State University Press, 1980.

Laub, George. Diary. Huntington.

———. Journal. Huntington.

Liston, Commodore P. Diary and Biography of Elizabeth Reeves Liston. Huntington.

McAllister, Daniel H. Journal. Huntington.

McAllister, John Daniel Thompson. Journal. LDS Church Archives.

Mace, Wandle. Autobiography. Huntington.

Massachusetts Secretary of the Commonwealth. *Twentieth Report . . . of Births, Marriages, and Deaths in the Commonwealth.* Boston, 1863.

Miles, Samuel. Life History. Washington County.

Nelson, William. Journal. Huntington.

Orton, Joseph. Autobiography. Bancroft.

Pratt, Parley P. *Key to the Science of Theology.* Liverpool: F. D. Richards, 1855.

Roberts, Brigham H., ed. *History of the Church of Jesus Christ of Latter-day Saints.* 7 vols. Salt Lake City: Church of Jesus Christ of Latter-day Saints, 1932–51.

Romney, Hannah Hood Hill. Autobiography. Huntington.

St. George City Cemetery Records. St. George Branch Genealogical Library.

Sketch of the Life of Adolphus Rennie Whitehead and Diary of Mary G. Whitehead. BYU.

Smith, Charles. Diary. LDS Church Archives.

Stout, Allen Joseph. Journal. Huntington.

Sudweeks, Henry. Diary. Huntington.

Talmage, James E. *A Study of the Articles of Faith.* Rev. ed. Salt Lake City: Church of Jesus Christ of Latter-day Saints, 1968.

Taylor, John. *The Government of God.* Liverpool: S. W. Richards, 1852.

Tullidge, Edward W. *The Women of Mormondom.* New York: Tullidge & Crandall, 1877.

Utah Irrigation Commission. *Irrigation in Utah.* Salt Lake City, 1895.

"The Verprecula" (St. George manuscript newspaper). BYU:

[Joseph Orton], "The Will," June 1, 1864.

[Joseph Orton], "Self-Government," July 15, 1864.

[George A. Burgon], article on conditions in St. George, Oct. 15, 1864.

[Guglielmo Sangiovanni?], article on conditions in St. George, Jan. 1, 1865.

[Guglielmo Sangiovanni], "A View of Dixie," Mar. 15, Apr. 1, 1865.

[Guglielmo Sangiovanni], "Association of Ideas," May 15, 1865.

[Guglielmo Sangiovanni], "Happiness," June 1, 1865.

[Guglielmo Sangiovanni?], "A View of Dixie," June 1, 1865.

Walker, Charles Lowell. *Book of Verse.* Bancroft.

Widtsoe, John A., comp. *Discourses of Brigham Young.* Salt Lake City: Deseret Book Co., 1925.

———. *Rational Theology.* Salt Lake City: Deseret News Press, 1915.

Woman's Exponent, Salt Lake City: Letter to the Editor, Oct. 15, 1872.

Wright, Louis B., and Marion Tinling, eds. *The Secret Diary of William Byrd of Westover, 1709–1712.* Richmond, Va.: Dietz Press, 1941.

SECONDARY SOURCES

Alexander, Thomas G., ed. *The Mormon People: Their Character and Traditions.* Provo: Brigham Young University Press, 1980.

———. "The Word of Wisdom: From Principle to Requirement." *Dialogue* 14 (Autumn, 1981): 78–88.

Alexander, Thomas G., and Jessie L. Embry, eds. *After 150 Years: The Latter-day Saints in Sesquicentennial Perspective.* Provo: Charles Redd Center for Western Studies, 1983.

Allen, James B., and Glen M. Leonard. *The Story of the Latter-day Saints.* Salt Lake City: Deseret Book Co., 1976.

Anderson, Nels. *Desert Saints: The Mormon Frontier in Utah.* Chicago: University of Chicago Press, 1942.

Ariès, Phillippe. *Western Attitudes toward Death: From the Middle Ages to the Present.* Trans. Patricia M. Ranum. Baltimore: Johns Hopkins University Press, 1974.

Arrington, Leonard J. "The Mormon Cotton Mission in Southern Utah." *Pacific Historical Review* 25 (1956): 221–38.

———. *Great Basin Kingdom: An Economic History of the Latter-day Saints, 1830–1900.* Cambridge, Mass.: Harvard University Press, 1958.

———. "An Economic Interpretation of the 'Word of Wisdom'." *Brigham Young University Studies* 1 (1959): 37–49.

———. "Persons for All Seasons: Women in Mormon History." *Brigham Young University Studies* 20 (1979): 39–58.

———. *Brigham Young: American Moses.* 1985. Reprint, Urbana: University of Illinois Press, 1986.

Arrington, Leonard J., and Davis Bitton. *The Mormon Experience: A History of the Latter-day Saints.* New York: Knopf, 1979.

Arrington, Leonard J., Feramorz Y. Fox, and Dean L. May. *Building the City of God: Community and Cooperation among the Mormons.* Salt Lake City: Deseret Book Co., 1976.

Arrington, Leonard J., and Dean May. " 'A Different Mode of Life': Irrigation and Society in Nineteenth-Century Utah." *Agricultural History* 49 (1975): 3–20.

Bean, Lee L., Dean L. May, and Mark Skolnick. "The Mormon Historical Demography Project." *Historical Methods* 11 (1978): 45–53.

Bean, L[ee] L., and Geraldine P. Mineau. "The Polygyny-Fertility Hypothesis: A Re-evaluation." *Population Studies* 40 (1986): 67–81.

Bean, Lee L., G[eraldine] P. Mineau, Katherine A. Lynch, and J. Dennis Willigan. "The Genealogical Society of Utah as a Data Resource for Historical Demography." *Population Index* 46 (1980): 6–19.

Bennion, Lowell "Ben." "The Incidence of Mormon Polygamy in 1880: 'Dixie' versus Davis Stake." *Journal of Mormon History* 11 (1984): 27–42.

Bennion, Sherilyn Cox. "The *Woman's Exponent:* Forty-two Years of Speaking for Women." *Utah Historical Quarterly* 44 (1976): 222–39.

Berg, Barbara J. *The Remembered Gate: Origins of American Feminism.* New York: Oxford University Press, 1978.

Blayo, Yves, and Louis Henry. "Données Démographiques sur la Bretagne et l'Anjou de 1740 à 1829." *Annales de Démographie Historique,* 1967, 91-171.

Bongaarts, John. "Why High Birth Rates Are So Low." *Population and Development Review* 1 (1975): 289–96.

Bourgeois-Pichat, J. "De la Mesure de la Mortalité Infantile." *Population* 1 (1946): 53–68.

Boyd, George T. "A Mormon Concept of Man." *Dialogue* 3 (Spring, 1968); 55–72.

Boyd, Mark F., ed. *Malariology: A Comprehensive Survey . . . from a Global Standpoint.* Philadelphia: W. B. Saunders, 1949.

Bringhurst, Newell G. *Brigham Young and the Expanding American Frontier.* Boston: Little, Brown, 1986.

Brown, Richard D. *Modernization: The Transformation of American Life, 1600–1865.* New York: Hill and Wang, 1976.

Buley, R. Carlyle. *The Old Northwest: Pioneer Period, 1815–1840.* 2 vols. Bloomington: Indiana University Press, 1950.

Burnett, John. *Plenty and Want: A Social History of Diet in England from 1815 to the Present Day.* Rev. ed. London: Scolar Press, 1979.

Burris, Evadene A. "Frontier Food." *Minnesota History* 14 (1933): 378–92.

Bush, Lester E., Jr. "Birth Control among the Mormons: Introduction to an Insistent Question." *Dialogue* 10 (Autumn, 1976): 12–44.

———. "The Word of Wisdom in Early Nineteenth-Century Perspective." *Dialogue* 14 (Autumn, 1981): 47–65.

Bushman, Claudia L., ed. *Mormon Sisters: Women in Early Utah.* Cambridge, Mass.: Emmeline Press, 1976.

Bushman, Richard L. *Joseph Smith and the Beginnings of Mormonism.* Urbana: University of Illinois Press, 1984.

Caldwell, John C. *Theory of Fertility Decline.* New York: Academic Press, 1982.

Campbell, Flann. "Birth Control and the Christian Churches." *Population Studies* 14 (1960): 131–47.

Chen, Lincoln C., Emdadul Huq, and Stan D'Souza. "Sex Bias in the Family Allocation of Food and Health Care in Rural Bangladesh." *Population and Development Review* 7 (1981): 55–70.

Coale, Ansley J., and Paul Demeny. *Regional Model Life Tables and Stable Populations.* Princeton: Princeton University Press, 1966.

Coale, Ansley J., and T. James Trussell. "Model Fertility Schedules: Variations in the Age Structure of Childbearing in Human Populations." *Population Index* 40 (1974): 185–258.

———. "Technical Note: Finding the Two Parameters That Specify a Model Schedule of Marital Fertility." *Population Index* 44 (1978): 203–13.

Daughters of Utah Pioneers, Washington County Chapter. *Under Dixie Sun.* Salt Lake City: privately published, 1950.

Davis, David Brion. "The New England Origins of Mormonism." *New England Quarterly* 26 (1953): 147–68.

Davis, James E. *Frontier America, 1800–1840: A Comparative Demographic Analysis of the Settlement Process.* Glendale, Calif.: Arthur H. Clark, 1977.

Degler, Carl N. *At Odds: Women and the Family in America from the Revolution to the Present.* New York: Oxford University Press, 1980.

DePillis, Mario S. "The Quest for Religious Authority and the Rise of Mormonism." *Dialogue* 1 (Spring, 1966): 68–88.

Drake, Michael, ed. *Population in Industrialization.* London: Methuen, 1969.

Dublin, Louis I., Alfred J. Lotka, and Mortimer Spiegelman. *Length of Life: A Study of the Life Table.* Rev ed. New York: Ronald Press, 1949.

Dykstra, Robert R., and William Silag. "Doing Local History: Monographic Approaches to the Smaller Community." *American Quarterly* 37 (1985): 411–25.

Eblen, Jack E. "An Analysis of Nineteenth-Century Frontier Populations." *Demography* 2 (1965): 399–413.

El-Badry, M. A. "Higher Female Than Male Mortality in Some Countries of

South Asia: A Digest." *Journal of the American Statistical Association* 64 (1969): 1234–44.

Embry, Jessie L. "Effects of Polygamy on Mormon Women." *Frontiers* 7:3 (1984): 56–61.

Evans, Richard J., and W. R. Lee, eds. *The German Family: Essays on the Social History of the Family in Nineteenth- and Twentieth-Century Germany*. New York: Barnes & Noble, 1981.

Faragher, John Mack. *Women and Men on the Overland Trail*. New Haven: Yale University Press, 1979.

Farrell, James J. *Inventing the American Way of Death, 1830–1920*. Philadelphia: Temple University Press, 1980.

Foster, Lawrence. *Religion and Sexuality: Three American Communal Experiments of the Nineteenth Century*. 1981. Reprint, Urbana: University of Illinois Press, 1984.

Gallman, James M. "Mortality among White Males: Colonial North Carolina." *Social Science History* 4 (1980): 295–316.

———. "Determinants of Age at Marriage in Colonial Perquimans County, North Carolina." *William and Mary Quarterly*, 3d ser., 39 (1982): 176–91.

Geddes, Gordon E. *Welcome Joy: Death in Puritan New England*. Ann Arbor: UMI Research Press, 1981.

Glass, D. V. Preface to "The Demography of the British Peerage," by T. H. Hollingsworth. *Population Studies* supplement to 18 (1964).

Glassie, Henry. *Folk Housing in Middle Virginia*. Knoxville: University of Tennessee Press, 1975.

Glover, James W. *United States Life Tables: 1890, 1901, and 1901–1910*. 1921. Reprint, New York: Arno Press, 1976.

Gottlieb, Robert, and Peter Wiley. *America's Saints: The Rise of Mormon Power*. New York: G. P. Putnam's Sons, 1984.

Greven, Philip J., Jr. *Four Generations: Population, Land, and Family in Colonial Andover, Massachusetts*. Ithaca, N.Y.: Cornell University Press, 1970.

Griffen, Clyde. "Community Studies and the Investigation of Nineteenth-Century Social Relations." *Social Science History* 10 (1986): 315–38.

Guest, Avery M., and Stewart E. Tolnay. "Children's Roles and Fertility: Late Nineteenth-Century United States." *Social Science History* 7 (1983): 355–80.

Guttentag, Marcia, and Paul F. Secord. *Too Many Women? The Sex Ratio Question*. Beverly Hills, Calif.: Sage, 1983.

Hafen, A. K. *Beneath Vermilion Cliffs (Historic St. George)*. St. George: privately published, 1967.

Haines, Michael R. "The Use of Model Life Tables to Estimate Mortality for the United States in the Late Nineteenth Century." *Demography* 16 (1979): 289–312.

Halttunen, Karen. *Confidence Men and Painted Women: A Study of Middle-class Culture in America, 1830–1870*. New Haven: Yale University Press, 1982.

Hansen, Klaus J. *Mormonism and the American Experience.* Chicago: University of Chicago Press, 1981.

Harrison, J. F. C. *The Second Coming: Popular Millenarianism, 1780–1850.* New Brunswick, N.J.: Rutgers University Press, 1979.

Hartman, Mary S., and Lois Banner, eds. *Clio's Consciousness Raised: New Perspectives on the History of Women.* New York: Harper & Row, 1974.

Hatch, Nathan O. "The Christian Movement and the Demand for a Theology of the People." *Journal of American History* 67 (1980): 545–67.

Heinerman, John, and Anson Shupe. *The Mormon Corporate Empire.* Boston: Beacon, 1986.

Henretta, James A. "Families and Farms: *Mentalité* in Pre-industrial America." *William and Mary Quarterly,* 3d ser., 35 (1978): 3–32.

———. *The Evolution of American Society, 1700–1815: An Interdisciplinary Analysis.* Lexington, Mass.: D. C. Heath, 1973.

Henry, Louis. *Anciennes Familles Genevoises: Étude Démographique, XVIe -XXe Siècle.* Paris: Presses Universitaires de France, 1956.

———. *Population.* Trans. Etienne van de Walle and Elise F. Jones. New York: Academic Press, 1976.

Hershberg, Theodore, and Robert Dockhorn. "Occupational Classification." *Historical Methods Newsletter* 9 (1976): 59–98.

Higgs, Robert. "Mortality in Rural America, 1870–1920: Estimates and Conjectures." *Explorations in Economic History* 10 (1973): 177–95.

Hirshson, Stanley P. *The Lion of the Lord: A Biography of Brigham Young.* New York: Knopf, 1969.

Hollingsworth, Harold M., and Sandra L. Myres, eds. *Essays on the American West.* Austin: University of Texas Press, 1969.

Hollingsworth, T. H. "The Importance of the Quality of the Data in Historical Demography." *Daedalus* 97 (1968): 415–32.

Ivins, Stanley S. "Notes on Mormon Polygamy." *Western Humanities Review* 10 (1956): 229–39.

Jameson, Elizabeth. "Women as Workers, Women as Civilizers: True Womanhood in the American West." *Frontiers* 7:3 (1984): 1–8.

Jeffrey, Julie Roy. *Frontier Women: The Trans-Mississippi West, 1840–1880.* New York: Hill and Wang, 1979.

Johnson, Rufus David. *J[oseph] E[llis] J[ohnson]: Trail to Sundown.* Salt Lake City: Deseret News Press, 1961.

Kammen, Michael, ed. *The Past before Us: Contemporary Historical Writing in the United States.* Ithaca, N.Y.: Cornell University Press, 1980.

Kantrow, Louise. "Philadelphia Gentry: Fertility and Family Limitation among an American Aristocracy." *Population Studies* 34 (1980): 21–30.

Kennedy, Robert E., Jr. *The Irish: Emigration, Marriage, and Fertility.* Berkeley: University of California Press, 1973.

Kern, Louis J. *An Ordered Love: Sex Roles and Sexuality in Victorian Utopias.* Chapel Hill: University of North Carolina Press, 1981.

Kett, Joseph F. *Rites of Passage: Adolescence in America, 1790 to the Present.* New York: Basic Books, 1977.

Kintner, Hallie J. "Trends and Regional Differences in Breastfeeding in Germany from 1871 to 1937." *Journal of Family History* 10 (1985): 163–82.

Knodel, John. "Natural Fertility in Pre-industrial Germany." *Population Studies* 32 (1978): 481–510.

Knodel, John, and Hallie Kintner. "The Impact of Breast Feeding Patterns on the Biometric Analysis of Infant Mortality." *Demography* 14 (1977): 391–409.

Knodel, J[ohn], and E[dward] Shorter. "The Reliability of Reconstitution Data in German Village[s]." *Annales de Démographique Historique*, 1976: 115–54.

Kulikoff, Allan. *Tobacco and Slaves: The Development of Southern Cultures in the Chesapeake, 1680-1800.* Chapel Hill: University of North Carolina Press, 1986.

Lamar, Howard R. "Statehood for Utah: A Different Path." *Utah Historical Quarterly* 39 (1971): 307–27.

Larson, Andrew K[arl]. *"I Was Called to Dixie": The Virgin River Basin—Unique Experiences in Mormon Pioneering.* Salt Lake City: Deseret News Press, 1961.

———. *Erastus Snow: The Life of a Missionary and Pioneer for the Early Mormon Church.* Salt Lake City: University of Utah Press, 1971.

Larson, Gustive O. *The "Americanization" of Utah for Statehood.* San Marino, Calif.: Huntington Library, 1971.

Leavitt, Judith Walzer. "Under the Shadow of Maternity: American Women's Responses to Death and Debility Fears in Nineteenth-Century Childbirth." *Feminist Studies* 12 (1986): 129–54.

Lee, Ronald Demos, ed. *Population Patterns in the Past.* New York: Academic Press, 1977.

Levine, David. *Family Formation in an Age of Nascent Capitalism.* New York: Academic Press, 1977.

———. " 'For Their Own Reasons': Individual Marriage Decisions and Family Life." *Journal of Family History* 7 (1982): 255–64.

Levison, Catherine Hofer, Donald W. Hastings, and Jerry N. Harrison. "The Epidemiologic Transition in a Frontier Town—Manti, Utah: 1849–1977." *American Journal of Physical Anthropology* 56 (1981): 83–93.

Livi-Bacci, Massimo. *A History of Italian Fertility during the Last Two Centuries.* Princeton: Princeton University Press, 1977.

Logue, Larry M. "Belief and Behavior in a Mormon Town: Nineteenth-Century St. George, Utah." Ph.D. diss., University of Pennsylvania, 1984.

———. "Modernization Arrested: Child-Naming and the Family in a Utah Town." *Journal of American History* 74 (1987): 131–38.

Lynch, Katherine A. "Marriage Age among French Factory Workers: An Alsatian Example." *Journal of Interdisciplinary History* 16 (1986): 405–29.

Lynch, Katherine A., Geraldine P. Mineau, and Douglas L. Anderton. "Estimates of Infant Mortality on the Western Frontier: The Use of Genealogical Data." *Historical Methods* 18 (1985): 155–64.

McCue, Robert J. "Did the Word of Wisdom Become a Commandment in 1851?" *Dialogue* 14 (Autumn, 1981): 66–77.

Macfarlane, Alan. *The Family Life of Ralph Josselyn, a Seventeenth-Century Clergyman.* Cambridge: Cambridge University Press, 1970.

Macfarlane, L. W. *Yours Sincerely, John M. Macfarlane.* Salt Lake City: privately published, 1980.

McGrath, Roger D. *Gunfighters, Highwaymen, & Vigilantes: Violence on the Frontier.* Berkeley: University of California Press, 1984.

McKiernan, F. Mark, Alma R. Blair, and Paul M. Edwards, eds. *The Restoration Movement: Essays in Mormon History.* Lawrence, Kan.: Coronado Press, 1973.

McMahon, Sarah F. "A Comfortable Subsistence: The Changing Composition of Diet in Rural New England, 1620–1840." *William and Mary Quarterly,* 3d ser., 42 (1985): 26–65.

McMurrin, Sterling M. *The Theological Foundations of the Mormon Religion.* Salt Lake City: University of Utah Press, 1965.

Madigan, Francis J. "Are Sex Mortality Differentials Biologically Caused?" *Milbank Memorial Fund Quarterly* 35 (1957): 202–23.

May, Dean L. "People on the Mormon Frontier: Kanab's Families of 1874." *Journal of Family History* 1 (1976): 169–92.

———. "The Making of Saints: The Mormon Town as a Setting for the Study of Cultural Change." *Utah Historical Quarterly* 45 (1977): 75–92.

Meeker, Edward. "The Improving Health of the United States, 1850–1915." *Explorations in Economic History* 9 (1972): 353–73.

Miller, Albert E. *The Immortal Pioneers: Founders of City of St. George, Utah.* St. George: privately published, 1946.

Mineau, G. P., L. L. Bean, and M. Skolnick. "Mormon Demographic History II: The Family Life Cycle and Natural Fertility." *Population Studies* 33 (1979): 429–46.

Mitchell, B. R. *European Historical Statistics, 1750–1970.* New York: Columbia University Press, 1975.

Modell, John, Frank F. Furstenberg, Jr., and Theodore Hershberg. "Social Change and Transitions to Adulthood in Historical Perspective." *Journal of Family History* 1 (1976): 7–32.

Monahan, Thomas P. *The Pattern of Age at Marriage in the United States.* Philadelphia: Stephenson-Brothers, 1951.

Mulder, William, and A. Russell Mortensen, eds. *Among the Mormons: Historic Accounts by Contemporary Observers.* Lincoln: University of Nebraska Press, 1973.

Muncy, Raymond Lee. *Sex and Marriage in Utopian Communities: 19th-Century America.* Bloomington: Indiana University Press, 1973.

Murphey, Murray G. *Our Knowledge of the Historical Past.* Indianapolis: Bobbs-Merrill, 1973.

———. "Nonresponse in Samples from Historical Populations: Observations on the Problem." *Social Science History* 8 (1984): 455–67.

Naismith, D. J. "The Foetus as a Parasite." *Proceedings of the Nutrition Society* 28 (1969): 25–31.

O'Dea, Thomas F. *The Mormons.* Chicago: University of Chicago Press, 1957.

Ohlin, G. "Mortality, Marriage, and Growth in Pre-industrial Populations." *Population Studies* 14 (1961): 190–97.

Olsen, Steven L. "Joseph Smith and the Structure of Mormon Identity." *Dialogue* 14 (Autumn, 1981): 89–99.

Pace, D. Gene. "Wives of Nineteenth-Century Mormon Bishops: A Quantitative Analysis." *Journal of the West* 21 (Apr., 1982): 49–57.

Parkerson, Donald H. "How Mobile Were Nineteenth-Century Americans?" *Historical Methods* 15 (1982): 99–109.

Pearson, Carol Lynn. *The Flight and the Nest.* Salt Lake City: Bookcraft, 1975.

Peterson, Charles S. *Take Up Your Mission: Mormon Colonizing along the Little Colorado River, 1870–1900.* Tucson: University of Arizona Press, 1973.

———. "The 'Americanization' of Utah's Agriculture." *Utah Historical Quarterly* 42 (1974): 108–25.

Poll, Richard D., Thomas G. Alexander, Eugene E. Campbell, and David E. Miller, eds. *Utah's History.* Provo: Brigham Young University Press, 1978.

Preston, Samuel H. *Mortality Patterns in National Populations.* New York: Academic Press, 1976.

Preston, Samuel H., and Robert L. Higgs. *United States Census Data, 1900: Public Use Sample* (machine-readable data file), 1st ICPSR ed. Ann Arbor: Inter-university Consortium for Political and Social Research, 1980.

Preston, Samuel H., Nathan Keyfitz, and Robert Schoen. *Causes of Death: Life Tables for National Populations.* New York: Seminar Press, 1972.

Quinn, D. Michael. "The Mormon Hierarchy, 1832–1932: An American Elite." Ph.D. diss., Yale University, 1976.

Rapson, Richard L. "The American Child as Seen by British Travelers, 1845–1935." *American Quarterly* 17 (1965): 520–34.

Richards, Ralph T. *Of Medicine, Hospitals, and Doctors.* Salt Lake City: University of Utah Press, 1953.

Robson, Kent E. " 'Man' and the Telefinalist Trap." *Dialogue* 3 (Spring, 1968): 83–97.

Rock, Paul. "Some Problems of Interpretative Historiography." *British Journal of Sociology* 27 (1976): 353–69.

Rutman, Darrett B. "People in Process: The New Hampshire Towns of the Eighteenth Century." *Journal of Urban History* 1 (1975): 268–92.

———. "Assessing the Little Communities of Early America." *William and Mary Quarterly*, 3d ser., 43 (1986): 163–78.

Rutman, Darrett B., and Anita H. Rutman. "Of Agues and Fevers: Malaria in the Early Chesapeake." *William and Mary Quarterly*, 3d ser., 33 (1976): 31–60.

———. *A Place in Time: Explicatus.* New York: Norton, 1984.

Saum, Lewis O. *The Popular Mood of Pre-Civil War America.* Westport, Conn.: Greenwood Press, 1980.

Schoen, Robert. "Measuring the Tightness of a Marriage Squeeze." *Demography* 20 (1983): 61–78.

Shepherd, Gordon, and Gary Shepherd. *A Kingdom Transformed: Themes in the Development of Mormonism.* Salt Lake City: University of Utah Press, 1984.

Shipps, Jan. "From Satyr to Saint: American Attitudes toward the Mormons, 1860–1960." Paper presented at the annual meeting of the Organization of American Historians, Chicago, 1973.

———. "The Principle Revoked: A Closer Look at the Demise of Plural Marriage." *Journal of Mormon History* 11 (1984): 65–77.

———. *Mormonism: The Story of a New Religious Tradition.* Urbana: University of Illinois Press, 1985.

Shryock, Henry S., and Jacob S. Siegel. *The Methods and Materials of Demography.* 2 vols. Washington: U.S. Government Printing Office, 1975.

Skolnick, M., L. Bean, D. May, V. Arbon, K. de Nevers, and P. Cartwright. "Mormon Demographic History I: Nuptiality and Fertility of Once-Married Couples." *Population Studies* 32 (1978): 5–19.

Smith, Daniel Blake. "Mortality and Family in the Colonial Chesapeake." *Journal of Interdisciplinary History* 8 (1978): 403–27.

Smith, Daniel Scott. "Parental Power and Marriage Patterns: An Analysis of Historical Trends in Hingham, Massachusetts." *Journal of Marriage and the Family* 35 (1973): 419–28.

———. "Population, Family and Society in Hingham, Massachusetts, 1635–1880." Ph.D. diss., University of California, Berkeley, 1973.

———. "The Estimates of Early American Historical Demographers: Two Steps Forward, One Step Back, What Steps in the Future?" *Historical Methods* 12 (1979): 24–38.

Smith, H. Shelton. *Changing Conceptions of Original Sin: A Study in American Theology since 1750.* New York: Charles Scribner's Sons, 1955.

Smith, James E., and Phillip R. Kunz. "Polygyny and Fertility in Nineteenth-Century America." *Population Studies* 30 (1976): 465–80.

Spicer, Judith C., and Susan O. Gustavus. "Mormon Fertility through Half a Century: Another Test of the Americanization Hypothesis." *Social Biology* 21 (1974): 70–76.

Stannard, David E., ed. *Death in America.* Philadelphia: University of Pennsylvania Press, 1974.

———. *The Puritan Way of Death: A Study in Religion, Culture, and Social Change.* New York: Oxford University Press, 1977.

Steffen, Jerome O., ed. *The American West: New Perspectives, New Dimensions.* Norman: University of Oklahoma Press, 1979.

Stolnitz, George J. "A Century of International Mortality Trends: II." *Population Studies* 10 (1956): 17–42.

Tate, Thad W., and David L. Ammerman, eds. *The Chesapeake in the Seventeenth Century: Essays on Anglo-American Society.* Chapel Hill: University of North Carolina Press, 1979.

Taylor, P. A. M. *Expectations Westward: The Mormons and the Emigration of Their British Converts in the Nineteenth Century.* Ithaca, N.Y.: Cornell University Press, 1966.

Thayer, James Bradley. *A Western Journey with Mr. Emerson.* 1884. Reprint, Port Washington, N.Y.: Kennikat, 1971.

Tufte, Virginia, and Barbara Myerhoff, eds. *Changing Images of the Family.* New Haven: Yale University Press, 1979.

Turner, Rodney. "The Moral Dimensions of Man: A Scriptural View." *Dialogue* 3 (Spring, 1968): 72–83.

Underwood, Grant. "Re-visioning Mormon History." *Pacific Historical Review* 55 (1986): 403–26.

Van de Walle, Etienne. "Household Dynamics in a Belgian Village, 1847–1866." *Journal of Family History* 1 (1976): 80–94.

Vinovskis, Maris A. "Mortality Rates and Trends in Massachusetts before 1860." *Journal of Economic History* 32 (1972): 184–213.

Walsh, Lorena S., and Russell R. Menard. "Death in the Chesapeake: Two Life Tables for Men in Early Colonial Maryland." *Maryland Historical Magazine* 69 (1974): 211–27.

Watkins, Susan Cotts, and James McCarthy. "The Female Life Cycle in a Belgian Commune: La Hulpe, 1847–1866." *Journal of Family History* 5 (1980): 167–79.

Watkins, Susan Cotts, and Etienne van de Walle. "Nutrition, Mortality, and Population Size: Malthus' Court of Last Resort." *Journal of Interdisciplinary History* 14 (1983); 205–26.

Wells, Robert V. *Revolutions in Americans' Lives: A Demographic Perspective on the History of Americans, Their Families, and Their Society.* Westport, Conn.: Greenwood Press, 1982.

Whipple, Maurine. *The Giant Joshua.* Boston: Houghton Mifflin, 1942.

Wiebe, Robert H. *The Opening of American Society: From the Adoption of the Constitution to the Eve of Disunion.* New York: Knopf, 1984.

Wilcox, Linda P. "The Imperfect Science: Brigham Young on Medical Doctors." *Dialogue* 12 (Fall, 1979): 26–36.

Woodbury, John Taylor. *Vermilion Cliffs: Reminiscences of Utah's Dixie.* St. George: privately published, 1933.

Wright, Carroll D. *The History and Growth of the United States Census.* Washington: U.S. Government Printing Office, 1900.

Wrigley, E. A. "Mortality in Pre-industrial England: The Example of Colyton, Devon, Over Three Centuries." *Daedalus* 97 (1968): 546–80.

Young, Kimball. *Isn't One Wife Enough?* New York: Henry Holt, 1954.

Zuckerman, Michael. "Dreams That Men Dare to Dream: The Role of Ideas in Western Modernization." *Social Science History* 2 (1978): 332–45.

Index

Note on the Author

Larry Logue, who received his Ph.D. in American Civilization from the University of Pennsylvania, has taught American studies at California State University and was a resident scholar at the School of American Research. He has published several articles on Mormon history. Currently, he is a visiting assistant professor in the History Department at the University of Oklahoma.